GOVERNANCE AND HUMAN RIGHTS

GOVERNANCE AND HUMAN RIGHTS

Edited by

Bharat Jhunjhunwala

KALPAZ PUBLICATIONS

DELHI–110 052

GOVERNANCE AND HUMAN RIGHTS
(Human Rights, Public Administration, Sociology)

Rs. 525

ISBN: 81-7835-124-2

Published with support of Motilal Bhimraj Charity Trust
732, Modern Society, Sector 15
Rohini, Delhi—110 085
Tel: 729-8589; 789-3673
E-mail: bharatj@nda.vsnl.net.in

Published in 2007 in India by
Kalpaz Publications,
C-30, Satyawati Nagar, Delhi-110052
E-mail : Kalpaz@hotmail.com
9212729499

Lasertypesetting at: Varsha Graphics, Delhi
Printed at: Mehra Offset Printers, New Delhi

Contents

PART II : HUMAN RIGHTS

Preface

Democracy is assumed to be the only 'correct' form of governance and Human Rights are considered to be inviolable. By implication it is assumed that the forms of governance practised by other civilizations are somehow irrelevant or outdated. Little is it realised that the practice of universal franchise is only two centuries old and that of human rights barely half century old while great living civilisations of India and China have survived for more than five thousand years and the Hellenic precursors of the Western civilisation are long dead. This book is an effort to develop a critique of these ideas from the *Sanatana* Indian perspective. The idea is not to lament about the glorious past of the Indian civilisation but to learn from our tradition to improve upon the Western ideas for the good of all human beings

The Western civilisation has conquered the East on the strength of its technologies—the canon, airplanes, computers and nuclear power. But it is faltering on social issues—obesity, suicides, domestic and child violence permeate these societies. The great danger before all human civilisation is that the East may unthinkingly give up its time-tested social organisation and blindly ape the West. At the same time the East has to realign itself with the new technologies and the increase in economic welfare, literacy and health status that the West has begotten to the people of the world.

There is a twofold task before us. One, we have to critique the Western social sciences to point out the unsolved problems and help them in their evolution. Two, we have to self-critique our own tradition to modify it in keeping with modern developments.

Motilal Bhimraj Charity Trust was established by my Late Great Grandfather Motilal Jhunjhunwala to promote education in his home district of Jhunjhunu in 1936. A programme was initiated in 1997 to encourage persons well versed in Indian tradition to develop critiques of the Western social sciences. A series of seminars were organised in this direction. The papers relating to Governance and Human Rights have been put together in this book.

We hope that this book will help the Indian social scientists to critically look at both the Western social sciences and our own.

Bharat Jhunjhunwala

732, Modern Society
Sector 15, Rohini
Delhi—110 085

Acknowledgements

The authors wish to thank Swami Shantidharmananda of Satya Darshan Ashram, Rishikesh who helped organise the first seminar of the series. It were the ideas that were unleashed during that seminar that led to the organisation of the subsequent ones.

Dr. Chhaya Rai had helped organize a seminar at Jalalpur where many papers included in this volume were presented. We are thankful to her. The participants in these seminars helped clarify the ideas and made a valuable contribution.

The authors of the papers contained in this volume have been kind to provide their ideas in writing. They have further helped in editing the page proofs.

Introduction

PART I : GOVERNANCE

Democracy in Indian Tradition

It is debatable whether 'democracy' in the sense of universal adult franchise was an integral part of the Indian tradition. K.M. Mathur argues that elections are mentioned in *Yajurveda* and B.N. Tiwari mentions many examples of similar nature. Chandrakant Shukla says that the king was selected by consensus implying thereby that though formal elections were not known yet the will of the governed was taken into account in the selection of the king. According to R.P. Gupta the king had to necessarily rule as directed by the people's assembly. Panchanand Misra opines that Indian monarchy itself was democratic in nature. These observations indicate that Indian institution of kingship was at best quasi in nature. The will of the governed was an essential pillar of governance.

The same scholars also assert that there was something higher than the political rulership. This may be called social consensus, will of the people, moral imperative, common good, or *dharma*. This social consensus stood above the king and the king lost legitimacy if he violated the same. There is a near total agreement that without such a social consensus or the establishment of *dharma* in the people's mind no democracy can function successfully. 'Pure' democracy, in the sense of adult franchise, is not complete without this complementary principle. And, if this *dharma* is established then the precise method of selecting the system of administration, i.e., whether a monarchy or democracy becomes less important.

In the Indian tradition the source of legitimacy of power, whether adult franchise or monarchy, was less relevant than the checks that were imposed on the use of that power. Modern democracy on the other hand, stresses the legitimacy arising from adult franchise but fails to recognize that legitimately acquired power can be misused.

The voter is often more occupied with his immediate problems and fails to elect those who can secure his long-term good. It can be seen that those who have worked hard for the people often loose in the elections and those who are unscrupulous win because they satisfy the immediate needs of the people. Good governance is not therefore, a question of the establishment of democracy. Democracy can sacrifice *su-rajya* on the high altar of *swa-rajya.*

The central issue is not that of establishment of democracy but that of the *dharmic* exercise of power. According to S.E. Bhelkey "the democratic pattern should be organized in such a way that it will generate self-regulating principles which will check the role of the individual." B.K. Swain avers that the emphasis in the Indian tradition was on stability which was seen as a precondition of people's welfare. And this stability could come only if the rulers exercised moral influence over the ruled. B.P. Singh, while criticising Nehruvian socialist democracy, asserts that politics is, correctly speaking, governed by religion and "to separate the political realm from the sacred and to make it sovereign is necessarily to run a politics of exploitation and oppression." Navlata opines that without a commitment to the people's welfare any administration would become oppressive. M.N.V. Nair, while eulogizing modern democracy, admits that elected representatives will stop misusing their power only if there exists a social consensus on the issue.

The central point of all these studies is that universal adult franchise, though welcome, is a second order issue. The primary question is that of a social consensus to secure public good. Without the establishment of such *dharma* every system, including democracy, can turn oppressive. Therefore, we must apply our minds more to the establishment of *dharma* rather than presume that the mere establishment of democracy is adequate for securing good governance.

We have had many instances of a democratically elected government becoming tyrannous. A democratic England exploited the colonies blatantly. Hitler came to power and retained it democratically. Dictators like Sukarno too were elected. Therefore, it is important for the society not to rest with the securement of democracy. It is more important to establish a social consensus about the nature of good governance and to energize the people to oppose a bad ruler whether democratic or monarchial.

Control of Power by People

Though Indian system of governance was nominally monarchial but it had many in-built systems of checking the exercise of power by the monarch. It was not autocracy.

Ila Ghosh points out on the basis of Kalidasa's *Raghuvansa* that one of these checks was guidance by the *purohita*. The public had a major role in controlling the king by techniques such as stricture, criticism, picketing and distrust. If the society fails to restrain the king by applying these various pressures then it has to bear the fruits thereof in the form of bad governance. The ascetic also had a role in controlling an evil king by pronouncing a curse upon him.

R.P. Gupta adds that war itself was a check upon a bad king. An evil king would loose the support of his people who would instead side with the challenger. In order to win the support of his subjects in a war, the king necessarily had to become soft and charitable. Presumably, the ancient system had assessed that the costs of war were less than the benefits that accrued from the good governance that was established as a result. Sovereignty then becomes a protection to bad kings.

S.E. Bhelkey points out that representative democracy does not work if all the people have their own personal interests as the objective. In that case the elected representatives too become interested in securing their own personal welfare rather than that of the public. The people have to be educated to take democracy as a duty rather than as a right which is the same thing as saying that *dharma* should be established.

The Spiritual Imperative

The motivation for the ruler to rule in a people-friendly way has to be moral or spiritual. It is possible for rulers to acquire power by evil means. Who knows how many Ravanas and Kamsas went unpunished.

The motivation for a ruler to govern his subjects in a benign manner cannot, therefore, flow from the desire to retain power. These has to exist a moral or spiritual imperative. A king has to be taught to secure his people's happiness because it leads to his own spiritual evolution, or because it is his *dharma* to do so. Thus, Navlata says that *tyaga* or sacrifice alone is the *mantra* of people's welfare.

Role of Brahmin

Another pillar of good governance was the Brahmin or the *purohita,* the former being independent and free of the system of kingship while the latter being within the same. The Brahmin and the *purohita* were to advise the king if he were benign. This point is explained both by R.P. Gupta and V.K. Hampiholi.

The Brahmin was to educate the masses about the misdeeds of the king if he were tyrannous and thereby galvanize them into action. Thus is said in *Manu Smriti* that the Brahmin's weapon is speech. By speech he galvanizes the people into action against a bad king.

It is the duty of the Brahmin to evaluate the politician's (Kshatriya's) conduct and take appropriate actions. There is no guarantee, however, that the Brahmin will indeed discharge such a role. But awareness will help. This is the key which determines whether good governance will prevail or not.

Generally the Brahmin was above the king. 'Above' here should be understood in terms of spiritual rather than political power. The Brahmin's ideal was that of voluntary poverty and abstaining from state patronage. Chanakya did propound that the king was above the Brahmin but that should be seen as an aberration.

R.P. Gupta also elaborates the view that the formulation of laws was the responsibility of the brahmin *(dharma guru),* not the Kshatriya. The king only implemented them. This would be tantamount to saying that the legislative was the Brahmin and the executive-judiciary the king. But the narratives such as those of Viswamitra and Vidura do not support such a system of governance; while that of Vasistha might. Perhaps these were ideals, not the norm.

There have been periods in our history when the society has become *adharmic.* Ravana, Kamsa and Duryodhana were all real. Thus, we should see our history as engaged in constant struggle between *dharma* and *adharma* rather than as an ideal from which we have fallen.

Possibly Brahmins like Bhishma and Drona became servants of the State and, therefore, were not able to resist the tyranny of bad kshatriyas. Their silence on the disrobing of Draupadi is a clear demonstration of the implications of the dependence of the Brahmin on the state. One reason for the decline of India would then be the decline of morality of the Brahmin.

There is a need for more detailed examination of the question whether the Brahmin controlled the Kshatriya from the 'outside' like Viswamitra and Parsurama; or from the inside like Vasistha and Drona.

The practice of truth by the Brahmin necessarily leads to his economic and political impoverishment. The Brahmin has to, therefore, reduce his material needs and live in voluntary poverty. Only then he will be able to control the politician.

Any 'organisation' of Brahmins, the Church, for example, is not able to discharge this function because it fights for the same powers and is subject to the same perversions that are inherent in any social organisation *(sangha)*, including the State. Any 'organised' effort by the Brahmins to secure good governance is, therefore, self-contradictory. The Brahmins have to discharge this role in an autonomous fashion as free individuals. Of course, they can evolve a consensus among themselves as by meetings such as at the *Kumbh Mela* but they have to be independent in their livelihood.

The learned *pandit* may or may not be a Brahmin. The *pandit* may be a Sudra (if he is pursuing his *bhoga vasana*), Vaishya *(vitta vasana)*, Kshatriya *(satta vasana)* or Brahmin (only if he is pursuing *swadhyaya vasana*). But because the *pandit* was perceived as the Brahmin, and he started accepting State patronage and his role as Brahmin stood negated. No Brahmins were left in the society who could restrain the state. This may have been one reason for the decline of India, for our succumbing to foreign rule and the continued inability of our Brahmins to speak the truth.

Democracy in the West

There is a need to appreciate that modern representative democracy has its origins in non-egalitarian societies such as those of ancient Greece. The *Magna Carta* was a Charter of Demands of the aristocracy.

R.P. Gupta points out that the monarchial system in India with the institution of the Brahmin or the *purohita* was fundamentally different from the monarchy in the West which was bereft of such a check.

We have seen how democracy in the West has often become anti-people. It is necessary to establish such *dharma* in the West that provides recognition to the role of the people, the spiritual imperative and the role of the Brahmin in securing good governance. Democracy by itself is a weak instrument for securing good governance.

Varna Vyavastha and Governance

Studies by Bharat Jhunjhunwala and Vidyaratna develop the role of *varna* system in securing good governance. Jhunjhunwala makes the distinction between *varna*, which is, at the very core, a psychological concept indicating the nature of one's inner desires and, therefore, his line of worldly action. *Jati*, on the other hand, is a mere classification of professions. The central model of Indian governance is that people are classified into four *varnas* according to their inner desires. The Brahmin is one who has transcended his desires of physical pleasures, wealth and power. He alone can think of the general welfare of the society in a dispassionate manner. Since his worldly desires have been fulfilled, he can face the wrath of a tyrannical king and yet galvanize the society into resistance. Vidyaratna similarly points out that *varna vyavastha* was a system of governance.

PART II : HUMAN RIGHTS

Duties Spontaneously Beget Rights

The Indian view stresses the performance of duties instead of demanding rights. If all individuals perform their duties, the rights of others are automatically secured. The mother's performance of her duty to feed the child begets the child's right to milk. If every human being demands his rights and does not perform his duties then the situation becomes unmanageable. Therefore, the main thrust should be to teach people to perform their duties. This point has been elaborated by Mala Pyasi who says that the sole right is to perform one's duty. A.K. Sinha argues that the *dharma* or responsibility of each individual is to serve other human beings. If, and only if, this is done then the rights of all human beings would be secured.

Vidyanand Jha, Sridhar Misra and G.S. Misra develop this

theme to explain that the rights are given only for the performance of one's duty. The student is given the right to go out of the house in order to perform the duty of learning in school. Discharge of duties spontaneously brings forth commensurate rights because duty cannot be discharged without them. The manager cannot manage labour without the right of transferring the workmen. The demand for human rights, therefore, itself implies that the duties are not being discharged. Thus, in the Vedic period we find no description of 'rights' but only of 'duties'. There is no sanctity of any right which is not attached to a duty.

There should be stress on the duties of the individual along with his rights, i.e., the exercise of rights should be made contingent on the discharge of duties. Individual rights should be conditional in this way.

Individual and Social Good

The Sanatana view is that the rights of the individual are subservient to the common good. "Give up one for the family, family for the village, village for the district, and whole earth for salvation." This advice was given by Chanakya to the king. It is related to the discharge of king's duties. It is not a voluntary code to be implemented by the individual but a rule for governance to be implemented by the State.

The human rights of five innocent villagers and their mother were sacrificed in the *laksya-griha* so that the Pandavas could survive and usher in good governance. Sita's human rights were violated when she was expelled by Rama without a hearing or any cognizable fault of hers.

Hemant Namdev builds on this theme by pointing out that present day violation of human rights are occurring because people have become individualistic, materialistic and self-centred. Unless there is a shift in the philosophical paradigm and the 'I' is made subservient to the collective, there will be no solution to the violations of human rights. Every individual is likely to trample upon the rights of others in the pursuit of his own self-interests. The beginning of the securement of human rights has to be made by inculcating the philosophy of 'non-I' or *dharma*.

Urmila Chaturvedi explains the Hindu view of women's rights by building on the concept of *rina* or debt with which every person is born. This approach is contrary to the Western view which posits that every human being gets some inalienable rights by the very virtue of being a human being. The Indian view seeks to make every person conscious of the rights of others by telling him that he has to discharge his *rina.* The Western approach asks him to demand his rights. It is not examined in the Western model as to who will give him his rights if every person is busy demanding his own rights.

The social consensus that it is the responsibility of the 'society' or the 'government' to provide these rights has to be examined. The securement of the rights of the individual then becomes contingent upon the discharge of the responsibility by the State. The Indian approach takes this further. It says why limit the responsibility to the State ? Let the responsibility be expanded to all society so that the violations themselves become few and the role of the State becomes negligible.

The Western view, furthermore, is that the protection of rights of the individual does lead to social good as has been argued by Ashu Pasricha. There is a need to study this question in detail. There is no problem as long as individual good leads to social good. But many situations can be conceived—such as *lakshya-griha* and Sita's being expelled—where there is a conflict between the two. There is a need to discuss whether such a conflict is real or has been created to establish a hierarchial, and often tyrannous, social order.

The precedence to social good over that of the individual rights could be construed to mean the establishment of a social order where the elite can define social good to further its own ends. Hitler, for example, persecuted the Jews in the name of social good. This problem, has to be dealt with by discharging the role of the Brahmin in securing good governance. Such failure of the Brahmin cannot be made the basis of negating the primacy of social good as has been done in the Universal Declaration of Human Rights.

The second way of solving the contradiction between the individual and the society is to search for higher values which would override the conflict. These 'higher values' are social consensus or *dharma* established by following the example of the sages.

Equality of Rights

The *Sanatana* tradition is based on discharge of responsibilities rather than demand of the rights of the individual. This translates into different—instead of equal—rights of the individuals. The classic example is that of Duryodhana and Yudhishtira being asked to determine punishment for a Sudra, Vaisya, Kshatriya and Brahmin for a similar crime. Yudhishtira meted out higher punishment to the higher *varna*. This was a clear negation of the concept of equality before law. The example has implications in the converse as well. In the *laksya-griha* the rights of the Pandavas took precedence over those of the innocent villagers.

One way of solving this dilemma would be to classify the people on the basis of their nature—*varna*—and then ensure equal rights to those of the same *varna*. Tarkesh Molia and B.K. Jha develop this theme. Molia shows that the Indian Constitution accepts such a classification and that the rights of persons of different categories are different. This becomes a vindication of a *varna*-type of classification. B.K. Jha explains that this classification is necessary for operational purposes of managing the society.

The alternative viewpoint is that there are certain basic needs—*bhaya, nidra, ahar* and *maithun*—which are common to all *varnas*. These constitute of human rights. These would be equivalent of 'natural' laws (in contradistinction to statutory or social laws). This view has been expounded by Uma Singh, Shweta Srivastava and Alok Tandon. Tandon also challenges the idea that human rights are culture specific.

This debate can only be resolved by dwelling deeper into the route to the securement of those rights. Granted that some rights are universal, how does the society go about fulfilling them? The next step requires that different.persons discharge their respective responsibilities which are themselves determined by one's temperament and capabilities. The question then becomes of getting people to discharge these latter responsibilities. The universal or basic rights are then automatically secured.

The Indian tradition stresses these latter responsibilities and also that the roles of different individuals are different. The Western tradition stresses the universal basic rights which are the result of the approach taken by the Indian tradition. It may be said that the Indian tradition secures the universal rights by stressing the differences between human being and their different responsibilities.

State and Human Rights

The Universal Declaration of Human Rights is a response to the misuse of power due to lack of a controlling mechanism. The problem was that of checks on power. The solution is consensus on social good—*dharma*—alongwith checks on power. Instead of bringing in these checks the Declaration has negated the concept of social good itself. D.K. Dixit develops this theme by pointing out that the UN Declaration is only a legal document. What is required is a moral code and consensus.

Shobha Misra points out that the *Sanatana* values can be built from the existing Constitution. Making changes in the Constitution is less important than building a social consensus of *dharma*.

Sri Krishna Agarwal points out that the ancient system of *panch* was much superior than that of paid judges of the present day. The *Sanatana* viewpoint here is that the judiciary is the state. The king dispensed justice. This implies that an organ of the State cannot control the State. The judiciary can be hijacked as Justice Chandrachud did during Emergency by sanctioning it. The fundamental problem is that the judge cannot be a Brahmin because he is under the control of the State. Vasistha—living in his *ashrama* free of State patronage—could tell Dasaratha to send Rama with Viswamitra; but Drona could not prevent disrobing of Draupadi. Thus, the judiciary may prove incapable of resisting the State at critical juncture. At that point the people would be helpless for they would not have, in the meanwhile, created alternative methods of control of the State.

An opposite viewpoint is that the judiciary is the protector of individual and social good. The Indian view is that the judiciary cannot control the State. If at all, it can control the bureaucracy. If the 'State' i.e., the Prime Minister, does indeed want justice to be provided but the bureaucracy, say the SHO of Police Station is tyrannous, then the judiciary can indeed intervene. Here judiciary or the National Human Rights Commission acts as a higher organ of the State keeping vigilance on another lower organ of that same State. This is a positive function of the judiciary. But it should not be confused with the control of the State by the judiciary itself.

Bharat Jhunjhunwala develops a critique of various clauses of the Universal Declaration from the Indian standpoint.

PART I
GOVERNANCE

1

Statecraft in Ancient India

V.K. Hampiholi

Role of Brahmin was central in making Kshatriya rule in public good.

Editor

"Happiness of the king lies in the happiness of the subjects. What is dear to himself is not beneficial to the king, but what is dear to the subjects is beneficial to him."

These aforesaid lines give the essence of governance. *Dharma* is a very comprehensive and almost all pervasive term in the history of Indian thought. It embraces and touches upon almost all aspects of human life. The Sanskrit term *Dharma* denotes duty, custom, moral laws, general laws, nature, righteousness and culture. It is derived from the root *dhr* (धृ) which means to hold together or to preserve. It is an adhesive and a cementing catalytic agent which holds mankind individually and socially intact. It maintains social stability and unites the individual with the society. It is a bond which makes individual and society interdependent and strikes an equilibrium between the two. Lord Krishna in the *Mahabharata* explains that *Dharma* is created for the well-being of all the creatures. Bhishma too echoes the same idea in *Shantiparva*. All that is free from inflicting any harm on any creature is *Dharma* in the true sense of the term. Its sole objective is to ward off harm and this single objective makes it comprehensive as it takes many a thing in its stride. Bhishma adds that *Dharma* is so called because it protects all; it preserves all that is created. Its very basis is positive. It is a two-pronged weapon. It protects those who protect it. It is doubly blessed. Those who inculcate and protect it, enhance it and they are protected by it in return. Those who flout it have to suffer. It is a never-failing friend on this earth and even after death. It is force of the force and power of the power. All the thinkers have extolled it as supreme in the world. It is altogether vital and indispensable for the good of the individual as well as of society. Our ancestors had realised its importance. They were inspired and convinced beyond any doubt that it is the only means to usher in peace and security in society and to maintain them. Thus, it is the sacred duty of each and every individual to uphold it for the welfare of society.

Concept of State

The term State is a technical word. According to Article 12 of our Constitution state includes executive as well as legislative organs of the Union and States. According to our ancient thinkers, State *(rajya)* was an organism of seven *(prakritis)* elements, viz., ruler, ministers, people, territory, treasury, army and friends or allies. According to modern writers, the essential features of the State are territory, population, government and sovereignty. When we compare these two streams of thought we realise that our ancient thinkers were more comprehensive. They left nothing to chance. They included those elements also without which modern four features of the State may crumble like a house of cards. They attached equal importance to treasury and allies. If we peep into this comparison we would find that the modern political thinkers think of the State statically and not dynamically. Their definition describes the state rather internally than externally. Hindu polity looks at the composition of the State not as a thing in itself but as one political entity in relation to many.

The seven elements of the State are called *angas* or *prakritis*. Almost all the thinkers consider the king to be the hub. He is the supreme being. So much so, Kautilya declares that he is the state. The *Shukranitisar* compares the seven elements to the organs of the human body, viz. the king is the head; the ministers are eyes; friends, the ears; treasury, the mouth; the army, the mind; territory, the hands and the people, the feet. Being the most vital organ of the State, the king stands on a higher pedestal. He is the head of the kingdom. Thus, his role in upholding *Dharma* is important all the more.

Importance of the King

Formerly all the people were comparatively righteous. They lived adhering to the dictates of *Dharma*. Hence there was neither punisher nor punishment. All were protected by *Dharma* itself. Change is the law of nature. Old order changes the yielding place to new. With the passage of time, a sea change came into human beings. *Moha, lobha, kama* very subtly crept into the very structure of man and started eating and corroding it like cankers. Man became selfish and self-centered. He left *Dharma* and started flouting the rules and regulations established by *Dharma* for his well-being and well-being of society at large. Feather light fetters imposed by *Dharma* became too heavy. Might is right pushed brotherhood in the background. Survival of the fittest perhaps became the order of the day. This let loose many ills. Weaker ones started playing second fiddle to their counterparts. Chaos was prevalent. There were chances of society to crumble down. Need arose to arrest this trend. The king was thus created to punish the wicked and to protect *Dharma*. He came into being to restore peace and harmony and establish equilibrium in society. He came forward to scatter the clouds of barbarism and bring about an era of stability and peace embracing all departments of human life. Manu, Kautilya, *Ayodhya Kanda, Shantiparva, Kamandaka* have used the phrase *Matsya Nyaya* to describe the bad and anarchic condition of society in the absence of a king. Absence of the sovereign at the helm of affairs created chaos, anarchy and everything went topsy-turvy. Rules of the jungle got the upper hand and pushed back all decency and rationalism. This slowly but surely ushered in an era of immorality and injustice. Morality sank to the fathomless chasms and justice evaporated in the thin air. Absence of a king thus creates untold difficulties. Ultimately it creates unrest in society. Intermixture of castes (*Varna Sankar)* may occur and it is sure to make a dent on purity in society. The very infrastructure of society trembles under the unholy burden of immorality and injustice. The society sits on the volcano of destruction. So the king is indispensable to uphold *Dharma*. He with sceptre and coercive power punishes the wicked and protects his subjects. Manu attaches all significance to this *Danda*, the coercive power of the sovereign. It is a must to govern, to protect and to play the role of a watchdog when people sleep unmindful of possible dangers lurking around them. The *Danda* is not only earthly but heavenly also.

It symbolises *Dharma* itself. Fear corrects and mends. Fear of the sceptre makes people act according to *Dharma*. *Danda* works wonders. The king is called *Dandadhari*. He governs and governs well with its help. All this displays the indispensability of a king and his coercive power. A State remains in existence only because of the presence of the king and the *Danda* with which he wields powers. The *Ramayana* describes the chaos created by the absence of a king. *Shanti parva* states that in the absence of a king *Dharma* disappears and there is blood flooding the drains, people killing each other. Dwelling in such conditions becomes well-nigh a mirage, a hoax, a deception. Manu states that king's absence accelerates the downfall of society and its virtual disappearance. All earthly comforts follow if there is a king. Bhishma advises that one should first secure a king, then wife and then wealth. In the absence of the king there would be neither wife nor any private property. *Danda* brings about order and other necessary things of society follow automatically. Thus, all the authorities on Indian polity emphasize the importance and necessity of a king in the State.

Duties and Responsibilities of the King

The authorities on Indian polity prescribe many duties and various types of responsibilities of the king. Protection of his subjects is his primary duty. Manu, Narada, Shukra and the like are of the same view. This protection is a comprehensive term. It goes beyond its literary meaning. It includes *prajapalan* also. Protection from internal and external aggression should be provided by the king. Royal officers, royal favourites, local thieves, enemies of the king, and so on pose internal aggression. External aggression emanates from the kings of neighbouring countries. Both these aggressions should be met with an iron hand. The king should blunt their sharpness and uproot their teeth. Moreover, he should ensure that his people follow the right path and they do not go astray. He is to see that they follow *Varna Dharma* and *Ashrama Dharma*. His role is that of a father who protects, guides and directs his children. The king's pleasure lies in the pleasure of his subjects. Personal happiness and comforts do not matter. Kautilya decries a pleasure-seeker king. The *Vishnudharma Sutra* installs such king on the highest pedestal who seeks his happiness in the happiness of his subjects and experiences pain in their pain.

Such a king attains fame both on this earth and in heaven after death. Bhishma opines that a king should protect his subjects like a pregnant woman who protects her foetus. She sacrifices her own pleasure and comforts. The king should play the same role. He should provide food, shelter and clothings to the destitutes, orphans, the aged, the infirm, the afflicted, the crippled, lunatics, widows and sufferers of diseases and calamities. He should give succour to them by all means at his disposal and try to minimise their sufferings to the maximum. So the responsibilities of a king are enormous. *Ramayana* puts forward Sri Rama symbolising all these aspects. Tears flowed down his cheeks when his people were in sorrow. Their smiles made his face radiant. *Ramayana* dubs a king a sinner if he does not protect his people after having taken 1/6th part of their income. The *Dharma Sastras* guarantee unseen fruits (अदृश्य फल) to a king who is the armour of his subjects. Manu says such a king will secure the reward of solemn sacrifices. Yajnavalkya opines that he will get 1/6th of merit (पुण्य) done by his subjects by protecting them according to what is just (न्याय). According to Angiras the king who protects his subjects need not do austerities and sacrifices.

Another important duty of the king is *Dharmaraksana*. He should act according to *Dharma* and goad his subjects to tread the same path. *Arthasashtra, Manusmriti, Yajnavalkya, Sukraneetisara* and other works lay down the daily duties of the king in detail. He should perform them diligently, convincingly and with religious fervour and gusto. He should set an example for his people. He should always remember that he is the architect of his age. Only his exemplary personality will inculcate the same vibrations in his people. His subjects will follow him in toto. Qualities of the people would be directly proportionate to the qualities of the king. The *Shantiparva* states that the king will create heaven and hell in his kingdom by practising *dharma* and *adharma* delete respectively. All the beings take shelter under *dharma* and *dharma* takes shelter under the king. The king's personal likes and dislikes cannot be the driving force behind his deeds (यथा राजा तथा प्रजा). He should remember that his subjects emulate him. He is their guiding star and path finder. Bhishma declares in the Shantiparva that the king is the maker of his age. He remarks that the concept of कृत, त्रेता, द्वापर and कलि depend on his conduct and character. He is identified with *Yugas*. This simply shows his importance and indispensability. According to Manu also, the concept of *Yuga* depends on the attitude of the king towards his duties. A sleeping king represents *Kali*; an awakened one stands for *Dvapra*; he represents *Treta* if he shows interest to act; if he is inactive he represents *Krta*. According to the *Sukraniti Sara* he is the promoter of his age by his *Dharma* or *Adharma* activities. There is neither the fault of *Yugas* nor the fault of the subjects for bad times. The fault lies squarely with the king. So he can make his tenure as कृतयुग or कलियुग by his conduct and by his attitude towards *Dharma*. If he is धर्मिष्ठ goodness of his subjects is guaranteed. Such subjects represent good age, i.e., कृत युग. Hence the role of the king is significant and indispensable. According to Narada, protection of the subjects, honouring the aged and the wise, looking into the disputes of the people and diligence in sarvadharm are the functions of the king. Atri opines that punishing the wicked, honouring the good people, increasing the treasury by correct means, dealing impartially with litigants and protecting the kingdom are considered to be sacrifices in case of the king. The *Visnudharmottara Purana* refers to similar types of sacrifices for the king. Manu advises the king to emulate the actions of Indra, the Sun, Vayu, Yama, Varuna, Moon, Agni and of the earth to uphold *Dharma*. The king should bestow benefits to his subjects like Indra who showers rain for four months. He should draw the taxes like the sun who draws up water with its rays. He should move everywhere like Vayu with the help of his spies and secret agents. He should act impartially and has no need to make any discrimination between friends and foes like *Yama*. He should punish the wicked like *Varuna*. He should be pleasing to his people like the moon. He should destroy his enemies like Agni and protect all his people like the mother earth. These eight-fold functions help him to uphold *Dharma* effectively in his kingdom.

The *Anushasnaparva* states that the king should construct boarding halls, tanks, temples, *stupas* and hermitage places for Brahmins. Pages of history boast of many kings who attached utmost importance to welfare activities. King Ashoka constructed hospitals for men and animals (2nd rock edict at Kalsi), alm houses, rest houses, watering places, shady trees on the highways and paid active attention to irrigation works (8th Girana Rock edict). The *Hathi-gumpha* inscription declares that the king Kharavela of Kalinga constructed embankments round the Khibira lake and renovated all public gardens. Welfare activities undertaken by the ruler make him *sarvapriya* 'सर्वप्रिय', (darling of all) and he becomes a beckoning light for posterity to come. Bhishma in the *Shantiparva* remarks that State welfare, good rains, sickness, calamities and fear among people owe their origin to the king.

In ancient times, the ruler was held responsible for untimely deaths in his kingdom, for famine, for excessive rain and for other natural calamities. In the *Ramayana* (VII. 70) a brahmin brings to the royal palace the corpse of his young and declares that the king Rama has committed *adharma* and this has resulted into the untimely and premature death of his young son. This shows that any sin committed by the king invokes wrath of the gods and it lets loose unnatural phenomenon to happen. Rama later on comes to know about *Sambuka* who was practising *tapas* violating the dictates of *Varnadharma* and kills him. So if the ruler does not keep a judicious watch on the activities of his subjects even then he commits sins. Sins committed by the subjects cast their inauspicious shadow on the personality of the ruler. He becomes a sinner by proxy.

A king should collect fair taxes from the subjects. He should not be a blood-sucker. In return he must maintain law and order. He should draw the taxes like a leech, a calf and a bee which suck their food little by little. The gardener culls and plucks flowers and fruits but in no way harms the plants; the bee sucks the honey but does not damage the flowers. In the same way, the king while collecting taxes should not cause any suffering to his people. He should levy taxes in proper places, at proper time and in proper form. He should take mild as well as harsh steps to collect taxes and in no way this should be coercive. The idea is his subjects should pay taxes willingly and think as their religious duty.

The administration should give birth to happiness in the good people and terror and unhappiness in the bad people. The king should impart punishment to the guilty and the wicked without any mercy. He should not hesitate in declaring the punishment and while doing so, an impartial image of the punisher should emerge. The king should be impartial and should look so. His relatives should not become a stumbling block in his path. King Sagar of Surya dynasty did not hesitate to drive out even his son Asamanjasa who enjoyed inflicting suffering on his subjects by throwing children in the Sarayu river for his amusement.

Satyavrata, who became famous as Trisanku afterwards, was leading a wicked life. He once entered the wedding hall of a Brahmin and carried away the bride by force. His father Aruna, the king, pronounced the punishment for his own son and exiled him from his kingdom. Thus, he preserved and protected *Dharma*. But it does not mean that the king should be rash in his judgement as it can have farreaching implications. He should consult his ministers and *purohita*. That is why in ancient India the judicial place was called 'धर्म स्थान' and judge's seat was known as 'धर्मासन'. The king should be extra careful and vigilant in sifting the grains from the chaff. There should not be an iota of doubt while dubbing somebody as an offender or a culprit. The king should examine the motive, the place and the time of the offence. The punishment must be according to the magnitude and severity of the offence. Punishment should be awarded to the actual culprits. Innocent should not be prosecuted as it may lead to repentance afterwards and it makes the king a sinner. He earns infamy and will enter hell. Rash judgement should be discarded. Vasistha ordains one day's fast for the king and three days' fast for the *purohita* when the king does not punish him who deserves punishment. He ordains three days' fast for the king and penance for the *purohita* when the king punishes the innocent. Justice delayed is justice denied. The king should not make the litigants wait for justice. He should be quick but not rash. The *Ramayana* narrates the episode of the king Nrda who was cursed by the Brahmins to become a chameleon as he was late to meet the litigants.

The Role of Spiritual Leader

The spiritual leader or *purohita* or royal priest occupied a prominent and influential position in ancient Indian political system. He was honoured as a spiritual leader, as a religious preacher and as a political thinker. In the *Rigveda* the *Purohita* is elevated to great heights. *Purohita* Viswamitra protected the Bharata clan. The Danastutis of *Rigveda* tell about gifts of the king to the *purohita* who have helped him in the battlefield. The *Atharvaveda* refers to a *purohita* engaged in a spell for success in the war. These references clearly indicate that the *purohita* was not a mere priest in the *Vedic* period. *Aitareyabrahmana* calls him Rashtragopa (राष्ट्रगोप), i.e., saviour of the kingdom. So much so, it states that he is half soul of the king. The *Satapatha Brahmana* states that a Brahmin may remain without a king but a king should not be without a Brahmin. The *Purohita* and the king are the two wheels of a chariot. Both are indispensable for the development of the kingdom and for upholding *Dharma.* According to Manu, a Kshatriya will not prosper without a Brahmin and vice-versa. Any ordinary man cannot occupy the seat of a *purohita.* The *Gautamasutra,* the *Yajnavalkyasmriti,* the *Apastamba Dharamsutra* require that the *purohita* should be well versed in the vedas, *itihasas,* Dharamashastras, astrology, the rites of propitiation contained in the *Atharvaveda,* and so on. He should be of a high family and endowed with all *vidyas* and good acts as stated in the shastras. Kautilya praises him sky high when he says that a king should honour his advice as a pupil honours his teacher, a son his father and a servant his master.

Most of the authorities of Indian polity do not include *purohita* among *amatya* or *mantris.* He does not come under the organism of the State. But one thing is sure that he enjoyed a status equal to that of the king. His knowledge and austerities put him on a higher pedestal and perhaps on the highest rung of the ladder of administration in a kingdom.

Responsibilities of the *Purohita*

The *Mahabharata* points out that *Yogkshema* (welfare), sustenance and good administration of the state depends on the king and the *Yogkshema* (welfare) of the king depends on the *purohita.* So the foremost duty of the *purohita* used to be the welfare of the king. He was a friend, a philosopher and a guide. Kautilya states that fire, flood, disease, famine, rats, wild elephants, snakes and evil spirits are great natural calamities. The *Purohita's* sacred duty is to assist the king to protect the people from those calamities. During the war he should go to the battlefield with ministers and boost the morale and courage of the soldiers to fight valiantly. Secondly, he should help the ruler in judicial matters. There was a time when he was held more responsible for not punishing the offender and punishing the innocent and this is evident from the fact that the authorities had prescribed severe *prayschit* (penance) for him. Still more, he as a religious head might advise the king to perform sacrifices for the welfare of the State.

The scriptures boast of many incidents where the *purohita* is shown rendering unflinching and tactical help to the king directly and indirectly to uphold *Dharma*. Vasistha was the *purohita* of the Surya dynasty. He helped Dashratha and Rama to preserve and uphold *Dharma*. He advised Dasratha to send Rama with Viswamitra and keep the words given to the brahmins to protect them. Dashratha could not ignore his advice because otherwise it would have been *adharma*. Again it was Vasistha who advised Kaikeyi to give ornaments to Sita. Kaikeyi treated his advice as a command. Again he explained the crucial situation and urged Bharata to take charge of the kingdom. He solved his dilemma. He accompanied Bharata to the forests to bring Rama back. He arranged the coronation of Rama. Thus, we see Vasistha, the *purohita*, was assigned the most important tasks and he performed them to the best of his ability and to the best satisfaction of all concerned. He performed his duties as per the norms of *Dharma*. Vasistha is the name of a *Gotra* or a family. That is why we read about many Vasisthas in the scriptures.

Samvarana was a king of Lunar dynasty. He was attacked by the king of Pancala. Clouds of war and aggression forced him to give up his throne. He lived on the banks of the river Sindhu. He approached Vasistha and implored him to become his priest. Vasistha helped him to regain his lost empire. Once the god of rains played hide and seek. His kingdom experienced no rainfall for 12 long years. The king looked towards Vasistha to salvage the situation. Vasistha brought rains with the help of his austerities. He became so dependable, indispensable and trustworthy that before going to the forests to do penance Samvarana entrusted the administration of the State to him. There he fell in love with Tapati, the daughter of Surya. Love torn and passion-starved the king returned to the kingdom. Vasistha knowing well his condition went to *Suryaloka* by his *yogic* powers and implored *Surya* to give his consent for the marriage of Samvarana and Tapati. Surya agreed to his implorings. It simply shows how tactfully and wisely Vasistha must have tackled the situation and without compromising *dharma* he must have put the case of the king before Surya.

Kalmasapada or Mitrasaha was another king of Solar (Surya) dynasty. Once he was cursed by Shakti, the son of Vasistha, to become a demon and roam in the forests for 12 years. The curse proved true and the king became a demon. He devoured all the sons of Vasistha. In his killing spree once he killed a Brahmin who was with his wife. Angirasi, the wife of that slain Brahmin, cursed the king, now a demon, that if he touched any woman in future he would die at once. Twelve years of trials and tribulations passed. Here once again Vasistha came forward for rescue. He met the demon, sprinkled holy water on him and brought him back to his original form. Afterwards he blessed him with a son.

Muchukunda was a celebrated king of Solar dynasty. Once he was defeated by Kubera. He meditated on Vasistha who helped him with his *yogic* powers to inflict a crushing defeat on the army of Kubera. Dhaumya was the royal *purohit* of Pandvas. When the Pandavas started for the exile and forest life he walked in front of them with *Kusa* grass in his hands singing *Yamasama* and *Rudrasama*. He advised *Dharamraja* to worship sun god. Dhaumya also advised Pandavas how to preserve pseudonymity in the Virata's capital. He performed the rites of *Agnistoma* and uttered the *Veda Mantras* for their prosperity when they started their life *incognito*. He prayed for the recovery of their kingdom and victory in the world.

Examples of *purohita* going to any length to assist their kings are in plenty. In the *Vanaparva* we come across a *purohita* who ventures to go to hell to fulfil his king's desire. Somaka was a generous king of Panchal. He had two wives and one son named Jantu. He craved for 100 sons from his 100 wives. He expressed his heart-felt desire to his *purohita* who directed him to perform a sacrifice and offer the young prince in the sacrificial fire. Unflinching faith and trust of the king in his *purohita* made him follow his advice literally and he was blessed with 100 sons. The *purohita* went to hell as he had directed the king to kill a child.

Our ancient literature is sprinkled with pure spiritual leaders. They were interested only in establishing and upholding *Dharma*. They advised and many a time made the kings swallow sugar-coated pills, bitter ones, in the form of warnings to maintain *Dharma* in society. Vyasa is one such figure. He was an ascetic but his role in upholding *Dharma* was unparalleled. He untied the mysterious knots of *Dharma* and explained its intricacies. Narada was also one such spiritual leader who very cleverly but innocently tried his level best to preserve and uphold *Dharma*. Mahavira, Buddha, Ramdasa of Maharashtra, Vidyaranya of Karnataka, and so on, were regarded as spiritual leaders. All of them influenced the contemporary political set-up and did a lot to preserve and uphold *Dharma*.

To conclude we can say without any hitch that the king and the *purohita* played vital roles. Peace and unrest, rise and fall, happiness and unhappiness in society were directly proportionate to the conduct, character and ideals of the kings and the *purohita*. Their mutual cooperation, coordination, understanding and qualities of head and heart went a long way in bringing about a good State. They were the harbingers of the very best in the kingdom, otherwise the death knell was imminent; chaos and anarchy were bound to arise.

Thus, we see in ancient India, government was not police. The government's function comprised in its entirety the whole of protective and disciplinary measures. It was the duty of the king to rule in accordance with the sacred and eternal laws and traditions. People were free in their conduct if that was consistent with the *Dharmic* code and preservation of order. The king was to ensure that the treasury was never depleted. An empty treasury is cankerous both for the people and the country. Enforcement of *Svadharma* by the ruler was to guarantee welfare of the citizens at large and to prevent social disorder. The relationship of the king with his subjects was paternalistic. There was gradualism in the imposition of taxes and that too in proportion to the increase in prosperity of the people. The king, wielder of the rod and preserver of the law, was himself restrained by this law. Thus, we see governance in ancient India was fully developed.

2

Kalidasa's Description of Checks on the Unrighteous Ruler

Ila Ghosh

The evil king was checked by the *Purohita,* his own training and the people.

Editor

With the dawn of human civilisation the institution of State underwent pangs of birth of its development and evolution. Trial and error has convinced humanity that democracy is the best form of government as it has superseded all other forms of government in different countries of the world. For human existence, preservation of human freedom, sanctity of human rights, social justice and economic parity, a democratic set-up is considered to be the most pliable form of government which is suitable to human aspirations and longings. To achieve the lofty ideals of human existence mentioned above the democratic set-up came into being in India after independence. But during the last two decades there has been a gradual erosion, decrease and dilution in the tendency for public welfare. An ever increasing phoenix of corruption amongst elected representatives, selfishness, hunger for power, criminal tendency, violent, recurring and expensive elections, and so on, have jeopardised and put a question mark on the very success and usefulness of this democratic set-up. The obvious question that arises out of this complex situation is whether it is possible to have checks on such corrupt and pleasure seeking tyrants.

Though this question is related to the twentieth century or the twenty-first century in particular, but this irritant has been racking the mind of man ever since he has bestowed the duty of his protection on the leader or the king willingly. It has created apprehension in the mind of man.

Through this write-up an endeavour has been made to find out a solution to this question peeping through the pages of literacy work of Kalidasa, the poet and dramatist of India. In reality he has created his famous great work *Raghuvansha* to present before the leaders and rulers the exemplary life of rulers with the noble ideals of public welfare embedded in them. It presents before us the lofty ideals of benevolent and friendly rulers. *Raghuvansha* begins with the very ideal qualities of the *Raghuvanshi* kings employed in the service and welfare of the people from time immemorial, e.g., racial purity, nonstop struggle till success, undisputed authority, crimewise punishment, being ever vigilant, storing of fortunes for distribution, measured speech, underlying truth, victory for glory, domestic life for lineage and abandonment of body through meditation. The epic ends with the untimely death of the king Agnivarsha caused by tuberculosis and his secret cremation in the very household park. On the one hand we have had great model kings like Dilip, Raghu, Az, Dashratha, Rama, Kush and Atithi and on the other, we have experienced the bitter reality of licentious and amorous kings like Agnivarsha. It is the aim of the poet to bring to the fore this contemptible, shabby and disgusting truth. But even after two thousand years the aims of the poet cannot be confined to such a presentation. This is certainly not the end of *Raghuvansha.* In reality the poet is warning tyrannical and licentious rulers that if they do not undergo self-reformation they would meet the same doom which the last ruler Agnivarsha of the great Raghuvansh dynasty met. They would have to lick the dust.

Reasons of becoming an Unrighteous Ruler

First of all let us have a look, through the eyes of the poet, at the reasons which transform a decently bred, sagacious and sensible king into a tyrant, amorous, liberative and unprincipled king. The reasons are:

1. Fortunes or Wealth. Intoxication evoked by fortunes and wealth puffs up ego and gives rise to various vices such as not to own and admit the wrongs done, to be indifferent to principles and stick to one's wrong actions with zeal and jealousy. These very vices showed their heads in the King Dushyanta. Thus, knowingly, he did not recognise Shakuntala. Ego makes man numb to all unpleasant information. In the same way, intoxication caused by fortunes makes the king numb to the sensation of right and wrong, justice and injustice, morality and immorality.

2. ***Too Much Passion for Love and Pleasure.*** This vice makes even a renowned and traditional king follow a wrong path. Knowing very well that elephant killing is prohibited as per scriptures, Dashratha shot a penetrating arrow on an unseen person, Shravan Kumar, after hearing a sound made by him. In this way he committed an abominable sin of killing the only support of his parents. Pleasure of hunting and the pride of being a good warrior made Dashratha a seeker of short-lived satisfaction of flesh and blood. Over-indulgence made him a murderer.

3. ***Perpetual Indulgence in Vices.*** Perpetual indulgences in vices makes the king completely charmed by them, so much so that he forget his duties. Such kings, seekers of the pleasure and satisfaction of the five senses, remain engulfed in the vices and luxuries and leave the administration in the hands of his ministers. Fondness of Dashratha for hunting, a pleasure game, made him insensible to take stock of the situation and put a check on his insatiable enjoyment in hunting.

4. ***Hereditary Trouble-free Kingship.*** Agnivarsha after inheriting a trouble-free and prosperous empire from his father Sudarshna thought it a means to vices. Easy come easy go. He forgot his duty to nurture the inherited empire because he thought it was God's bounty. So he did nothing to maintain the *status quo* of what he had received from his father. Nadir was bound to come. Agnivarsha started moving towards a gradual but sure downfall. Fortunes received effortlessly became the cause of his indulgence in vices. Public welfare was the first victim and bad became worse.

Steps to Curb the Unbridled Activities of a King

The following steps can go a long way to cut such rulers and administrators to size and to check their unbridled activities :

(a) Advice, discipline, learning, courtesy and education. Learning and counselling were vital in moulding an able administrator and they did play a significant role in bringing back an astray and fallen administrator on the right track. A would-be king was exposed to social and physical sciences, weaponry, scriptures and epics. He was made adept in the art of state-craft. This sowed the seeds of an able ruler and thereby as future well-wisher of his subjects. This grooming made the future king win over all temptations and vices. Hidden and indestructible knowledge of scriptures and sobriety were the sureties of public good. Kautilya has illustrated this by citing examples of various renowned kings namely Dandakya Bhoj, Videh Karal, Sauveer Raj Azbindoo, Ravana, Duryodhana, and so on, who fell easy preys to temptations and vices and had to suffer the consequences. They failed to rule well and perished. They paid no heed to advice and counselling. They thought themselves above the shortcomings of flesh and treated themselves invincible. They flouted all principles and trampled the green grass of righteousness to its pale death. They suffered and met their doom sooner or later. So much so they became villainous characters of history. This shift in their character establishes the importance of advice, discipline, learning, courtesy and education.

(b) Religious instructor, family priest, adviser and minister. Religious instructor, family, priest, adviser and minister played a vital role in counselling the ruler and make him weigh all pros and cons of the matter and then take decision. They helped in keeping the king well principled and never allowed him to trespass the limits which might harm the general public. They worked as the extra head and heart of the king. These able helpers helped him in the smooth running of the affairs of the State. Kautilya played a vital role and an unparalleled part to build the Maurya Empire. The throne went to the ablest person as per the assent and advice of these able advisers. King Dashratha used to go for hunting only after seeking the advice of his ministers. The stricken and confused Dushyanta consulted the priest and solved his dilemma to come out of his oblivion when he had failed to recognise Shakuntala.

(c) Public. General public is instrumental in keeping even the despots in check. In monarchy as well as in democracy the rulers find it difficult to flout public opinion. Powers have been entrusted in the hands of administrators to rule well for the betterment of the people. Rulers are only trustees. If they act contrary to this, public wrath erupts. This public wrath is the ultimate controller. A sagacious ruler wins the heart of the public by his extraordinary qualities of head and heart. Then nobody can uproot such a king. If a ruler, who is only a trustee, gets swollen by the powers he wields, he is either finished by the public or he goes in the clutches of the enemies. But one thing is certain that he is finished. Beauty and brawn cannot stern the ongoing currents of public wrath.

Peoples Ways of Expressing Public Wrath

According to Kalidasa, people express their anger, wrath and dissatisfaction through various ways. They are:

(a) Stricture, blame, censure. Public accusation and censure unleash great power to keep the ruler in check. Sri Rama himself acknowledges it as a potent weapon in the hands of public. A public accusation and censure forced Sri Rama to renounce his innocent wife Sita and send her to the jungle. Even an upright king Sri Rama found it difficult to swim against the currents of public opinion. He had to bow to the expectations of his people. Public censure helped the king named Az to do his duties and reject the idea to die after the death of his beloved wife Indumati. In the interest of his people he did forego his personal whims and desires. So the very fear of public accusation and blame makes a ruler duty-conscious.

(b) Criticism. Intelligentia could criticise the misdeeds of the king and express its anger and disagreement. Balmiki expressed in no uncertain terms his anger and disagreement when Sri Rama renounced Sita. She herself criticised the step taken by her husband simply to appease public sentiments. Certainly such open and healthy criticism gives jolts to the ruler and he tries to reform. Healthy criticism shows light and it helps the ruler to think over the steps he has taken. It makes him wiser. It pricks his conscience and rational point of views may prevail ultimately. The king is after all a human being, and as such, may become emotional and sentimental. Criticism comes handy for his rescue and he gets guided by his brain and not by heart. In *Abhigyanshakuntlam* the wrong deeds of the king were criticised in the context of Shakuntala's refutation. The king was given a sugar-coated dose :

> "O King, must you insult the saint who has given you
> his daughter and increased your grandeur !"

Indirectly these were sarcastic remarks emanating from truth and thus had their impact. Look at the penetrating satire hidden in the words when the king was further confronted :

> "A person who has never practised knavery is a liar a person's words who is past master in wickedness are valid proofs."

Thus, healthy criticism can prevent the ruler from passing strictures against a gentleman who is under clouds of unfounded suspicion because of some rash and irrational public opinion.

(c) Picketing and Protest. People were free to sit in protest before the palace doors to register their distrust, anger and anguish against the administration. We come across such instances in the reign of Sri Rama. A Brahmin whose only son had met an untimely death took the corpse and placed it on the ground before the palace doors. He started shouting and put the blame for that untimely death on the ruler. He had the guts to protest against the inefficiency of the ruler and his wrong deeds which had provoked the gods and their wrath came like a bolt from the blue in the shape of untimely death of the son of the Brahmin. It was the belief of the people that unnatural things could never happen if the king was righteous and upright. The picketing and protest was to make the ruler vigilant.

(d) Curse. Curse uttered by the down-troddens is powerful enough to destabilise any government. Crying Andh Muni hurled the curse on Dashratha and the king accepted it without any hitch. This very curse might have caused ripples that destroyed the very foundations of Ayodhya and made it splendourless and brought about the end of the great Raghuvansha dynasty. Impact of a curse is directly proportionate to the purity of heart of the down-troddens.

(e) All Consuming Energy and Fire of Ascetic. According to Kalidasa, peace loving ascetics have all consuming energy and fire. When provoked they unleash that heavenly energy and fire. This fire can consume even the king who dispenses justice and awards punishment. Offsprings of the King Sagar were eliminated by this fire. This very energy caused Priyavanda to take birth as an elephant. This latent heat punished Shakuntala for trespassing her limits as she had invoked the wrath of an ascetic by ignoring his presence. King Dilip remained issueless because of the curse hurled by an ascetic when his latent energy was provoked. Crime committed, willingly or unwillingly, cannot go unpunished.

(f) Distrust. A king bereft of public trust and faith cannot remain on the saddle perpetually. Vote of confidence can make or mar any government in a democracy. The ruler too has to win the trust and faith of his people from time to time. To win this trust Sita had to enter the fire and ultimately enter and disappear in the earth's womb. Sri Rama asked Sita to win over the trust of the people of Ayodhya regarding her character as because the people did not trust the fire-test which she underwent in Lanka in the presence of Rama and his army. Thus, we see a ruler has to win over the confidence and faith of his people time and again and it can be a continuous process.

(g) Natural Calamities. Nature hurls her curses in the shape of famine, flood and epidemics. When people fail and find themselves helpless to put checks on the tyrants and the corrupt rulers, nature comes for their rescue. Natural calamities are warnings to the ruler to mend his ways and rule with the force of principles. Indians have deep-rooted faith that when the cup of sins committed by man gets filled upto the brim, repercussions flare up. Reactions take the shape of natural calamities. The ruler is responsible for the good conduct of his people. He is to see that people in general live a righteous life. Indirectly it is the duty of the ruler to be righteous and dutiful. It is a two-way traffic. Like ruler, like subject. The ruler is responsible for immoral and unethical acts of his people. The poet goes a step further when he says if blossoms do not bloom and change into fruits in nature even then the ruler is to blame. He is at fault. All this is incorporated in the epics to stress the role of the ruler to run the administration smoothly.

(h) Regulation, Destiny and Fruits of the Deeds. Indians have staunch faith in the presence of some overseeing power controlling the affairs of this cosmos. Man can reach lofty heights and be like God. This all pervasive power awards fruits according to the deeds done by human beings. A king is not above the law. Laws to punish the ordinary people are equally applicable to him and if he flouts principles and goes morally and ethically corrupt, fate regulates everything. Kalidasa gives expression to this great Indian philosophical idea time and again in his poetical works. Immoral kings cannot survive the regulations of nature. Their dynasties disappear into thin air for want of heirs. King Dilip got heirs to perpetuate their dynasties only after purifying themselves of the sins committed. Misdeeds done by the rulers render their spouses barren. This is natural justice. The death of Agnivarsha sounded the death knell of his great dynasty.

Look at the end of the glorious Raghuvansha dynasty. With the passage of time, the glory and splendour of this dynasty changed into a flutter of the dying lamp. It could extinguish any time. Regulations by the overseeing Power convert glory into dust. Principle-flouter Agnivarsha failed to get any heir in spite of having many wives. The king is never dead. To save the kingdom from anarchy, a successor is a must. So his pregnant wife was enthroned with the hope that in due course of time she would deliver a heir. Seeds are sown with the hope that they would sprout and this earth would be green once again. Hope sustains life. Man proposes, God disposes. Misdeeds and bad actions cannot bear fruits. This way the poet's works give message and warnings to the unbridled State authority to impose self-imposed fetters and regulate itself according to moral and ethical laws and be the saviour and well-wisher of the general public.

Our democratic set-up is under stress. We elect our representatives with the hope that one day something good would turn up. The wife of Agnivarsha may deliver a righteous heir to the throne. People are still optimistic. The future and success of democracy lies in the righteous actions of the elected representatives. Unfortunately these representatives have turned into power hungry, vice-seekers, corrupt and selfish to the core. Criminal tendencies have cropped up in them. A vital question arises—is it possible to put checks on these corrupt representatives? Is it possible to put a fence around their unbridled behaviour and conduct? This is a question to ponder over. This stark reality crops up in all ages. This dilemma faces the people invariably. Even dynastic grandeur, greatness, glory and popularity cannot save a corrupt, power hungry and swollen-headed ruler. Agnivarsha from the illustrious Raghuvansha dynasty met his nadir because he flouted principles and natural regulations. Fire of the wrath of people consume any and every unrighteous ruler. Public welfare should be enthroned at the top in the heart of a ruler. If this is not so, he is doomed. Through his writings Kalidasa gives a pat to the upright rulers and warns the corrupt ones. Scanning done by him of the various unrighteous rulers has given us a crystal clear picture of the maladies marring the lives of these rulers. He has also short-listed some harsh methods to counter these maladies so as to bring about a transparent administration and establish a welfare State. He has very clearly put forward duties and rights of the ruler and the ruled.

3

People's Voice in Vedic Political System

Chandrakant Shukla

The king was selected by consensus and people's views were given due consideration.

Editor

When we hear the word State, a certain image of an institution appears in our mind. The initial, albeit undeveloped form of this image is found in the Vedic period. The extended Aryan family which was also called *Griha* or *Kul* can be considered to form the basis of the Vedic State. A number of related households, i.e., the *Grihas* or *Kuls* together constituted a village. A group of several villages was called a *Vish* and these *Vishs* collectively formed a *Jana*. The area occupied by the *Janas* was called a *Janapad*. These *Janapads* can be accepted as an equivalent of the modern State. The word *Rajya* or State does not specifically occur in the Vedic period and the actual word is *Rashtra* or country. Reflecting on the word *Rashtra*, Rahul Sanskrityayan writes: "The *Rashtra* and *Janapads* were synonymous in meaning. *Janapad* implies the importance of the *Janas* while the word *Rashtra* accords importance to the noble men. The head of the *Rashtra* was called *Raja*, i.e., the king. The other words for *Raja* used in the Vedic period are *Samrat*, *Swarat*, *Shas*, *Ishan*, *Bhupati*, etc. (*Rigvedic Aryans* 123-24).

Selection of the King

A specific procedure was adopted in the Vedic era for selection of the king and it was superior than even the modern democratic system. The king was selected through a consensus of the people. The institution which provided a forum for conducting deliberations amongst all the people of the *Vish* was known as *Samiti.*

Samiti was the supreme and all powerful body. Almost everyone attended its meeting and when someone's name was proposed he was chosen as the king if there was unanimity. In view of the limited population and smaller geographical area occupied by a state it was feasible to adopt this method in those days.

Distinction between Sabha and Samiti

Apart from the *Samiti* there was another institution which was called *Sabha.* No clear distinction has been explained between the two at any place. It, however, appears that the *Samiti* was an institution formed by all the people of the state while the *Sabha* consisted only of selected representatives. Differentiating between the two institutions, A.B. Keith writes:

> The *Samiti* was the assembly of the people to do business of tribals and the *Sabha* denoted the place of assembly which served besides as a centre of social gatherings.
>
> *Cambridge History of India,* Vol. I, (p. 96)

The political power was vested in the *Samiti* while the *Sabha* was a representative body of the learned members of the society with very little political authority. These two bodies may be compared with the Lok Sabha and Rajya Sabha of our present parliamentary system or the House of Commons and House of Lords of the British. In later times corruption raised its ugly head in the *Sabha* and it has been mentioned by Patanjali in his work. The word *Sabhya* (civilized) is derived from *Sabha* itself. Thus, notion is that civilized person is one who participates in the meetings of the *Sabha.* According to Patanjali, the word *Sabha* cannot possibly have a feminine form because the woman who goes to a *Sabha* will not remain civilized any more. A somewhat modified form of the *Vedic Sabhas* can still be seen amongst some tribal societies of Chotanagpur.

The Rights of a *Samiti*

According to the *Rigveda* (10-191) and the *Atharvaveda* (6-64), the *Samiti* used to deliberate over the affairs of the State. It was a very powerful body which kept a check even on the kings. Political issues of all kinds were discussed in this forum and every member was free to express his opinion. But it was always kept in mind that nothing remained under dispute at the end. Maximum effort was made to arrive at a decision through consensus.

Any citizen could become a king if chosen by the *Samiti.* Kings were selected in much the same manner as a president or a prime minister can be selected in the modern democratic nations from amongst the citizens. When the people had selected someone as a king, they presented him with an armlet made of Palash wood. It was called a *Mani.* The six categories of the highest officials and scholars, also known as the makers of the nation, were: the treasurer, chief of the military force, the priest, *Gramani* or village chief, the diplomatic representative and the spy. The prominence was, however, given to the chief of the military, the priest and the village chief. They worked together with the king in performance of the administrative duties. The kings were also given a royal crown. It was made from the skin of a lion, a tiger or a crocodile. His special insignia also figured on the crown. There is a historical significance of the use of the skin of the above mentioned animals for making a crown. It was supposed to be a way of reminding the king that he too must become courageous like these creatures (*Atharvaveda,* 4.8.4).

According to the *Rigveda* (10-173) and the *Atharvaveda* (8-87, 80), the citizens bestowed all love and affection while appointing a king. They told him to remain firm like the mountain and Indra. "Just as the heaven is the earth, the world and the mountains have fixed positions, may this king, the representative of the people also establish himself firmly" is how the prayer goes. The gods—Varuna, Indra, Agni and Brahmanspati—were invoked to seek a long life for the king: "May you rule here for one millennium as an able king" (*Atharvaveda*-3.4.7). The people used to say to the king that you defeat the enemies without any restriction and vanquish the pride of all those too who behaved like enemies. Everyone respects you and the *Samiti* appoints you for the well-being of all.

The king was also coronated after his appointment. The rituals which formed a part of this ceremony have survived till today in some form or other in the religious and social events. The king used to take a vow during the coronation ceremony that he would work towards providing care, food, security, etc., to the people. He would establish a rule of law and punish all the offenders.

Duties of the King

Duties of the king were of a far more complex and difficult nature. His primary duty was to conduct battles and protect the people from aggression. During the times of peace, he was actively involved in creating harmony amongst the people. His duty included settlement of disputes and to provide justice. He was also duty bound to work for inculcating religiousity amongst his people and for seeking their participation in various rituals, etc.

It was the *Dharma* of the king to be present in the meeting of the *Samiti*. Only one who fulfilled this prerequisite was considered as a true king (*Rigveda* 9.92.6).

Taxation System

The king was the main responsible person for collecting the taxes in the Vedic era. He was assisted in this task by the head of the households and the village chief. The *Vish*, i.e., a single group of villages, has also been referred as *Balihut* or that which collects taxes. It is, however, unknown as in which form this tax was collected. It appears from the text of the *Atharvaveda* that the wealth of the whole nation was considered to belong to everyone and the king was expected to protect this wealth and other proceeds (*Atharvaveda* 5.4.4).

Removal of a King

It can be inferred from the Vedas that if the king was not able to rule properly, the *Samiti* had the right to depose him. However, if the people were to repose confidence in his gain, he would be made the king once more. Despite this, it also appears that the kingship was hereditary. Often, the appropriate successor in the royal linkage had his name proposed by the State council and the people used to accept it.

Relevance in Today's Times

Thus, we see that kings were elected through a very simple process in the Vedic era but once appointed, he had to shoulder many responsibilities. Though he was the king, people had the right to remove him from the kingship if he deviated from his duties. This is exactly the chief shortcoming of the present day democracy. If we compare the prevailing democratic system with the monarchial system of those days, we can say with confidence that the latter was far more superior. Admittedly, the modern democratic system has provisions for effecting a change in the government through popular vote, they have not turned out to be effective in actual practice. The reason for this lies mainly in the vast size of the State in terms of area as well the population apart from a growing greed for power and posts. The small states of the Vedic times made it possible for all citizens to assemble together for taking the decision for deposing a king. It also seems the primary reason when Plato considered that ideally the population of a state should be 5040. This number might have been further lower in the Vedic period. Switzerland still provides for election of all the officials of a canton through a similar process whereby all the people collect at one place for this purpose. The public has a right to recall these officials if it feels unsatisfied with their performance by repeating this process. The constitution of Switzerland has incorporated these processes known as referendum or recall. The Swiss cantons are quite small in size and it is somehow possible to manage his system. It is, however, simply impossible to adopt it in big states. Nonetheless the Vedic system can be modified after giving the matter a serious thought and the experiences gained so far are also kept in mind and appropriate conclusions are drawn. It is possible for the big State to absorb its qualitative features. The Vedic system may be accepted in various forms like the Gandhiji's dream of *Ram Rajya* or an administrative system based upon the village *Panchayats*. The positive merits of the Vedic system, if incorporated effectively in the governance of modern India would surely enable it to develop into a model, ideal State. In any case the dream of achieving the *Ram Rajya* or the Ideal State cannot be realised unless the aberrations of the present day democratic system are eliminated. One cannot, therefore, dispute the necessity of a reconsideration of these issues on the basis of the Vedic system and later day expenses.

4

Bhisma's Description of Democracy

Brajakishore Swain

Monarchs in the Indian tradition sought cooperation of the people hence functioned as a democracy.

Editor

During the time of the Mahabharata and in the periods preceding and succeeding to it, the essential value of a democratic order was not altogether unknown in spite of the fact that the monarchical system of government was the order of the day. It is beyond doubt that democratic norms operated in a disguised form in the polity both in the enactment and execution of law and its judicial interpretation. Adequate measures were prescribed and adopted both for the prevention and eradication of administrative and legal lapses. Ordinary law of the land was sufficient to deal with eradication, whereas amendment of the existing convention required a popular mandate. These democratic norms very often remained suppressed under the might and majesty of the royal grandeur, but at the same time it is also true that people, in those days, enjoyed ample freedom, scope and privilege to contribute their administrative experience, constitutional wisdom and political consciousness to the decision-making process. It is interesting to mark that people embraced monarchy without bothering the least for democratic system of governance. Democracy remained in the domain of ideas without getting a chance to enter the world of reality.

The system of government operating under the name of monarchy was of a different kind. It was not a synonym for tyrannical rule resulting in oppression of the people. Rather it was purely value-based and stood for an altogether different connotation from what it implies today. By laying emphasis on the aristocratic background of the ruler, his individual merit apart, the society strove to create the ruling class, which by tune, temperament, education and training, was fit to shoulder the onerous task of nation-building. It is a matter of regret that nowadays scant respect is shown to those qualities at the time of recruiting the higher scholars of civil service or offering ministerial berth to politicians.

Things degenerated with the passage of time as follows:

(a) *First,* the ruling class started interfering in the social life of the individual which the rulers of the Mahabharata age left totally untouched. The centre of gravity began shifting from the polity to the individual—the rulers of the period attaching more importance to royal vanity and the consolidation of their individual authority. In the process the sacrosanctness of rulership was destroyed.

(b) *Second,* in modern times the ruler resorts to actions to hoodwink the ruled even by distortion of facts which was quite unthinkable in the days of Mahabharata. Rather hard facts were made to reach the people in a way which may be called a sort of referendum in modern times. This degeneration is the direct consequence of the devaluation of political institutions and lack of true leadership on the part of modern politicians entrusted with the responsibility of shaping the destiny of the nation.

In the *Mahabharata,* Kubera, while giving his political discourses to Yudhisthira, has made the latter acquainted with the great democratic tradition of India of that period. Subsequently, Bhishma followed this view of Kubera. The present study is an attempt to give a bird's eye-view of the present-day relevance of that great tradition.

Bhisma was excellent and invincible both in the art of war and the science of government. A great rationalist and unparalleled sentinel of national unity and integrity he has chosen the State and not the individual as the focal point of his political thought. As he has put it, whatever may be the purpose of the ruler, he must have some weaknesses for democratic way of life. Under the monarchical form, the ruler poses as the representative of God on the earth whereas in a democratic system he poses as the servant of the people, with whom the real power of governance resides. In this context many intricate questions may arise regarding the purpose of the polity and the stability thereof. Therefore, with great caution Kubera has used *lokatantra* in place of *ganatantra* as the more appropriate nomenclature for a popular government. *Ganatantra* rests on in quantity and majority whereas in *lokatantra* there is a positive tilt towards values. To be specific, he is more interested in the legal side of the administration while he has greater faith in the principles of morality. In this system of government law and morality are complement and supplement each other. There is a particular growth of realism buttressed by idealism. In case of a clash between the two—realism and idealism, the former is generally given precedence, but it becomes quite difficult to preserve its value for the posterior generation. At this critical juncture it is necessary to formulate a set of pragmatic rules which, while being realistic in character meet the exigencies of the hour, also take care to keep idealism intact. But at times the ruler is forced to make some sort of compromise with values or principles of morality to save the polity and society from immediate decay or devastation.

Five Pillars of Democracy (*Lokatantra*)

Kuber (followed by Bhisma) prescribes five pillars on which the edifice of *lokatantra* should stand.

Though *lokatantra* had greater fascination for Kubera than *rajatantra.* He is suspicious about the stability of the former and that is why in the whole political discourse he attaches primary importance to the fundamental issue of political stability—the issue which haunts all conscious citizens of this country all the time. He has termed this administrative stability as *dhrti.* According to him, since democracy stands on freedom of speech and expression it is not unlikely that there may be difference of popular opinion on any particular issue. While trying to create public opinion for developmental schemes the ruler may face this difference even in a very violent form. But if this difference is constructive and suggestive in nature, it must be taken cognisance of irrespective of whether it is on the safe side of idealism or not. But it does not imply that the State is bound to accept all such suggestions or criticism. For the greater interest of the polity these can be accepted and implemented within the frame-work of legal principles, social customs and traditional conventions. Or else the stability of the State will face serious challenges and, as one knows, political instability will make people restless. Thus, instead of giving them the time and opportunity to think about the State and its future, frequent change of government will lead to a breakdown of the whole political structure. A harmonious balance between realism and idealism is the only solution to this fundamental issue of any polity.

Second, efficiency (means stability) is indispensable for *lokatantra.* But it is the other name of cruelty in the lexicon of politics. Indians need no illustration of this hard reality of politics when instability has made many efficient rulers cruel and thereby unacceptable to the people. But the efficiency of Kubera's description is not confined to the exhibition of military valour or the ability to maintain internal order by suppressing crime. It rather stands for the popularity of the ruler—how far is the ruler acceptable to the masses by his people-oriented programme and objective and his real strength rests on the love he begets from the people over whom he rules. Kubera further clarifies that people-oriented administration leads not only to popular support but to political stability as well. Efficiency, according to him, is rather a stepping stone to stability if properly used by the ruler. In trying to define the word in concrete terms he says that administration is efficient where the ruler exerts tremendous moral influence on the people, the ruler and the ruled move together in the same direction and the latter are capable of appreciating the deeds of the former by their wisdom. Lack of coordination and understanding between the two leads to *coup d'etat* and the result is obvious.

Then comes the question of *national integration* at the third place which may create surprise in modern minds that how could such a vital issue be put in the third position by no less a person than Bhisma whereas in modern times it gets precedence over all other aspects of our polity. Here a distinction between the meaning of this word and its modern connotation needs illucidation. For us today, the term national integration is confined to the maintenance of territorial sovereignty in a defined geographical area only whereas for Bhisma it signified things far beyond and much above the physical level. It was rather a synonym for a sort of emotional and physical cohesion between man and man that contributed immensely towards the achievement of a such goal. Of course, in the ancient agrarian society such an attachment of man with man was easier than the present day industrial society since the former was based on mutual cooperation while the latter, for its onward march and even sustenance, depends upon cut-throat competition. To make things more complex for a just social order, the present governments seem to take keen interest in the industrial sector even at the cost of agriculture. The government along with the machinery was entrusted with the responsibility of implementation of the programmes of the State, encourage industrial and technological growth with special emphasis on the financial aspects. As a result of this the agricultural sector suffered a lot since they take the former as more profitable than the latter, and a greater sign of development to compare with the world economic standard. The consequence was obvious—the most vital element of any stable polity, i.e., emotional bond among citizens was nipped in the bud. For the modern State national integration is a precondition of stability but for Kubera (or for Bhisma) it was *vice versa*. Stability, according to him, is the fertile soil on which the delicate plant of liberty can ground when watered by the efficiency of the government.

The fourth elementary feature of *lokatantra* is the performance of policies and their acceptability to the people. Of course, Kubera is not opposed to the use to harsh State measures in response to the exigencies of the time; but he reiterates that such measure should be adopted with a broader perspective so that at no point of time should any action be construed as the will of the brute majority where the whisper of the minority has not been heard. Second, the State should not confine its activities merely to the preservation of *status quo* which is totally detrimental to the growth of any developing economy like ours; rather steps should be taken in such a way that the nation can march forward on the path of progress and prosperity while maintaining an ideal and harmonious balance between the immediate need of the people and the ultimate goal of the polity.

Last but not the least Kubera talks of security as an essential feature of any polity worth the name. But his definition of the term is totally different from that of modern policymakers—it was, to him, always defensive rather than offensive. He opines that an exhibition of military prowess against a neighbouring State is in no case an indication of international civility on the part of a State. Foreign policy should rather be the accumulated expression of the cultural heritage and historical tradition of a State which, in all normal welfare States, preach peace and harmony in international relations. Moreover, closer cooperation and clear understanding between neighbouring States strengthen the internal stability of each individual State. Kubera proceeds further by saying that even in case any civilised State is forced to fight a defensive war the spoils thereof should be treated as the private property of the victor; rather it should find a place in the relief-fund of the State to meet the calamitous situations.

Thus, in sum, it is quite pertinent that the lines containing the definition of *lokatantra,* according to Kubera, need to be maintained for rather a clearer understanding of what it actually stood for:

Yudhiṣṭhira dhṛtir dākṣyaṃ deśakālaparākramāh
Lokatantravidhānanām eṣa pancavidho vidhiḥ

—Mahabharata 3.159.1

युधिष्ठिर घृतिर्दाक्ष्यं देशकालपराक्रमाः।
लोकतन्त्रविधानानामेष पञ्चविधो विधिः ।।

—महाभारत ३.१५६.१

5

The Moral Imperative in Good Governance

Navlata

> Welfare of the people can only be secured when the rulers and administrators serve with an attitude of *tyaga* and public good. This moral imperative is central to good governance.
>
> *Editor*

The world is a very complex place to live in. The means are not in tendem with the ends. On one hand, we want to reach lofty heights and aspire to realise the dream of one world government but on the other hand, we are too much attached to materialism and individual selfish interests rule supreme. We are living with contradictions. We are being burnt by the heat of the fire we have ourselves kindled to enlighten and warm ourselves. The traditions, the ideals and the institutions of the past are our rich legacy. Our *Sanatana Dharma* is not a thing to be put on and put off like Sunday clothes. It permeates the whole fabric of our life. Glamour and glorification of material prosperity has modified our aims and ambitions. A new orientation has been given to Indian life. The ideal now admired is that of success or the ability which produces success. This cult of success has dazzled our eyes and we have started looking down upon the old and eternal values. Moral values have lost their charm and we consider them baseless and care not for them. Science has shattered our faith in God and with this eternal values have received a crude jolt. We are too absorbed in material pursuits to strive for spiritual heights. Our faith in ourselves, in God and in everything else has been shattered to pieces and scepticism has enveloped us completely and not an aperture is left for fresh air of eternal values to come in and rejuvenate us. Even policies to influence national consciousness are seen with suspicion. They fail to inspire confidence. Politics of self-appeasement has cast a slur on the names of the leaders. India ranks number six amongst the most corrupted nations of the world. Known as the store-house of truth, knowledge, morals and unity India has fallen in the fathomless chasms of degradation.

It is highly regrettable that hyperbolic slogans to ameliorate the condition of the masses have remained hollow slogans. They are ideals but hollow within. Doubt has gripped the masses in general. Government has lost confidence and faith of the people. Dirty and cut-throat competition to acquire more and more material gains has given a blow to values of life which are prerequisites for individual and national progress and prosperity. Eternal *Sanatana* values are the very basis of happiness, prosperity and existence of the entire universe. In this sentient and practically lifeless world man is the centre of all thinking. *Sat* is the nature of matter. All efforts of man are directed towards salvation and bliss. Even inferior creatures are nurturing 'swadharma'. Expression of *Sat* is *Dharma*. Values and *Dharma* are one. The ideal of *Dharma* symbolises the eternal values. Testimony of this fact is the conduct of the best of men. God Krishna says in *Gita* (3/21):

> "Whatsoever a great man doeth, that other men also do;
> the standard he setteth up, by that the people go."

In developed and developing nations and especially in India which has spiritual background, eternal values are the very basis of man and the whole biological creation. Actions, deeds and conduct of the creamiest of the creamy layer become *Lokadharma*.

Man by nature wants to reach higher and higher rungs of progress. This continuous upward march is his rising. Man meandering through mundane and earthly honour reaches the zenith of heavenly glory and this is called salvation. This is the final stage. Reaching there man has nothing more to reach. Acquisition of this perfection is installation of *Sat*. Unattached enjoyment and renunciation have in their womb the seeds of salvation. Totality and completeness of life lies in the homogenous amalgamation of worldly attainment and other worldly attainment. Unattached enjoyment and renunciation ultimately bring man to that stage where the entire world looks like a family to him. Internationalism, plugging the gap between individual and the whole and devoid of differences of castes and creeds, does display that picture of the world where confluence of harmony, compassion and love drench the minds of men with the ideas of world peace, world well-being and oneness. *Sanatana* values inculcate such feelings. The ultimate path is there but we are to tread it.

Philosophers of other nations do believe consciously or subconsciously that eternal values are indispensable for the all round well-being of the entire world. Kant and Plato do define *Shiva Sankalp* in the context of moral values.

In every society social arrangements and codes of conduct have been drafted to control and circumscribe human conduct. The basic social set-up in the Indian tradition in based on the division of *Varnas* and *Ashramas.* People intellectually sound, having leadership qualities and highly developed sensibility were entrusted the responsibility of running the system. It was expected of the rulers to establish an administration ever-engaged in the activities of welfare of the public and thereby lay the foundation of such a stable, free and fearless society where everybody had equal opportunities to express his or her heart out as per social decorum and norms. The aim of this government was not self-service but service of the people. In ancient India, the king was the fountain head of authority who by appointing trustworthy officials used to have close contact with the masses and worked for their benefit and well-being. There was practically no difference between monarchy and democracy. It was because the king was a fatherly figure and he looked after his subjects as a father looks after his offsprings. He ruled justly and earned their unflinching confidence, loyalty, unconditional support and cooperation. In spite of being the centre of power he ruled with the concurrence of his ministers and secretaries and never went beyond his limits. He remained circumscribed by the sense of his duties. Detailed study of such a rule and governance is available in *Ramayana, Mahabharata, Manusmiriti* and Kautilya's *Arthsastra. Manusmiriti* propounds that destruction befalls that State where unrighteousness rules. Where truth is stifled nature's wrath comes down like a bolt from the blue. Gods hurl down their venom and calamities and sufferings visit that kingdom in succession. The whole administrative machinery including the king are equally responsible for this. It clearly depicts that both the king and the people are equal participants in administration. Is it not democracy? Kautilya gives full importance to the opinions and suggestions of the State officials and recommends that the king pays appropriate attention to them. Officials are the ears and eyes of a king. Kautilya has depicted the picture of a society where all round development—social, economic, political and spiritual—can be guaranteed. By doing so he has presented guidelines and codes of conduct for the ruler, his ministers, his officials and the public in general.

The present democratic superstructure owes much to Kautilya's *Arthashastra.* The difference is that we have a totally people-oriented political set-up whereas in the past there was limited monarchy. Values are part and parcel of both the systems. Different thinkers have given us different definitions of democracy. All opinions agree at one point that the best set-up is that where public welfare is supreme. The responsibility of the governed is not less in any way. Without public awakening and vigilance, the administration cannot realise its goals easily. Democracy is a confluence of similar values and united efforts put in by the government and the public. Without their coordination and mutual participation, protection of public interest, provision equal opportunities to all, utilisation of human resources to the maximum and in the best possible manner and the creation of a congenial and healthy social environment wedded to values is not possible.

Democracy is by the people, of the people and for the people. The best thing about it is that the ruler is from the very public. First of all he is a member of the society and then the administrator. He is well versed with the needs and problems of the general public as he can feel their pulse easily. He can solve them accordingly. This is possible only when the administrator considers himself to be a public servant and not a boss to wield the rod of authority. This requires a plethora of qualities. He should be upright, honest, righteous, humane, wedded to values, just, transparent and truthful. Determination, objectivity and not subjectivity are second to none. Success of a government lies in its ability to use minimum of economic resources and show maximum output. Able, efficient, diligent and selfless officials are the brain and spinal chord of a democracy. One can evaluate governance by examining how much responsible and awakened the masses are. Success of governance is directly proportionate to the degree of coordination between people and government. Democracy is a delicate plant watered by collective awakening of the people and government policies. Good governance through the expression of human moral values plays a vital role in the installation of *Sat*. Value neutrality in public administration is not-desirable.

Faith in truth and moral awakening are natural to man which impart him the sixth sense to distinguish between what is wrong and what is right. But many external forces and emotional human flaws do influence his conduct. This implants the seed of moral, social and economic crimes. These flaws are lust, anger, arrogance and malice. They kill the spirit of *Sanatana* values. State controls play their part at this juncture. Through direct and indirect programmes, media, workshops, camps and other means public and national awakening is sought to be created. It awakens the whole machinery and common people from their slumber and they once again become vigilant. The State also reminds people of their obligations. To eliminate social and economic crimes the sceptre does use its authority. Harsh measures become indispensable in the case of moral turpitude. Discerning intellect and wisdom here comes for rescue. Every effort is made to keep the society intact and protect the well-established social set-up. The organisational structure of Indian society is faultless in principle but there are many complications and contradictions in practice. This results into corrupt administration and unrestrained politics and is reflected in people's moral degradation. In such an atmosphere it is very difficult for a honest, morally sound and principled administrator to work with dignity and honour. For a corrupt official it is a matter of shame and self-analysis because public welfare is the moral and constitutional responsibility of officials. The second practical difficulty is stringent control of government on administration. Generally political influence and concealed pressure do not give the official a free hand to implement the schemes in such a way as to benefit each segment of society. Such a difficulty occurs mostly at the time of economic frauds. The veil of greed covers everything and especially public welfare fades into nothingness. In the guise of public service, officials fill their own coffers and become parasites. For their self-interests they do not hesitate to exploit the nation. When this happens it causes heart-burning and revolt in the hearts of the people. Unconsciously moral values get a collective beating and get eroded.

To realise the goal of 'well-being for all', discerning wisdom, insight and self-discipline are indispensable. Good and bad governance can make or mar a society. A society which is submerged in the fulfilment of self-interests thinks of attainment of materialistic gains by hook or by crook as the end all of values. Disintegration of domestic and social structure and problems of crimes and treason are taking hideous proportions. It is a contagious disease and administration is not left untouched. Appeasement of political leaders and misuse of the authority of the official and official machinery consume much of the efficiency of the government.

Everything is not lost. This is not the end of the tunnel. A small segment of administrators are still engaged in public service and are performing their duties faithfully and sincerely. Such officials fall prey to the wrath of their superiors and corrupt colleagues. They are mentally tortured and subject to all kinds of harassment. Instead of some rewards and public appreciation they are hounded and put in tight corners. In such a mesh of immorality it is difficult for the upright officials to save their skin. They either opt out or fall in line with their colleagues. The system stagnates and starts emitting foul smell. Honest and upright public servants languish in jails while the perpetrators of corruption flourish and enjoy life. It is something to ponder over. Good administrators should not be allowed to feel depressed and crestfallen.

Determination, will-power and stability of character are badly needed today. The noble words, 'truth always wins' inscribed on the Ashoka Chakra should jolt the dead conscience of the corrupt officials. There is need to pursue whole-heartedly the path of duty and the ideals set before governance. Today the police department is the most corrupt and degraded force in India. The oath undertaken at the time of entry into service to serve people honestly and sincerely is blissfully and conveniently forgotten. The ideals of 'परित्राणाय साधूनाम' should decorate the walls of the police stations. This ideal should merge with the very personality of the police officials. Police force should be an exemplary force.

Without changing the environment the idea of individual and national rise is unthinkable. Success of democracy and values depends on impartial and just administration. Men selecting administration as their fields of activities must keep in mind the following points :

1. The aim of governance is the all round well-being on social, economic and psychological levels.
2. Public awakening and their participation in administration should be welcomed.
3. In the administrative culture there should be forceful merger of service, time bound action and discipline.
4. Comprehensive knowledge of the problems and their solutions should be the second nature of the officials.
5. Constitution is ideal of administration but human welfare is supreme.

Every action done with wisdom, devotion and faith is the harbinger of self-satisfaction. Worldly disruptions, hardships and inconveniences are insignificant. Simple life, natural conduct, compasssionate and sympathetic attitude along with steadiness in dispensation of justice and care for eternal values in place of transitory gains are medals of an officer.

All round corruption is a deep-rooted menace, that has eaten into the vitals of society, distorted all values and made mincemeat of morality, truth and virtue. Ironically instead of fighting against the menace of corruption, our political leaders declare it a world-wide phenomenon and accept it as something inevitable. *Sanatana* values are moral imperatives. They are codes of conduct so to say. Welfare of the general public can only be secured when political bosses and administrators serve with an attitude of renunciation and detached enjoyment. Moral flavour is indispensable for good governance.

6

Checks and Balances of Governance in Ancient India as per the Mahabharata

Ram Prasad Gupta

The king in the Indian tradition was controlled by the Brahmin as well as the people. Indian monarchy was fundamentally different from the Western democracy. It was quasi-democracy.

Editor

We have been receiving oral knowledge from time immemorial. Variations in the same are inevitable. Distortions creep in unnoticed. Authentic and recognised volumes are difficult to find with the passage of time. *Manusmriti* was shorn off its verses and today we have only 10,000 *slokas* (verses) left whereas in the beginning there were one lakh *slokas*. The language pattern and combination of words went through a sea change and this must have altered the meaning also. Many old manuscripts have disappeared. Similarly *slokas* have been added to the *Mahabharata*. Discrepancies have percolated in these *slokas*. This trend certainly lessens the sanctity of *granthas* (volumes). Anyhow, strangely enough, our sacred *vedas* stood the test of time and distortions failed to make any impact on them. Their religious tinge acted like an armour which protected them from any change.

Literature reflects its age as it is embedded deep in its contemporary conditions. It is a mirror of society. *Mahabharata* was written after 2800 years of the actual battle having been fought. Still everything looks authentic. It speaks of acumen of the writer.

Epics cannot be history—merely, facts and figures. Imagination does play its part. Contemporary society supplies the subject matter but the wings of poesy can transport the writer to the fathomless past and the ravelled future. Poesy transcends the limits of time and space but the events of the *Mahabharata* are not figments of imagination. Ancient literature makes us acquainted with all aspects of human life.

Limits of Institution of Kingship

The King was not the law maker. He was to implement the law. In ancient India rules and regulations, laws and codes were framed by learned Brahmins. We have *Yagyavalkya Smriti, Prashar Smriti, Manusmriti, Vashistha Smriti,* and so on. Administration was the prerogative of the ruler. He implemented laws as per the guidelines propounded by the law makers. He could never assume the mantle of a dictator. We had 'Limited Monarchy'. The king (executive) and the learned Brahmins (legislative) had separate functions. Even then there was complete harmony, cooperation and coordination. The king could overrule if the laws were not as per the directives given in the contemporary *Smritis.* Good administration and glorious monarchy were guaranteed by the active coordination between the king and the Brahmins. *Purohita* too played a vital role. He was the chief adviser, guide and philosopher. In *Satyuga,* the king was non-existent as only the learned people inhabited the earth. There was no need of a governor. Mutual preservation of Dharma protected the masses (*Shanti Parva,* 59/14). Indian wisdom considers Dharma as the king of kings. Change is the law of nature. With the passage of time criminal tendencies got the upper hand. Then there arose the need of a king and administrator to uphold *Dharma* and to administer various punishments to the criminals, unrighteous and wicked people. It was a sort of contract. The king was elected to protect his masses, the country and the people willingly paid taxes. The ruler was a fatherly figure. Indian scriptures allow dismissal, exile and even death penalty to a despot. *Dharma* was the guiding spirit both for the governor and the governed. The king was always accountable and *dharma danda* (punishment) was always on his head. He could not be arbitrary and self-willed. It was obligatory for him to act according to the ordinances of *Dharma.* A punisher could be punished with the same *danda* with which he punishes others. Thus, we see a despot had no place in the Indian polity.

The *Mahabharata* boasts of perhaps the best definition of democracy—happiness of the king lies in the happiness of his people. His benefit lies in whatever is beneficial for his people. His interests do not exist (*Anushashan Parva,* 145). The king is responsible for everything (good or bad). No excuse can exempt him from his duties and responsibilities. He is to administer with the help of the Brahmins. These words are uttered by Kunti in the shape of a message to Yudhisthira. *Shanti Parva* is largely based on politics. Duties of a king are described in detail. *Anushasan Parva* and *Sabha Parva* depict rights and duties of the ruler. Thus, we see that chances of a king turning into a despot were dim. In other countries the monarch was the all in all. Church representing *Dharma* was there but it itself tried to assume more and more rights and powers of a governor. But in India the *Purohita* and the learned Brahmins never tried to wear the mantle of the king. The *Prajapati* did not confer this right on the Brahmins. Brahmins would keep checks but not rule. All powers were not concentrated into the hands of the king. Decentralisation of powers was accepted. For years this arrangement worked well.

Election of the King

The king should be from the *Kshatriya* class but kingship was not the inborn right of the eldest son. Eligibilities were given due respect and any flexibility was considered. If the eldest son fulfilled the requirement only then he was enthroned, otherwise the throne passed on to somebody more capable and more eligible. The king had to pass through one more channel. Approval of the *Purohita* and consent of the cabinet and Assembly was mandatory. Thus, kingship was not a dynastic prerogative. Selection and election of the king went side by side. So the crown prince (future king) could not afford to be arrogant and rude, self-willed, voluptuary or dissolute. Traits like prowess, splendour, firmness, dexterity, generosity, wisdom and the like were the ornaments of the crown prince. National Assembly representing all the regions of the country and all the segments of society was asked to put its stamp of consent on the selection of the would-be ruler. This Assembly was a bridge between the king and the masses. In this way kingship was a perfect synthesis of dynastic ruler and elected ruler.

It is written clearly in *Satpatha Brahmana* that a self-willed king is deadly like a wild animal who can chew his own masses. (13/2/3/7-8).

There was provision of punishment both for the king and the subjects just to make them aware of their duties. There was no belief of divine rights. The king too was accountable and answerable. *Rajdanda* was created to uphold *Dharma* and to protect creatures. A king who cannot protect his people has no right to be on the throne (*Shanti Parva,* 89/10). The laws which enthrone a king become the cause of his destruction if he manipulates them to exploit and torture his subjects (*Anushashan Parva,* 145). Only knowledge makes a man wise and not years. If the people are wise and learned the king does not exploit them. Protection is a two-way traffic. The king protects the people and in return is protected by them (*Shanti Parva,* 130-32).

Sri Rama was declared crown prince only after the advice of Vashistha and the consent of the cabinet and it was endorsed by the assembly. Sri Krishna was also an elected ruler. He was not a king by birth. Tradition of election was prevalent in Yadavas. In Europe monarchy was generally hereditary and the monarch always acted according to his will. He was the earthly agent of God and the entire authority was vested in his hands. The saying – 'king does no wrong'—depicts absolute authority of the king. It was the contrary in India. Here *Purohita* and Brahmin were symbolic of checks on the ruler. There was complete and harmonious synthesis of powers of the king and those of Brahmin. The king who flouted and violated ordinances of the scriptures could not keep his throne intact. Non-cooperation by the masses and displeasure of the Brahmin proved very dear to him. He could be dismissed and even put to death if he went unrighteous. So the king left no stone unturned to rise to the occasion and perform his duties well.

Oath Ceremony

The oath ceremony had a special significance. Here the king used to take oath to protect his people, work for their prosperity and uphold Dharma. Brahmins, people's representatives and the Assembly used to bless him and take oath to assist him and protect him. This declaration on the part of the king became part and parcel of his conscience and it always brought him on the right path whenever he went wrong. The oath ceremony gives us a glimpse of contract theory of the West. The oath is called *Sruti* in the *Mahabharata*. Under the oath the king took the duty to nurture his kingship and to maintain and protect the established laws of the land if they did not go against the *'dandaniti'*. After the oath ceremony the people used to say 'Amen' just to display their oneness with the ruler.

Yudhishthira asked Bhishma as to how the institution of kingship had originated. The king was not an exceptional human being. Then what caused the difference between a king and an ordinary man? Why did all the people feel sad when the king was sad? Bhishma told him that in the beginning there was no king. People protected one another with *Dharma*. When *Dharma* lost its grandeur there arose the need to have a king to uphold *Dharma*. Thus, the institution of the kingship was created. Gods suggested the name of *Viragas*. He refused to become the king. His three successors were protectors. Venu was the fourth protector. He started ruling but soon became self-willed. Then his subjects put him to death. Then came Prithu who took the oath to act as per the ordinances of *Dharma* and *Dandaniti*. He was a successful ruler (*Shanti Parva* 59.102). A king respecting *Dharma* cannot be self-willed. Thus, we see that the oath taken by the king at the time of coronation was itself a deterrent because it was taken in the name of *Dharma* with all sincerity and honesty. Moreover, from time to time the king used to declare that he would abide by his oath all his life. He collected revenue and taxes and in this way took a portion of the wealth of his subjects. For any trial and tribulation, crimes, anarchy and sins he was held responsible. So he always performed his duties well and worked for the welfare of his subjects.

Strangely enough we do have exceptions. In spite of many bindings, ordinances of the scriptures and fear of the Almighty we did have despots. Ravana and Kamsa are glaring examples. These are exceptions only, otherwise *Dharma* was the king of kings. Power corrupts the individual and absolute power corrupts absolutely. Intoxication produced by power can have a damaging influence but intoxicated kings are few and far between in our ancient history. Pleasures hidden in powers make a man blind to all worldly and other worldly relations. Kamsa was the maternal uncle of Sri Krishna and the son of King Ugrasen. He put his father behind the bars and tried his utmost to kill his nephew. He followed *Adharma* just to perpetuate his rule. Ordinances of the scriptures could not inspire any respect in him. Just look at the result. He was killed by Sri Krishna and the people heaved a sigh of relief. Rama killed Ravana not because the demon king had abducted Sita. Hanumana was powerful enough to bring back Janaki by himself. Had he done so no demon would have been killed. Rama's aim was to eliminate the whole unrighteous class of demons. Sita did come back but only when demons were killed. Yadava dynasty sank under its own weight when it became indifferent to *Dharma* and found pleasure in wine. Duryodhana went against all ordinances of the scriptures and Mahabharata's great and bloody battle was the result. The Pandavas had to kill the unrighteous Kauravas to uphold *Dharma. Niti, Danda niti* and ordinances of the scripture were very influential but if somebody flouted them willingly he was put to death. Adherence to *Danda niti* and ethics helped India to reach the zenith of the leaders of worldly and other worldly achievements. Scriptures and weapons were used simultaneously. The Brahmin, the *Purohita* and the cabinet told Ashoka the Great that he had no right to squander away State wealth for the propagation of Buddhism. So we see that the minister used to express their views openly and without any hesitation and fear. They performed their duties and warned the king if he was misusing his rights. This tradition perhaps originated during the *Mahabharata* era. Vidur, Prime Minister of the Kauravas, used to express his dissension openly and boldly. Bhishma, Dronacharya and Kripacharya also behaved like this, but they could not gather strength enough to dethrone the king and this lapse on their part brought their death.

Thus we see that Brahmin, scriptures and *Smritis* provided checks on the king. They maintained balance of power. The saying—king does no wrong – does not fit Indian polity. The ruler commanded all reverence, allegiance and confidence only when he acted according to *Dharma*. The moment he did something wrong and contrary to the established moral and ethical codes of conduct he had to abdicate. Even death penalty could be imposed upon him. So no king could dare to go against *Dharma*, ordinances of scriptures, right advice of the *Purohita* and right voice of his subjects.

There were small States in India during the *Mahabharata* era.

They used to fight with one another and establish matrimonial relations also. They fought not to deprive one of his freedom, but to simply established their suzerainty over others. Empire expansion was not the aim. Expansionistic policy came into being only when Kautilya was at the helm of affairs. Earlier sovereignty and independence of a defeated State were never infringed. Wars took place but they were *Dharma Yudhas*. Thus, neither an emperor nor a king could afford to be despotic. Despotic tendencies could excite revolt by the subjects and it would attract the neighbouring king to invade and dethrone the despotic ruler. If the emperor went despotic smaller kings would rise against him and the masses would follow in their steps.

Krishna says in no ambiguous terms that if the king is unrighteous, his company should be given up. He should be removed and dethroned and another person from his dynasty should be enthroned (*Bhisma Parva*, 59).

In the *Mahabharata* checks and balance were profusely visible in the following ways:

1. The king was not a law maker. His duty was merely to implement the laws.
2. The king was elected. Appointment of the Crown Prince was endorsed by the *Purohita* and then by the Assembly comprising of representatives of people. Disapproval could be there.
3. The king used to take oath to act according to *Dharma*. From time to time he used to declare that he will be true to the oath taken.
4. At the time of coronation the king implored people for their cooperation. He promised them protection and happiness.
5. Independence was never infringed upon.
6. The king was not above law. Ordinances of scriptures propounded due punishment for him if he went wrong and surpassed the limits of his rights and forgot his duties.

Thus, we see the traditions prevalent in the *Mahabharata* era laid emphasis on balancing the powers of the State. Separation of powers between the ruler and the Brahmins made the location of responsibility easy. Every effort was made to discourage concentration of power in one hand. Different organs of the government interfered in the functions of one another in such a way that it made all the organs quite balanced. The doctrine of checks and balances prevented despotism from spoiling the spotless clothing of the *Dharma,* ordinances of scriptures, moral and ethical laws and codes of conduct.

No doubt we are breathing in a democratic set-up and there is no place for a monarchy. Our elected representatives can be challenged and they can be shunted out by the masses. But power can pollute any mind. If we adhere to checks and balances which are advised in the *Mahabharata,* we can realise our dream of ideal democratic set-up. Tradition and codes of conduct prevalent in the lore are more relevant today. The need is to adhere to them boldly, courageously, with all sincerity and honesty.

7

Eternal Values, Democracy and Human Rights

Acharya Vidyaratan

> *Varnashrama* is based on good of all. It alone can be get justice to the poor
>
> *Editor*

Virtues that Sustain the State

The Vedas present a beautiful synthesis of worldly and spiritual prosperity. The 'Prithvi Sukta' of the *Atharvaveda* propounds elaborately basic elements for national prosperity and progress. Very truly the Vedas are universal and comprehensive. The verse from the *Atharvaveda* states:

> *Satyam breeht rit umgram, deeksha, taph, Brahma, yajna, prithveem dharyanti'sa no bhootasaya, bhavyasya patni, urum lokam prithvi nh krinotu.*

The verse enumerates seven virtues that sustain the State. They are: truth, righteousness, devotion to a cause, hard labour or perseverance, determination to surmount obstacles in the path of greatness, sacrifice of selfishness and valour. These traits can make a nation impregnable, impenetrable and developed all round. The nation can reach the zenith of progress. If these virtues combine in each and every person, the whole world can rise to touch the lofty heights of progress. Material progress, peace and prosperity, comforts, happiness and all round welfare would creep in unnoticed. Thus, it is altogether necessary to know in detail about these virtues. Homogenous amalgamation of these virtues guarantees greatness. Balance between worldly and other attainments assures all round advancement.

Another verse of Yajurveda goes as follows:

Esha vasyam idam sarvam, yat kinch jagtyam jagat,
Tein tayaktein bhunjitha, ma gridha kasaysvitam dhanum.

One supreme ruler pervades this universe. He is the moving spirit. So find your happiness in renunciation. Do not covet wealth of others?

This verse enunciates four principles. (1) The supreme ruler pervades this universe; He is omniscient; (2) The universe is moving and not stationary; The Supreme Being is the cause of motion; (3) He is master of all; everything belongs to Him. (4) So enjoy with the feeling of renunciation as man is enjoying His bounty. So do not covet the things. This verse contains the philosophy of life. Strict adherence to these principles will go a long way in bringing about democracy in the real sense of the term. Enjoyment in renunciation is the theme. But it does not mean that man should sit idle. He is to act but without attachment.

The governor and the governed should possess basic elements of *Dharma*—truth, justice, benevolence, renunciation, perseverance, law-abiding will and non-violence as it would enhance their faith in the Almighty. It does not mean that we should bow meekly before exploitation, terrorism, wolfish tendencies and unrighteousness. We should have capacity to contain all these anti-social elements. To destroy and eliminate these anti-social elements we should have weapons at our disposal. We should kill if need be but with compassion. In a democratic set-up based on *Dharma* there is no place for communalism. Dissension should exist but it should be serious and well thought up. Dissension for the sake of dissension should be discarded and discouraged. Moreover, it should not leave the path of *Dharma*, cooperation and welfare of the people.

The sermon of Sri Krishna given in the *Gita* is an eye opener—

"Thy business is with the action only, never with the fruits; so let not the fruit of action be thy motive, nor be thou to inaction attached" (2.47).

Today the situation is topsy-turvy- where people try to relish the fruit with no action. Our scriptures and *Shastras* stress upon duties only and not on rights as rights follow duties automatically.

Rights and duties go hand in hand. They are interdependent. Rights we cherish and duties we have put in the dust-bin. Chaos is the result.

Excessive indulgence has pushed celibacy *(Brahmacharya)* in the background. Population is increasing at a rapid speed. People think that it is their right to produce children. But they do not realise that it is their sacred duty not to overburden the limited resources of the earth. The condition is going from bad to worse. The future is dark.

Primary needs of life are five in number: (1) clothing; (2) food; (3) shelter; (4) medical aid; and (5) higher education. In *Varnashrama* money is not given much importance. It lays stress on renunciation and performance of duties. It gives due importance to selfless service, donation and faith. *Varnashrama* propagates use of money only after proper distribution. Democracy in the real sense is depicted by this system. Truth, non-violence, non-stealing, perseverance, *Brahmacharya,* renunciation, purity, satisfaction, study of scriptures and worship of the omniscient are the virtues assimilated in this system. These virtues, if embraced with sincerity and serenity, can remove many ills of society.

Manusmiriti holds renunciation to be supreme. It can culminate into the ideal of 'entire world is a family'. Dignity of *Shudra* is inherent in *Varna* system as *Varna* is not by birth but by deeds. It is not a mere institution made by man but it is a law discovered. Its hidden meaning and potentialities should be explored and utilized for the good of society. Evil is not in the law or in the institution itself, but it lies in the doctrine of superiority and inferiority which are added to it. *Varna* institution does accept right to property but with some checks. Man should donate his wealth for different welfare schemes. This makes him a trustee only. While satisfying his ego it will impart him spiritual happiness which a man gets after performing duties.

Competition encourages hard work and better work. Consumers are benefitted the most. *Varna* system encourages healthy competition and produces expertise. Bolshevism gives importance to materialism whereas *Varna* institution presents synthesis of worldly prosperity and spiritual prosperity. Here spiritual part is more important as it culminates into bliss, i.e., salvation.

8

Elections in the Indian Tradition and Good Governance

Krishna Mohan Mathur

Good governance consists of the rulers being committed to the welfare of the people. The exact form of the constitution is less relevant than this moral commitment.

Editor

Swami Vivekananda once said: "I consider that the great national sin is the neglect of the masses and that is one of the causes of our downfall. No amount of politics would be of any avail until the masses of India are at once more well-educated, well-fed and well-cared for."[1] Democracy in India has established itself firmly and deeply in the soil during the last fifty-four years. Indians have reaffirmed their strong commitment to democratic polity.[2]

The Yajurveda

It is indeed a matter of great pride for all the Indians to find that in Yajurveda, there are some references of elected assemblies. In ancient India, there were several democratic republics and there are various references of their existence in *Yajurveda, Mahabharata, Manusmriti, Arthashastra* and Buddhist literature. In Yajurveda, *Dharma* (religious obligations) of rulers have been specified in many places and it has been laid down that such a ruler will be an elected one who will administer justice with the help of an elected assembly (Chapter VII, Verse 45). In Chapter VIII, Verse 50, it emphasized the good conduct of a ruler is a pre-requisite of the common good in the following words: "Virtuous and prosperous king, be knowledgeable about your conduct as a protector of the learned and impeller towards our progress and prosperity. Be in control of your passions and conduct yourself in a righteous manner. Be a friend to us. Know your conduct as laid down by all sages.[3] There are many instructions and guidelines for the elected rulers. Yajurveda's Verse 43 of Chapter XX says, "*Vidya Sabha* (Assembly of learned people), Dharma Sabha (Assembly of spiritual leaders), and Rajya Sabha (Assembly of political administrators) are the three organs of the government. These people should provide justice and solutions of problems, should consist of well-qualified persons fully constituted to manage the affairs of the State with prowess and skill and to maintain the common good (righteousness) of the government." In *Yajurveda* there are clear proofs of elected kings whose conducts were founded on humility, discipline, and high moral values. Verse 2 of Chapter IX follows these words: "O king, elected by an assembly of learned and wise people for carrying out the duty of the state, I accept thee who is knowledgeable, practices *yoga,* full of humility, leader among leaders, expert in science and is kind. The administration is thy mainstay. Thou has been elected by the people. I accept thee." The above words clearly state that kings used to be elected. Yajurveda contains a large number of instructions to the king to preserve the common good by acting in a moral and virtuous manner.

Mahabharata

In the *Mahabharata* there are innumerable instructions for the administration of the society.[4] In *Shanti Parva,* Bhishma, the grandfather, has given following main instructions:

1. Brahma, the lord of creation, has devised *Dharma* (righteousness) for the care and well-being of all; it is the duty of a king, to follow and advance the dictates of *Dharma* (Chapter XC, Verse 9).

2. The eternal duties of the rulers are to make the subjects happy, to observe truth and to act sincerely (Chapter LVIII, Verse 11).

3. The foundation of good governance is *Dharma* (right courses). The rulers have to uphold it and to act in accordance with the common good, must not act unjustly or unethically so as to secure their private good through selfishness (Chapter LXXXV, Verses 16-17).

4. If the rulers do not behave appropriately, they all will surely go to hell along with destroying the moral basis of governance (Chapter LXXXV, Verses 16-17).

5. A king, guided by righteousness *(Vyavaharen Shuddham)* and devoting his life in the service of his subjects, acquires fame and immortality both here and hereafter (Chapter LXXXV, Verse 20).

6. The main purpose of a king is to protect *Dharma* and to bolster righteousness, and to be free from indolence and desires One should know that a king is the defender of all *(Lokasaya Rakstula)* (Chapter XC, Verse 3).

7. According to *Anushashan Parva,* if the ruler ignored his responsibilities and was unjust or offensive, the people had a right to rebellion, even regicide was accepted and the people were free to kill such ruler 'as a mad dog.'

8. In *Shanti Parva,* the concept of good governance and good law and order implies that a newlywed beautiful bride laden with ornaments and attractive clothes may walk across the market place at midnight unescorted without any fear or risk to her.[5] The fundamental principle of governance of ancient polity required every function to preserve both society and State.[6]

Bhagawat Geeta

The *Bhagawat Geeta* contains a lot of instructions which can form the foundation of good governance for the protection of the common good. In Chapter XVI, Verse 24, Lord Krishna said : "One ought to understand what is duty, and what is forbidden in the commands laid out by the *Shastras* (scriptures). Knowing such rules and regulations, one should behave as ordained by scriptures." He emphasized *Dharma* in Chapter XVIII, Verse 30 and said: "O Partha! that understanding by which one knows what ought to be done and what ought not to be done, what is to be feared and what is not, what is obligatory and what is permitted, leads to the righteous path (Sattviki *Pravritti*)[7]. In Chapter XVIII, Lord Krishna explains the art and science of using power for the welfare of the society *(Loka Sangraha).* In *Geeta,* Lord Krishna has held that personal character and conduct of the highly placed people is generally emulated by others and therefore they must set high examples of *Nishkam Karma.* In Chapter III, Verse 21 it is said that whatsoever a highly placed person does, the same is done by others as well, whatever standards he sets, people follow (Chapter III, Verse 25). Public servants have to ensure common good *Sarva Loka Kalyankari Karma* and *Sarva Hitey Ratah* by maintaining feeling, protecting and defending people's interest and public property without allowing it to be destroyed.[8]

Kautilya's Vision

Kautilya's vision of governance, enunciated about 2300 years ago bears striking resemblance to the modern welfare State model in respect of ideology, ideals and socio-administrative structure. Kautilya in his treatise *Arthasashtra* (written circa 300 B.C.) has observed: "In the happiness of his subjects lies his happiness, in their welfare his welfare, whatever pleases himself he shall not considered as good, but whatever please his subjects be shall considered as good" (Chapter XIX, Verse 39). In this book, the foremost duties of the State are to protect and promote *Dharma* and to defend the community against enemies without any disorder. Kautilya suggested checks on public officials to prevent the growth of criminal tendencies in them.[9] In *Arthashastra*, a number of indicators of good governance have been enumerated and some of them are as under:

1. King must merge his individuality with duties.
2. Civil servants, like greedy children, need to be watched and guided but not controlled or enticed.
3. Good governance should avoid extremes without missing the goals.
4. Disciplined life with a code of conduct is to be led by ministers and the king.
5. Kings and public servants must be given reasonable fixed salaries and allowances.
6. Law and order should be the chief priority of governance.
7. There should be punitive measures against corrupt officials and preventive measures for wrong doers.
8. Periodically there should be replacement of ministers by good ones.
9. Qualities of leadership, intellect, energy, good moral conduct should be the criteria for selection of public servants.
10. There should be pursuance of good governance even amidst instability.[10]

Manusmriti

In *Manusmriti* it is said that Brahma has created the king to be the protector of the *Varnas* (based on occupation) and public order (common good) so that they discharge their several duties according to their *Dharma* and rank (Book VII, Verse 35). It is further said that conducting himself and even intent on discharging his prescribed royal duties, a king shall order all his officials to work for the good and welfare of his subjects (Book IX, Verse 324). We can notice that there is a moral and ethical tone in setting various instructions for the good governance of the kingdom.

The great epic *Ramayana* also contains many basic principles of statecraft and governance. An effective spy system, system of prompt justice, welfare of the people and high character of administration are some of the principles which can be applied in modern age with great benefits. In India, good governance is always visualized as *Ram Rajya. Ram Rajya* was conceptualized as an ideal governed State where the government became an instrument to achieve ends such as peace, economic prosperity, justice, dignity, maintenance of law and order etc., and establishment of rule of *Dharma*.

Whether People Control the Government or are They Governed by the Government?

In a democratic society, governed by a written constitution, theoretically, it should be government of the people, by the people and for the people. In India, after independence, constitutionalism and planned economic development have been two major landmarks in the process of our governance. There have been periodical elections and people have changed the governments which were disliked by them. People in a democratic society are not merely "customers" and "clients" of the government having some *quid pro quo* relationship, they are also "masters" and "citizens" who are found by mutual obligations and are entitled to enjoy public infrastructure provided by the government, such as roads, communication systems, courts of law, monetary system, public sanitation, medical and health facilities and good drinking water. It is due to non-feasance, over-feasance and malfeasance that people have started feeling that they do not control the government. A democratic government is the product of its people's choice and can legitimately claim people's support. George

Washington, the first President of the United States, once said, "Respect for its (government's) authority, compliance with its laws, acquiescence in its measures, are duties enjoined by the fundamental maxim of true liberty." How many Indians are committed to the fundamental duties enshrined in the Constitution? Governments function through bureaucracy in large democracies. In most developing countries bureaucracy is suffering from a large number of serious maladies. Democratic governance demands that government must not only be representative of the people but also responsive to their needs and problems. The public image of bureaucracy in India is one of inaccessibility, indifference, procedure-oriented, poor quality and sluggish, corruption prone and unaccountable for results. Moreover, political instability, proliferation of political parties, criminalisation of politics, growth of political parties in large number, corruption and lack of work ethics are some of the ills of Indian political system today. In democratic system people control the government through parliamentary control and judicial and quasi-judicial reviews.[11] An effective grievance redressal machinery can go a long way in controlling bureaucracy. So far except exercising their right of voting, there has been absence of vigilant and active citizenship. Empowerment of citizens in general and vulnerable sections in particular through decentralization, grass-root functionaries (delegation), dispersal of politico-administrative power (democratization) and debureaucratisation are essential for good representative governance. In democracy, representatives of the people should continue to be accountable to the masses.

Tyranny of State Power

State tyranny can take some of the following forms:

1. Death penalty without proper trial.
2. Depriving persons from their human rights and doing injustice to people through mal-administration or poor governance.
3. Taking away and depriving people's inherent dignity of human being.
4. Curtailment of civil and political rights without legal sanction and in violation of international covenant on civil and political rights [General Assembly Resolution 2200 A (XXI) of 10th December 1966 and entry into force on 23 March 1976].

5. Abuse of powers by the State against fighters of conscience and politicians.
6. Use of third degree methods of interrogation by the police and law enforcement authorities.
7. Custodial rapes, harassment, custodial violence and deaths.
8. State of violence against citizens and law abiding people.
9. Miscarriage of justice by criminal justice system, judicial delays and corruption.

While exercising state authority, public servants at times commit atrocities, injustices and unjustified curtailment of liberty of the people. *The Times of India* on 20 October 1999 brought out a news "TADA vanishes but the ghost lurks." Although TADA has been withdrawn in 1996, Assam has nearly 1000 TADA related cases yet to be disposed of, leaving hundreds of men languishing in captivity. The height of State tyranny and harassment is evident from the fact that only 14 persons have so far been convicted under TADA in the State since 1991. Despite 26,000 arrested persons having been made on this count, only 4 out of a total of 1,237 TADA related cases were wound up with conviction orders. Even after three years after the TADA Act was revoked, there are 400 odd cases where the police is yet to give its final report.[12]

In several other States TADA has been used to fight the smugglers, drug peddlers, Naxalites (as in Andhra Pradesh) and the underworld operators in Gujarat.[13] Use of third degree methods of interrogation, fake encounters, custody rapes and deaths, other police excesses are now being monitored by the National Human Rights Commission (NHRC) and regular annual reports are being placed before Parliament. During 1993-94, there were 34 custodial deaths and 61 cases of police excesses reported by the NHRC. Recently Human Rights Commission of Punjab has put the police in the dock charging it with raising a militant outfit—Tigers of Sikh Land—and falsely implicating seven former militants in it. The commission found that top police officials of Punjab were bent upon proving that the border was not free from the menace of terrorism.[14]

The latest figures on custodial deaths in India have been as follows:

1995-96	444
1996-97	888
1997-98	1029
1998-99	1297

There are various methods which can contain State tyranny against the people. Behaviour of the police officers at grass root level needs to be controlled by more effective supervision. The police can be made more accountable by adopting four categories of controls namely, (i) Organisational control or intra-departmental control; (ii) Governmental control; (iii) Political control; and (vi) Societal control.[15]

Humanizing the police behaviour is an important need of the hour. The role of the people, voluntary organisations and social action groups in making legal aid meaningful, effective and purpose-oriented can go a long way in containing the tyranny of the State.[16]

A free media, an independent judicial system and effective human rights organisations like Amnesty International are some of the important vehicles for stimulating public opinion and building an atmosphere where State tyranny is not allowed to be perpetuated.[17] Social justice must be ensured by prompt and effective criminal justice system. Liberty lies in the hearts of men and eternal vigilance is needed for good democratic governance.

India's Historic Experience with Democracy

Mahatma Gandhi dreamt of *Ram Rajya* in India after independence. Vinoba Bhave struggled for creating equalitarian and just civil society by his "Bhudan Movement". Jai Prakash Narain attempted to usher in "Total Revolution" as an alternative form. As an alternative to present corrupt and ineffective administration, we should have an effective parliamentary system which has a public service management based on *Dharma* (righteousness) and social justice, creating synergy between public and private sectors, developing transparent and accountable administrative system, harnessing modern information technology, reorienting public servants to greater sense of dedication and service and combating political and administrative corruption at all levels. We should get a "mission-driven government". We have to educate the masters (masses) so that as enlightened citizens they have respect for the government's authority and through effective voting and presentative system they select good representatives as their leaders. Good governance needs a proper government which respects the aspirations and needs of the people.

By giving the BJP-led omnibus alliances a comfortable working majority in the 13th Lok Sabha, the Indian electorate has reaffirmed their firm faith in the democratic system. Even after 54 years of independence, poverty, illiteracy, over-population, shortage of drinking water, corruption, collapse of criminal justice system, unemployment, rising crimes and criminality are challenges to our democratic system. It is, however, generally said that there is nothing basically wrong with the democratic system, the fault lies with the people who operate it. However, this argument ignores the following facts: (i) the people who are operating the system are largely the products of this system; (ii) the system is for the people and not the other way round, it has to be adjusted to the needs of the people; (iii) we cannot keep waiting for angels to descend, our people cannot be changed or others imported to work the excellent system; and (iv) both the system and its operators are responsible for the failure. If parliamentary democracy and individual freedom are to endure and representative institutions made impregnable, constitutional, legal, economic and political reforms have to be brought about in an integrated manner. There is no alternative to representative democracy in India, but certainly wide sweeping reforms are urgently called for. What we need is awakened citizenry and an activist populace who can build up public opinion for reforms. The most potent sign of hope is the government's 'National Agenda' for governance which has been further reenforced by the Prime Minister's address to the nation recently. Machiavelli has rightly observed: "There is nothing more difficult to take in hand, more perilous to conduct, more uncertain in its success than to take the lead in the introduction of new order of things."[19]

An action plan for an effective and responsive government had been prepared by Department of Administrative Reforms and Public Grievances, Ministry of Personnel, Public Grievances, Government of India for (i) making administration accountable and citizen-friendly; (ii) ensuring transparency and the right to information; and (iii) taking measures to cleanse and motivate civil services.[20] Prime Minister Shri Atal Behari Vajpayee has said, "If it is true that people are the king in a democracy, then we cannot have an administrative machinery that lords over the citizens. In a country, where a majority of the people are victims of poverty and unemployment, etc. we have to have an administrative system that has a heart, that feels for the poor, and a mind that cares for their needs... public administration cannot deliver good things to public unless the political leadership firmly upholds people's and nation's interests to be supreme."[21] It is necessary that the entire political and administrative machinery, from top to bottom, must work with a sense of mission and a result-oriented approach for "closing the gap between people's aspirations and government's performance". In my view the strategy to retrieve Indian administrative system from present ailments needs many-pronged reforms:

1. Political reforms and constitutional reforms.
2. Judicial reforms including reforms in law.
3. Administrative reforms with a view to modernization.
4. Socio-institutional reforms.
5. Human resource development, character building and leadership building through educational reforms and introduction of ethical-moral values for administration. Education should be our top priority.
6. Introduction of religious teachings to public administrators, politicians and the people.
7. Decentralization of power and authority and empowerment of the local-self bodies and the people.
8. Enforcement of accountability at all levels and adoption of Lok Pal bill.

Conclusion

Originally State and good governance may have been synonymous with *Dharma* but later State started using coercive power and became tyrant and oppressive. In India, scriptures emphasized rule of *Dharma* for good governance. After independence, there has been a seemingly elusive goal of good governance and thinking about enlightened vigilant citizenship. Good democratic governance of a civil society is not a finished product but it is a dynamic concept. The discursive shift can come when the political, social and economic milieu has a spiritual, moral and ethical base. There are a lot of promises and assurances made by the politicians during election times but their performance and action are totally different. The contradictions in discourse and reality are wide enough to escape notice of any sensitive scholar. Good governance implies presence of rule of law, transparency and openness in administration, accountability, presence of honest and efficient government and promotion of basic human rights of the common man. The major reality of the post-independent India has been assertion of the people's will and preservation and maintenance of democracy and freedom of thought and expression. India has maintained governance in a democratic framework but it has failed to solve number of pressing challenges and problems. Criminalization of politics, pervading corruption in administrative and political system, mass unemployment and poverty, population explosion, rising inequalities and disparities, politicization of administration, fissiparous tendencies of caste, tribe, religion, language and class, erosion of moral values, terrorism, insurgency and low-intensity conflicts are some of the main problems. The present system of governance has failed on several fronts, the major ones being vision and mission, education, character, values and integrity, nationalist spirit, fracturisation of political parties and criminalisation of the socio-economic system. These challenges need a new approach, and strong political will supported by an enlightened and dedicated public administration and popular support of the Indian masses. Albert Einstein observed, "The significant problems we face cannot be solved at the same level of thinking we were at when we created them. A paradigm shift in thinking and perception are needed. "In governance, there is a need to bring in *Dharma* for happiness and welfare of all "*Sarve Bhavantu Sukhinah*". There is an urgent need to operationalise this ancient wisdom through a restructuring of our socio-economic political system so that administrators focus their efforts for undertaking their duties with a view to ensure universal welfare *(Sarva Loka Kalyankari Karma)*, maintaining and protecting each and every one in the creation *(Sarva Lok Sangrahamevapi)* and securing universal care for all and every one *(Sarva Hitey Ratali)*.

NOTES AND REFERENCES

1. For a systematic treatment of this theme see Rajni Kothari "Towards Intervention", Seminar No. 269, January 1982, Annual Number.
2. For elaboration and details see Beni Prasad, *State and Government in Ancient India*, K.P. Jayaswal, *Hindu Polity*, R. Shama Sastry, Kautilya's *Arthashastra*, Mysore Printing and Publishing House, 1967, V. Subramaniam,

Administrative Legacy of Ancient India in Relation to Modern Public Administration, *Indian Journal of Public Administration,* Jan-March 1996, Vol. XLII No. 1.
3. O.P. Dwivedi, Common good and good governance, *Indian Journal of Public Administration,* July-Sept. 1998, Vol. XLIV, No. 3, p. 260.
4. *Ibid.,* pp. 260-61. *Mahabharata* published by Gita Press, Gorakhpur, 1988, Shanti Parva, Chapter 90.
5. Shanti Parva (Dutta) LXIX; Quoted by Dr. K.M. Mathur in *Management of Internal Security and Related Issues,* Gyan Publishing House, New Delhi, 1995, p. 9.
6. P.B. Gajendragadkar, The Historical Background and the theoretical basis of the Hindu Law, *AIR Journal,* Feb. 1993, p. 19 (21).
7. Dr. Radhakrishnan Commentary on Bhagwat Geeta. Also O.P. Dwivedi—"Administrative Theology, Dharma of Public Officials ": *Indian Journal of Public Administration,* Vol. 36, No. 3, July September 1990, p. 840.
8. Bal Gangadhar Tilak, *Shri Bhagavad Geeta Rahasya,* Poona, Tilak Brothers, 1902.
9. Aradhana Parmar: *A Study of Kautilya Arthashastra.*
10. R. Shamasastry, *Kautilya's Arthashastra,* Mysore, 1929. K.P. Jayaswal—*Hindu Polity,* 1968; Umesh Kumar, *Kautilya's Thought on Public Administration,* National Book Organisation, New Delhi; L.N. Sharma and Susmita Sharma—"Kautilyan Indicators of Good Governance", *Indian Journal of Public Administration,* July-Sept. 1998, Vol. XLIV, No. 3, pp. 265-71.
11. R.B. Jain, Citizen's Charter—An Instrument of Public Accountability: Problems and Prospects in India, *Indian Journal of Public Administration,* July-Sept, 1998, Vol. XLIV, No. 3, p. 362.
12. For full detail see Mrinal Talukdar "TADA Vanishes but the Ghost Lurks." *The Times of India,* New Delhi, 20 Oct. 1999, p. 5.
13. For number of TADA cases in badly affected States—consult Dr. K.M. Mathur's, *Crime Human Rights and National Security,* Gyan Publishing House, New Delhi, 1996, p. 226.
14. Ajay Bharadwaj—Rights Panel Puts Police in the Dock—*The Times of India,* New Delhi, Oct. 20, 1999, p. 9.
15. K.M. Mathur, *Management of Internal Security and Related Issues,* Gyan Publishing House, New Delhi, 1995, p. 225.
16. The Supreme Court—Hussamara Khaton vs State of Bihar, AIR, 1979 SC 1361; Kishore Single vs State of Rajasthan AIR 1981, S.C. 1597.
17. K.M. Mathur's *Indian Police—Role and Challenges,* Gyan Publishing House, New Delhi, 1994, pp. 86-112.
18. Subash C. Kashyap, Towards Good Governance: Need for Political Reforms, *The Indian Journal of Public Administration,* July-September, 1998, Vol. XLIV, No. 3, p. 323.
19. Sydney, Machiavellie—A Discussion—Granada Publishing House, 1971.
20. For details, consult document 1 special number on Towards Good Governance—*Indian Journal of Public Administration,* July-Sept. 1998, Vol. XLIV, No. 3, pp. 626-60.
21. Address of Prime Minister on March 29, 1999, *IIPA Annual Report,* 1998-99, pp. 42-43.

9

Democracy in the Indian Tradition

B.N. Tiwari

> Indian governance had people's voice built-into it in many ways though nominally it was mostly a monarchy.
>
> *Editor*

Before delving deep into the subject matter it is essential to penetrate the smoke screen covering the terms democracy, public and social welfare and eternal or primeval values or *Sanatana Mulyas* and know their true meaning and see them in their true colours. It is very easy to define democracy. It is acknowledged that democracy is a government by the people, of the people and for the people. The phrases 'by the people' and 'of the people' may not hold good because democracy today is representative form of government. Participation by all the people in the functioning of the State is well-nigh possible. But the phrase—'for the people'—is significant. This phrase leads us to public or social welfare. The object of both organisation and administration is to control human and material resources. Success of administration is ultimately tested by the welfare of the masses. State activities cover the entire gamut of social, economic, political, religious and cultural life of the people. In the ancient Indian culture we come across the term—*Yogaksema*—well-being or welfare that includes happiness and prosperity, akin to the aims of a welfare State. The primary source of power is allegiance and devotion of the people towards State authority. So interests of the people come first. Kautilya says:

> In the happiness of the subjects lies the happiness of the king and in what is beneficial to the subjects of his own benefit.

> What is dear to himself is not beneficial to the king, but what is dear to the subjects is beneficial to him.

Democracy and public welfare or social welfare are interlinked. Where public welfare is considered to be supreme there cannot be autocracy or dictatorship or any form of government except democracy. Public welfare implies governance by moral and ethical laws. A king who follows codes of conduct and is punished by the same *danda* which he wields cannot be an autocrat. His tenure is but a form of democracy. It does not mean that a dictator or a king cannot establish a welfare State. He can establish a welfare state but only when his regime is for the people. This brings us to the values of governance. The ruler should observe the highest ethical standards. He should not be arbitrary and his powers are circumscribed by the *Dharmic* code. He is virtuous and self-restrained. He protects his people and looks after them and their welfare. Powers vested in the politicians and bureaucrats are not for self-aggrandisement but for doing social good. They must give due respect to sacred laws and traditions. The relationship of the ruler with his subjects is paternalistic. Powers wielded by the State are a sacred trust. In the administration of justice, principles of immediacy and equity must be followed. If you want to help mankind you must take your own pleasure and pain, name and fame and all sorts of interests and make a bundle of them and throw them into the sea. All these are eternal values.

Our ancient treatises on laws expand these eternal values. *Ram Rajya* was a regime for the people. Our ancient *Shastras* lay stress on the dictum—*Sarve Bhavantu Sukhinah,* i.e., happiness for all and this happiness is hidden in welfare of all. Thus, any form of government is akin to democracy if it is for the people. Moral and ethical laws, *Dharmic* codes propounded by our scriptures indirectly guarantee a government for the people and that government is not anything else but democracy.

What type of government should there be? Which is the best form? What should be the aims and ideals of effective governance? What standards should be adopted to establish a true democratic set up? How to bring *Ram Rajya?* All these questions have been vexing the minds of scholars, politicians, statesmen and the people from time immemorial. Indian thinking on this question has been greatly influenced by Srutis, Smritis, Upanishads, Puranas and, of course, the Vedas. Influence of these scriptures has been farreaching. Impact of these holy works is clearly visible not only on human beings, family atmosphere and society but also on administrative set-up. Our treatises on laws, scriptures and established moral values have been the directive principles for the formation of efficient government. Right from the dawn of civilisation, the question of just governance has remained the subject of deep pondering and serious thinking. In the Vedas we come across references to self-rule, democracy, republics, and so on. In the Vedic period, self-rule was considered to be the best. In common language it is called *Ram Rajya*. It is said that self-rule is that where most of the people abide by the rules and laws, where there is no place for narrow-mindedness and where the government is run with the consent of majority. It is said in the *Atharvaveda* that nation, its strength and splendour are interlinked. These features will be wanting in dependent nation. General consent and national unity are essential for national entity and prestige. *Swetasvtar Upanishad* says—"Unity is the harbinger of strength. Oh God! Protect us, nurture us fully. Our knowledge should be splendid. We should live in harmony and love without any malice." It is clear that eternal truths are propounded in our ancient treatises and these truths give us clues to define self-rule or democracy accurately.

On the contrary, Western scholars try to prove that self-government or democracy is the gift of Christianity. Lord Brice in his famous book *Essays on Reform* describes democracy as the gift of Christianity as its tenets have been propagating the message of equality of human beings before God. Just ponder over the indications of the *Yajurveda* and *Atharvaveda* where it has been desired—"Let your resolutions and minds be same. So live in harmony thereby." These words certainly depict oneness of human beings. Penance by the sages brought the dawn of nationalism. For its propagation codes to be followed were designed. In ancient Indian literature meaning of nation and nationality are clearly depicted. The words nation and nationality have been several times used in the Vedas. In the *Yajurveda* we come across a prayer, an incantation to a deity for the welfare and prosperity of nation. The incantation also provides us with a vivid definition of nation—a large group of people residing in a specific territory, believing in the entity of the omnipotent, omnipresent and omniscient Nature, who give priority to the intellect and respect learned men, who have the ability and capacity to safeguard the territory from external attacks, internal disturbances and natural calamities and can guarantee welfare of all citizens of a nation. In English language nation means—a particular race or multitude having the same origin, same language, same history and same political system. Thus, we see the definition depicted in the Vedic incantation is much more comprehensive.

Whether we use the word 'Self Rule' or 'Democracy' or 'Republic' it hardly matters. But Indian wisdom points out to one and only one motive of an ideal governmental set-up and that is welfare of all. Before the progress of State the *Mahabharata* describes an ideal set-up of a society comprising no punishment or punisher. Protection to all. Advice given by Bhishma to Yudhisthira in *Shanti Parva* is relevant even today—the king whose conduct is pure and moral standard is very high and who remains engrossed in the welfare of people and subjects gets name and fame, immorality and eternity. Here also once again we see that stress is given to well-being and welfare of the people. *Shanti Parva* and *Anushasna Parva* and treatise on politics by Yagyavalkya are testimonies to this truth. All of them have emphasized that the king should work for the goodness of his people and should not impose his own will on them. Advice given to the rulers of India by Kautilya in *Arthashastra* presents the same feeling—"In the happiness of the subjects lies the happiness of the king and in what is beneficial to the subjects lies his own benefit. What is dear to himself is not beneficial to the king, but what is dear to the subjects is beneficial to him." Man is a rational creature. Man who is not proud of his body and whose all actions are selflessly directed towards the welfare of the entire world, and any killing done by his body and senses seen through worldly angle is not killing in reality because absence of passion, selfishness and egotism, cannot cause killing of any creature. Work done without ego is non-work. Such a man is not bound by sin. Such work done without egotism for the welfare of the people but involving a killing has the sanctity of scriptures. Welfare of people is supreme. The frenzied king in whose kingdom the subjects remain riot-stricken at the hands of scoundrels loses his name and fame, span of life and grandeur. To give relief to the unhappy person is the supreme duty of the king.

Basis of good administration is good conduct and devotion to *Dharma*. The king, his ministers and officials who have taken the oath to work for public welfare faithfully and dutifully and not to indulge in unethical ways and malpractices to satisfy their personal interests, take charge of their offices for the growth of *Dharma*. If they do not perform their duties properly, they not only defy and spoil the moral image of the administration but themselves will end up in hell.

The state of nature was one of bliss and peace. It was an idealistic state. People conducted themselves righteously very willingly. They respected and cared for the comforts and freedom of others and they all spent their lives for harmony and love. But this state could not go too far because of selfish attitude, human greed and lust. These tendencies destroyed the blissful state and created a chaotic society. When the anarchy became unbearable people appointed Manu their first king to check misconduct through appropriate measures of punishment and make freedom and peace effective. The State was the outcome of a need to establish a system whereby the welfare of the entire community could be guaranteed. Kuber advised Yudhisthira that patience, proficiency, time, place and labour are the signs of democracy. Prudence, progressiveness, morality, equality, freedom are the basic criteria of democracy.

We have two types of democracies: Direct democracy and Representative democracy or Indirect democracy. Direct democracy was prevalent before evolution of the State. It existed in the city states of ancient Greece and the smaller republics of ancient India, in the cantons of Switzerland and in the smaller segments of Indian tribals. This type of democracy is still prevalent. Representative democracy (indirect democracy) is another type. In it, the entire multitude or the majority wields the power of government through their representatives elected from time to time. Later on, because of increase in population, direct democracy became impractical. It became impossible for the entire populace to sit at one place, to take decisions and thereby run the government. This gave rise to representative democracy. It rose from the ashes of direct democracy. In the ancient history of India we have description of smaller republics where almost the entire populace ran the government and discussed issues concerned to the State administration unitedly and in harmony. In Lichhbi

Republic under Bajji Sangha, there were 7707 people including the king. Their assembly meeting was held in a hall named Santhagar. Almost all the people participated in Sangha. Resolutions were passed not by the majority but unanimously or the decisions were left to a smaller committee for '*Panch* decision'. Gautama Buddha while organising *Buddha Sangh* kept this democratic set-up of the republics in view. These republics domains were small. Kapilvastu, Lichhbi Republic and other smaller republics are worth mentioning in this context. The Magadh empire annexed them and assimilated them in it. Direct democracy of Athens was superb and unparalleled. There was complete harmony and coordination between the individual and the whole community there. Such an example of direct democracy is very hard to find in history. Still these small democracies could not face the onslaughts of time. They died and lost their identity. Athens was consumed by the Macedonian empire and the smaller republics in India came under the Magadh empire.

According to Manu, the founder of rules of conduct based on the *Vedas,* if the king does not exercise his power of *danda* justly, it is likely that the powerful will devour the weak as the larger fish swallow the smaller fish. If the king exercises his power of *danda* justly and impartially people will prosper and they would be able to carry on their duties smoothly. But if the king himself is lustful, unjust and of mean and low feelings, he is punished with the same *danda.* So a king who is just with the danda is honoured. If he is severe with the rod he becomes a source of terror to the subjects and the king mild with the rod is despised. *Manusmriti* and *Sukrasmriti* propound that the sacred duty of the king is to work relentlessly for the welfare of the people. *Rajdharmanusasan parva* of the *Mahabharata* advocates this very idea. It is the king's moral duty to give relief and happiness to his people. Protection of truth and sincerity of conduct are qualities of a king.

India has a long democratic tradition. Its dawn is in the Vedas. Indian history, culture and philosophy owe their beginning to the Vedas, wherein tradition, the dawn of kingship and monarchy were the outcome of people's democratic thoughts. In the beginning there was neither the king nor the subjects. All were bound by morality. But with the passage of time when the strong started torturing the poor, there arose the need of an authority which could force everybody to live life as per the dictates of *dharma* or ethics so that all could enjoy peace, prosperity and get justice. The masses chose the king so that he could coerce each and everybody to follow the path of righteousness and mete out punishment to those who violated the code of conduct.

Gautam Buddha was born in a republic. He had the experience to administer the republic. His experience is still relevant and significant for the success of democracy in any State or country as it was in his times. The use of the words *Sangh* (Confederation, Assembly) and *Gana* (Community, Union) started in his time. The word *Gana* gets a place in *Acharung Sutra* of Jains also.

Republics of Gandhar, Punjab and Sindh fought well with the army of Alexander, a Macedonian king. Greek historians have described extensively the republics in India existing before Christ. Continuous development of the institutions like *Panchayats* at village level, unions of craftsmen and city committees is more important than the tradition of republic. Sir Charles Metcalfe, the then British governor of the United Province (now Uttar Pradesh) had compared the village *Panchayats* with small republics.

Monarchy in ancient India was based on the pattern of social contract and this system or arrangement was in vogue thousands of years before Rousseau and Voltaire. It was the duty of the king to establish a reign of moral laws and justice. He did not interfere in the social, spiritual, religious and economic life of his subjects. He used to wage war to uproot immorality, crime, misconduct and injustice but his motive was never to expand the frontiers of his empire.

The gist of the oath which a Hindu king takes at the time of his coronation is—"let all the people of my empire prosper and I act according to the *Dharma*. In my kingdom cows be safe, Brahmins be free from anxiety and worries and people of the entire world be happy." The reign of Ravana was considered to be the worst at that time. He had defeated the kings, plundered them, abducted their womenfolk but kept only that woman in his *harem* who got enamoured to him. The sage Balmiki had written this. In the eyes of the Aryans and hermits, Ravana was the most wicked. But he did not seize the kingdom of other kings and he never raped any woman. He did have the blemishes of plundering kingdoms, abducting women and keeping the enamoured women in his harem. The sages could not tolerate all this. Rama attacked Ravana to uproot immorality, misconduct, cruelty, villainy and wickedness.

To defeat the enemy and to establish an Aryan set-up and legislation was the sole motive of war at that time. Rama had not plundered Lanka. He did never enter this island. He left Vibhishna free but under the suzerainty of the Aryan set-up. To destroy one's freedom was not the policy in those days.

Whenever we talk of democratic set-up, we proclaim to bring about *Ram Rajya.* It was in existence when there was monarchy in Ayodhya. But today its eternal values seem to be a far-fetched idea. Tulsidas has described such propitious and friendly set-up of monarchy in the Uttar Khand of *Ramcharitmanas.* Laski suggests that rights are always circumscribed by duties and public welfare is clearly depicted in this friendly monarchy. Propitious reign of Rama made him *Maryada Purushottam.*

During the reign of Sri Rama all had an easy access to medical aid and other facilities. There was economic prosperity and no poverty. All the people were healthy and beautiful. There was amiability and love amongst all castes and creeds. Educational and cultural facilities were universally and easily available. There was parity between man and woman. In those days there was no gender disparity and discrimination. The masses were righteous and virtuous and followed moral codes and standards. Patriotism was in the air. Unity and harmony were omnipresent. The king respected public opinion and used to sort out contradictions and aspersions pertaining to himself and his family giving due weightage to public opinion. Sri Rama himself renounced his devoted wife respecting sarcastic remarks of an ordinary individual.

There has been a perpetual influence and impact of religious, moral and eternal values on Indian administrative set up whether it be republic, democracy or autocracy. The masses were the hub of authority. Democracy is not an acquisition of authority by a few but an acquisition of ability by all to resist authority when it is so abused. Real power emanates from the multitude. This conviction can be a great deterrent and can prevent any leader, king and administrator from becoming despotic, unrestrained, self-willed and indisciplined. All roads of administration lead to public welfare. The aims of the government should be directed by the eternal doctrine of *Satyam, Shivam, Sundram.* Its motives should be revolve around life, environmental, economic, social, political, administrative and cultural qualities. Prof. O.P. Dwivedi has classified eternal values in which Indians have great faith into nine groups: basic freedom; human rights and duties; representative democracy; rule by justice; equality and equal respect to all religions; federalism; non-communalism; secularism and security of minorities. These are very significant constituents of a democratic set-up. Transparency and morality are essential in administration. These eternal values are indispensable.

In the middle ages, the church propagated and established successfully the belief that the king was an emissary of God and he was not accountable to the masses but only to the Pope or Bishops. It displays that State-sovereignty was based on religion and was being directed and guided by it. This belief personified religion and circumscribed its domains. In the treatise *Aguttar nikaya* of Buddhist philosophy, a question was asked as to who is the king of the king? The answer was—king of king is *Dhamma (Dharma)*. Here *Dhamma* does not point out towards a person or an institution, but to high standards to perform duties. The king was accountable to the moral and ethical codes of conduct and not to the person or the institution. We come across many legends regarding monopoly wielded by people like Chanakya, sages and other teachers with respect to powers of the State. They were not autocrats. They were themselves checked and censored by moral and ethical codes. In the middle ages, representative form of government came into vogue. Beginning of this set-up can be considered to be the dawn of modern democratic form of government. Representative system gave rise to Parliament. With the passage of time Parliament went on assuming more powers and almost all functions of the State were performed according to its consent and directions.

In the *Sanatana* tradition historical importance of democracy is always to be reckoned with. Manu's polity having peculiarity of subtle thoughts, serious research, rightfulness, natural religious inclination and moral and ethical codes is better than western polity in many ways. Sir Charles Metcalfe had said that the Aryan politics not only influenced the big State but also its influence ushered in a system of democratic form in village that those people used to solve their problems themselves preventing them from visiting bigger courts. So while being subjugated to all pervasive State power they existed as free and happy individuals.

In fact, democracy or democratic government is one where the subject is both the ruler and the ruled. The subject constitutes its representative assembly and everyone has equal right in its election. One amongst them is elected chairperson and is given state powers for a particular fixed period of time. This form of government is not devoid of fear in spite of being very sweet in the beginning. The king was the head of representative assembly. Like a doctor well versed in medical knowledge the king adorned the assembly. The fear, however, was that the king may become an autocrat.

Diversity of knowledge is natural. So it is indispensable to take into consideration trivial and insignificant power and exalted and significant power. If the people are given the right *in toto* to administer the State there is every likelihood of disorder at a later stage. This very right will become a noose for them because so long as the people remain just, religious, learned, prudent and diplomatic, there remains peace on all fronts in the State. If this is not the case, then money, lust for power, intoxication of state power lead to disorder as happened in the Roman empire.

In the beginning kingship started in the shape of democratic institution in India. The king was elected by the people. Even when the king and the institution of kingship became hereditary, the king had to administer with the advice and cooperation of the assembly and the committee of councillors. Importance of these democratic institutions can be gauged from the fact that in the Vedic literature they are called two daughters of Brahma *(prajapati)* one was the congregation of the masses and the other constituted of prominent citizens.

Democracy is not merely a form of government but a life-style in itself. It is based on the conviction that man is a rational creature and his specific individuality must be accepted and respected. Therefore, he must have the right to express his views and thoughts and influence his society and administration. Giving due respect to the freedom of other people he should have the freedom to mould his life socially, politically and economically as per his aspirations.

10

Caste as a System of Governance

Bharat Jhunjhunwala

Caste System is designed to secure good governance.

Editor

Not a day passes by without some leader or the other exhorting the people to combat the 'dark forces of casteism threatening the fabric of society'. Perhaps the situation is not as clear as it seems. The *jati* system had its merits and democracy has actually deprived the people of those rights. It appears that what might be the denouncement of the people is being projected, and accepted, as their empowerment.

An old farmer of Jodhpur once explained how the society was organized by *jati.* Every adult had a profession—*Kurmis* practised agriculture, *Yadavas* bred cattle, *Sonars* made ornaments, and so on. The *jati* panchayat of each of the professions set the rules of the trade—quality, price and other commercial terms—by consensus. It also delivered justice. Any unsatisfied member of the *jati* could approach the larger panchayat of 100 villages and continue doing so until the king arbitrated on the matter. A *Kumhar* not satisfied with the distribution of earth from the village tank could insist that *kumhar* panchayat be called to decide the matter. His call for justice involved no expenditure and was decided by the people of his own profession.

The situation is similar to the governance of the modern *jatis* of doctors, lawyers and chartered accountants. The Medical Council of India frames the basic rules within which each member of the profession of doctors has to ensure—that he will not display a signboard, that he will not deny treatment on the grounds of religion and caste, that he will not do the business of selling drugs, and so on. The State Medical Council is their panchayat of first recourse. Not satisfied they may approach the Medical Council of India. As last recourse a doctor may approach the Supreme Court—an organ of the king.

Just as a doctor values his registration certified with the MCI so also a milkman was proud of his membership of the *jati* of *Yadavas*. His Yadavahood was his route to security and justice and access to the king. His *jati* was his empowerment just as the MCI is for a doctor.

Now every young lad got automatic membership in the *jati* of his father. Nothing unusual. After all, Rishi Kapoor gets spontaneous admission into the *jati* of actors and Rajiv Gandhi to that of politicians. If one wished to change his profession then it was up to the host *jati* to grant admission or not. Nothing unusual again. It is up to the *jati* of doctors—the MCI being its apex organ—whether to admit a member of the *jati* of lawyers.

In periods of technological change new *jatis* would be formed—software engineers, for example—and old ones would disappear. These periods have always been difficult. And this is what we are grappling with presently. The industrial revolution and the expansion of the service sector has created new *jatis* and many old ones have started disappearing. In this period of transition, inter-*jati* mobility is essential. Birth-based determination of profession does not work in periods of technological change. Thus, 'caste' has become a 'dark force' and it was rightly rejected as a method of governance.

Our people have been organized in *jatis* since time immemorial. We think of *jati* because *jati* was the source of livelihood, security and justice. True, it had become corrupted in many ways. The harassment faced by Ambedkar was only because the system had lost its inner vitality and had been hijacked by a few upper castes for their personal aggrandizement. *Jati* had to go and it went. But in the process we have also deprived ourselves of profession-based security, governance and justice.

We need to think afresh which is better; area-based or profession-based governance. What we need is perhaps an amendment to the Constitution. Let us give the freedom to every young lad to choose his professional association as he turns 18. And, let us make profession-based constituencies. Let a Yadava represent the interests of Yadavas in the Parliament. Let the software engineers decide whom they want to represent them. Geographical constituencies do not make sense for those elected are not accountable to any profession whatsoever.

We threw away the baby with the bath water. We deprived the individual of his rights under the *jati* system and handed him a scrap of paper on which he affixed a rubber stamp every five years. And, the fun of it all is that it is being called empowerment. It is thus that our people continue to think in terms of *jati*. Perhaps wisely so for they recognize the emptiness of the vote and long for the power that they had through their *jati* panchayats.

11

The Democratic Nature of Indian Monarchy

Panchanand Misra

> The basic model of Indian governance is that of decentralisation. Coalition governments are a welcome form of the same decentralisation.
>
> *Editor*

The history of India since the advent of the Buddha reveals that there were seven republics and sixteen kingdoms. Amongst the seven republics, Kapilvastu and Lichavi were most important. The administration was democratic in the modern sense of the term. Amongst the sixteen kingdoms, the most important were Koshal, Awanti, Vatsa and Magadh. These small republics were soon amalgamated in the neighbouring kingdoms and there emerged monarchies. Ultimately the Magadh empire became all powerful. That paved the way for the Mauryas, the Guptas, the Vakatakas, and ultimately the sharp rule of Harshavardhan.

Thereafter began the Muslim invasion of India. The Sultanate rule led to the establishment of autocratic rule of the Sultan. Then came the Mughals who established a very strong empire in India and the climax was reached during the despotic rule of Aurangzeb.

The Mughals were followed by the European traders and ultimately, the East India Company emerged all powerful. But the power of the East India Company was taken away. This led to the establishment of a powerful British empire in India.

The British were anxious to learn about the history of India and the customs and traditions of the people so as to lay down the empire on a firm footing. It was Vincent Smith who wrote the history of India and developed the theory that India would disintegrate as soon as the central government became weak. This led to the development of another myth of oriental despotism. That provided the philosophy of establishing a strong central government in India and, therefore, the Governor General of India emerged as the grand emperor.

In order to fulfill the aspirations of the people of India certain constitutional concessions were given leading to the establishment of a representative government and provincial autonomy. On the one hand certain powers were given to the people, more and more power was given to the Government and the Governor General on the other.

When the country was partitioned and India became independent, the framers of the Indian Constitution were also convinced with the ideology of centralisation of power otherwise the country would further disintegrate. Gaining experience of working in the British parliamentary system, the framers framed a Constitution after the British model of a parliamentary democracy in India. They established a Union of States with a very strong Centre. When a few members of the constituent assembly suggested a Constitution based on village *panchayat,* they were very strongly silenced by Dr. B.R. Ambedkar who regarded the villages as the cause of regionalism, localism and the ultimate ruination of India.

However, India had basically been a decentralised State. The Centre constituted of the central sovereign power. It collected tributes and sent army when called for. In all other respects the provinces were autonomous. At local level, democracy was accepted in the village *panchayats.* This system of administration was not basically changed either by the Sultans or Mughals. Rather when Harshavardhan attempted to ignore the local aspiration and led to strong personal rule, the country disintegrated and soon came under the control of the Muslims. When Aurangzeb also attempted to establish autocratic rule, the decline of the Mughal empire began. The overcentralisation of the British power also led to their having to lease India.

Therefore, the Indian historical experience has been of decentralisation of power, giving due respect to regional and local aspirations which the country had developed during the thousands of years. This idea had been forgotten during the two centuries of British rule in India. India is a vast country with great diversity. During the first four decades of India's independence there had been a trend towards centralisation of power. The dominance of one party at the Centre had virtually brought about party leadership deciding the fate of the provincial leadership disregarding the wishes of their own constituents. During the last decade the concept of one party rule has been rejected by the electorate resulting in a coalition government at the Centre.

As a matter of fact we have suffered from the 'myth of oriental despotism' of Vincent Smith who had created the idea of a strong Central government in the interest of British imperialism. The myth of oriental despotism in fallacious. Even with the decline of republics and emergence of monarchy in India, the pattern of government was not absolute monarchy as illustrated in Kautilya's *Arthashastra.* The ideal monarchical system was the Mauryan administration which was a mixture of monarchy, aristocracy and democracy. Decentralisation alone can fulfil local aspiration and satisfy regional identity.

The parliamentary democracy of India has now grown on the Indian soil and has discarded the British model of two-party system. The Coalition Government has come to stay in India which is really the embodiment of true federalism of peculiar Indian tinge. Therefore, there is the need to recognise local aspirations and undertake decentralisation of power. In spite of all the diversities we all belong to our motherland, i.e., India. The devotion to our motherland is the essence of our Indian cultural heritage that has sustained our culture throughout the vicissitudes of time and space. Lack of this devotion is the cause of all our sufferings and agony. All the ancient civilisations of the world have perished but we alone have survived because of this devotion to our motherland and our spiritual values. Let us justify this pride through the great Indian poet, Iqbal, and his faith in the immorality of the destiny of our great, historic, and ancient country, which he sums up in these beautiful lines:

Yunan-o-Misr-o-Roma sab mit gaye jahan se;
Baqi abhi talak hai nam-o-nishan hamara,
Kuch bat hai ke hasti mit-ti nahin hamari;
Sadiyon raha hai dushman daur-e-zamana hamara.

(Greece, Egypt and Rome have all disappeared from the surface of the earth; but the name and fame of India, our country, has survived the ravages of time and cataclysms of ages.)

12

Materialism, Spirituality and Democracy

Bhola Prasad Singh

> Marxist and liberal thinkers try to create social harmony within a materialistic ideology. This is impossible. Social harmony can only be established on the basis of religion.
>
> *Editor*

After independence, one of the main issues that has constantly animated the intellectual debate is the issue of the role of *Sanatana* or Hindu way of life—its world view, its metaphysics, its norms and rituals. A powerful group of Westernised intellectuals has taken upon itself the task of defending minoritism and debunking the Hindu way of life as retrogressive and harmful for the unity of secular India. Secularism is its *mantra* and Western ideologies, especially liberalism and Marxism, provide it with the food for thought. The ideas of the first prime minister of India Jawaharlal Nehru are its guidelines as all of these secularists, whether of Marxist or liberal hues, swear by the name of Nehruvian secularism. Jawaharlal Nehru's writings and speeches abound in stringent criticisms of Hinduism. For example, while talking to K.N. Katju on 17th November, 1953, Nehru said, "In practice, the Hindu is certainly not tolerant and is more narrow minded than almost any person in any country except the Jews." He gave a clean chit to minority communalism by terming it as "honest communalism". He once remarked, "Honest communalism is fear, false communalism (Hindu communalism) is political reaction." It was Nehru's fond belief that India cannot be secular unless Hindu communalism is curbed. The establishment of a "secular State and society are vital if India is to survive."[1] These views of Nehru are the main premises of the present secularists of India which can be seen in the columns of journalists like Prafulla Bidwai, Arvinda Das, Rajdeep Sardesai, Amulya Ganguli, Veer Sanghvi and host of others and in the writings of Marxist and liberal historians of JNU and Delhi University. The writings and views of these Marxists and liberal journalists and professors are staple food for the actions and programmes of caste mobilizers like Laloo Prasad Yadav, Mulayam Singh, Kanshi Ram and communist politicians like Jyoti Basu, Surjeet Singh and others.

Secularist Attack on Hindu Cultural Nationalism

Indian secularists call themselves either liberals or Marxists but they use the same language, same cliches, same jargon and the same ideological premises while damning the Hindu Dharma. The dividing line between liberals and Marxists is very thin in the Indian context and, in reality, as will be shown later in the discussion, Marxism is in fact "inverted liberalism" Examples of some pet themes with which they try to debunk Hindu way of life can be given below:

1. Secularists of liberal school advance the argument that the advocates of Hindu cultural nationalism have hijacked a tolerant liberal religion and are trying to convert it into Christianity. But in another breath they also say that these people believe in the *sati* and rigid caste system.
2. They present electoral figures to advance the argument that majority of Hindus do not support cultural nationalism. But they quickly contradict this argument by saying that middle class educated households are coming under the spell of Hindutva philosophy.
3. They ridicule and condemn the values and norms contained in ancient Indian history and culture and want to replace it by Western values and ideas. In fact they have little or distorted knowledge of Hinduism and ancient Indian history and philosophy.
4. They decry cultural nationalism as stifling and injurious to minority's religious and cultural aspirations and talk of cultural pluralism by giving examples of the so-called 'melting pot' model of American secular nationalism. This shows that they have either very poor information about

American society or they deliberately present America as a model of secular society by suppressing the reality. Prof. Gautam Sen has rightly remarked that, "The implicit premise that the US is not a religious society or that it treats its minorities fairly is a rubbish. Heaven forbid that India treat its minorities with the same callous disregard shown by US society towards its black citizens."[2]

5. They put forward this audacious lie that "Hindus and Muslims were largely amicable in the past and that contemporary Hindu cultural nationalism is provoking enemity which previously existed only on the margins." According to Gautam Sen: "In this rewriting of history there is no mention of imperial conquests by the Arabian and the Turkish Muslim invaders, and of abduction, slavery, forced conversion, mass murder *(katl-e-am)* and desecration of holy places. It is quite amazing that Pakistan and Bangladesh do not figure in this history of serenity in the Indian subcontinent and the population figures constantly being brandied about. They highlight overwhelming Hindu dominance but do not mention the religious roots of terrorism in Kashmir and North East; the causes of Indo-Pakistan wars; whose underlying reasons are more religious and less political; the role of *Mujahideens* and ISI agents; the Organisation of Islamic Countries support to Pakistan on Kashmir; the hostility of Bangladesh despite India's help to it in attaining independence."[3] Instead they talk of military mismanagement and intelligence failure in Kargil war, about the uselessness of nuclear weapons and about pacificism at the cost of India's security because they have to attack a government which upholds nationalism.

These are some of the themes with which Indian secularists attack cultural nationalism and *Sanatana* way of life in the name of liberalism and Marxism.

Symbiosis between Liberalism and Marxism

The unity between Liberal and Marxist secularists against *Sanatana* way of life is not unnatural as both spring from the same sources. These are children of European materialism and semitic religions. The structural similarities between Islam and Marxism are striking; both believe in one prophet Muhammad or Marx; both believe in one book, *Koran* or *Das Capital*; both believe in one aim, establishment of communist society or Umma. A detailed analysis of these similarities between Islam and Marxism is the subject matter of a separate article and this will not be attempted here. Similarly, the difference between Liberalism and Marxism are that of tactics of distributing wealth and title of ownership of property otherwise both are materialists and imperialists in nature. This fact will become apparent in course of the unfolding of this article. But it will not be out of place to quote some of the ideas of Eric Fromm who is regarded as one of the most brilliant leftist intellectuals of Europe but now he is completely disillusioned with European materialism of both Liberal and Marxist varieties.

Eric Fromm speaks of two modes of living; one is the mode of 'having' which is equivalent to Hindu view of *Bhog*. It is the materialist mode of living. The other is mode of 'to be', that is the mode of transforming oneself from an ordinary living being to a perfect human being. Because both Liberalism and Marxism are materialist ideologies they emphasise the 'mode of having'. Eric Fromm writes: "Socialism and communism quickly changed from a movement whose aim was a new society and new man into one whose ideal is a bourgeois life for all, the universalized bourgeois as the men and women of future."[4] This mode of having has failed and so its both versions, Liberalism and communism, have also failed because this mode is based on three values:

(a) unlimited production;
(b) absolute freedom; and
(c) unrestricted happiness.

All these three materialistic values have produced unwholesome consequences for human life because unrestricted satisfaction of all desires is not conducive to well-being, nor is it the way of happiness or to attain maximum pleasure. (i) This value has produced large-scale crime, pollution and fragmentation in developed industrial societies. (ii) The liberal individualist dream of being the independent masters of one's life ended when one awakened to the fact that we have all become cogs in the bureaucratic machine with our thoughts, feelings and tastes manipulated by government and industry and the mass communication that they control. (iii) Economic progress has remained restricted to the rich nations and the gap between rich and poor nations has ever widened, and the poor countries have fallen prey to the designs of comprador class. (iv) Technological progress has created ecological danger and the danger of nuclear war which may put an end to all civilization and the possibility of all life.[5]

The so-called intellectuals of the capitalist industrial societies and the representatives of the comprador class of the developing societies proclaim the indispensability of liberalism and flaunt two psychological premises in its support. They are: (a) the aim of life is happiness (following Bentham and J.S. Mill), i.e., maximum pleasure defined as the satisfaction of any desire or subjective need a person may feel; and (b) that egotism, selfishness and greed are the systems which generate it and help function. These are essential for progress and harmony in the long run. This premise is based on social Darwinism. The first premise is based on utilitarianism of English School of Liberals which was rejected in its very heyday but the liberals of today are again advocating it.

As to the second premise that greed ultimately leads to harmony is a premise upon which the conflicting theories of different types are based and which forms the main plank of the social mobilization theory. It is patently injurious to social harmony. According to Eric Fromm, greed and peace preclude each other. Criticizing Marxist theory of class struggle as the engine of social change, Fromm comments: "The pretense of the communists that their system will end class struggle by abolishing classes is a fiction; for their system is based on the principle of unlimited consumption as the goal of living. As long as everybody wants to have more, there must be formation of classes, there must be class war and, in global terms, there must be international war. Thus both Liberal and Marxist theories are destined to be enimical to the establishment of social harmony of domestic as well as international levels."[6]

Secularist View of History

Secularists of both liberal and Marxist varieties speak of progress, modernism and development, etc. In their view *sanatanism,* because of its roots in the ancient Indian past, has no relevance for modern India, which has to follow the path of Western industrialized nations if it wants to achieve the status of a modern secular nation State. The ideas of progress and modernism are rooted in a particular notion of history, the hallmark of which is the denigration of past.

This notion of progress is fully developed in Hegel's philosophy of history, according to which history of man always evolves in linear direction. This is called the linear view of history. According to him history is the manifestation of spirit or *weltgeist* which is marked by catastrophies, defeats and triumphs and every decline and rise leads to the next higher manifestation of the spirit. Thus, man's social, economic, political and cultural life can be explained according to this assumption and those aspects of man's life which are not susceptible to the explanation of this assumption are treated as accidents and chances. Hegel's notion of "oriental despotism" and Marx's idea of the "Asiatic mode of production" are examples of accidents and chances because they defy the explanation offered by Hegel's dialectics of development and Marx's historical materialism. According to German scholar Golo Mann, Marx adopted Hegel's idea of the progressive manifestation of the spirit by replacing Hegel's "worlds" (civilizations that can be understood by means of their spirit) by social classes which were produced by the development of economic forces of production and production conditions.[7] According to Marx, one ruling class succeeds another thereby exploiting the large majority of men for its own profit until the industrial proletariat seizes power, annihilates class rule and destroys the State. The idea of a historical progress gives Marxists an unbounded hope for future and helps them to reject past as constituting the different stages of barbarism. It gives them impetus to debunk the cultural and religious heritage of mankind in the name of progress and modernity.

As a result of this linear view of history, the colourful multi-dimensionality of the past is either ignored or deliberately misinterpreted and instead as Golo Mann remarks, "a grey monotony of production statistics and economic conditions"[8] are presented in a prosaic manner.

"History", according to Golo Mann, "denotes both aggregate of past events and the activities of historians, i.e., their perception, presentation and precepts. The past comes to life only if one knows it in detail, investigates it and interprets it without any preconceived notions and ideological predilection".[9] But Indian secularists of liberal and Marxist schools adhere to Marxist approach of the materialistic interpretation of history with its idea of progress, of modernism and development and they share common prejudices against *Sanatana Dharma.* They repeat Marx's views against Hinduism. Two quotes from Marx's writings are presented here to show that like many westerners (a) Marx was deeply antagonistic to Hindu way of life; and (b) Marx had a false and inadequate understanding of Hinduism. Failing to evaluate the meaning of religious symbols Marx writes that "Hindu religion brought about a brutalizing worship of nature, exhibiting its degradation in the fact that man, the sovereign of nature fell down on his knees in adoration of Hanuman the monkey and, Sabala, the cow."[10] Further, while praising capitalism as the penultimate stage of development of human civilization and its takeover by communist revolution as the highest stage of development he equates Hindu civilization with barbarism. He writes, "When the great social revolution (communist revolution) shall have mastered the bourgeois epoch, the market of the world and the modern power of production (created by capitalism) and subject them to common control... then only will human progress cease to resemble that Hindoo pagan idol who would not drink the nector but from the skull of the slain." Both of these quotations betray Marx's prejudices and poor knowledge of an ordinary ignorant westerner against religion and culture. Most secularists of India also betray the same ignorance about Hindu cultural and religious symbols.

In fact, in relation to Asia in general and India in particular Marx and Engels were no better than the ordinary imperialists of their time. In his writings Engels appears to share Cecil Rhode's imperialistic notion of "white man's burden" when he says, "European proletariat would have to take over the colonies and temporarily lead them autocratically towards modernization since they may not be able to do it themselves."

In fact, both Marx and Engels were the supporters of British imperialism in India. Justifying British colonialism in India Marx says, "can mankind fulfill its destiny without fundamental revolution in the social state of Asia. If not, whatever may have been the crimes of England she was the unconscious tools of history in bringing about the revolution." Thus, Marx shares Cecil Rhode's idea of "white man's burden". The Indian secularists are the true heirs of their Western masters. In the language they write, the ideologies they advance, and the value they profess they appear to be completely cut off from their cultural roots.

The Hegelian unilinear view of history which the secularists share with the Western intellectual forefathers, was rejected during Hegel's lifetime itself. It was soundly and forcefully rejected by many schools of historiography, one of which was called "historicism" in Germany. Its main proponent Leopold Von Ranke declared that every system, every historical development, endeavour and decision was unique and, therefore, must be interpreted as the product of circumstances, not in accordance with the place it occupied in the history of "progress". According to Ranke every epoch is 'equivalent from God' and that no age is better than the preceding age solely because it is later. Similarly, both Oswald Spangler and Arnold Toynbee rejected the idea of universal history and continuous progress. The works of both these philosophers of history are distinguished by an abundance of images, figures, detailed assessments and even striking predictions which a very few committed secularists and Marxist historians can match. Ideological drudgery can never replace imagination and creativity.

The dogma of dichotomy between tradition and modernity is the fashion of secularists of both tribes. They forget that we can not cut history with a hatchet into the past and the present because past always recurs in present. J.D.M. Derret has rightly remarked that, "Tradition is that element in the present which represents (or re-presents) the past." This is a guideline that no creative historian can ignore. By imaginatively examining tradition of a society a historian can assess the merits and failings of the past of a society because tradition always looms large on the collective psyche of a society. Through tradition past advances towards us and becomes the present. Therefore, to exclude the tradition along with spontaneous, irrational, pathological and human elements from history and to reduce it to the operation of economic and social forces leads a historian to a type of intellectual impertinence which is precisely being shown by secularists of India today.

Western Ideologies and Secularist Propaganda

With the transfer of power from the British imperialist government to the West-oriented Nehru government, the secular propagandists started dominating the intellectual space in India. Under the agencies of Nehruvian secularism they started advocating a mix of liberal, democratic and Soviet models of development for India. Both of these models were anti-tradition and anti-culture and emphasised Western values and outlook. Gandhism, which is a truely temporal version of *Sanatana dharma*, with its emphasis on *Ram Rajya*, rural upliftment, decentralization of power and non-violent State and society, was rejected by his heir-apparent Nehru in Gandhi's own lifetime. Gandhism appeared unpalatable to the Westernized elite led by Nehru because they saw the solution of every problem in either Liberal or Marxist approaches. As a result, as J.D. Sethi remarks. "He was deserted by his closest co-workers. His senior colleagues ignored his advice. Congress leaders were too anxious to get to power even if it meant running roughshod over Gandhi." Further, as Ved Mehta says, "Few of Gandhi's followers caught his vision and fewer still followed through with the experiments with Truth." Gandhism was thus aborted by the same people whom Gandhi himself anointed as his heir and with this the hope of establishing a genuine Indian political system was also aborted.

The Nehruvian mix of Liberal and Marxist approaches has fixed the framework of governance in India. As a consequence, from the very beginning of Independence, our policy planners have been moving back and forth in the alloy of Western theories and approaches alternating between liberal capitalism and communist totalitarianism forgetting that capitalism and communism, despite their confrontations, are deeply rooted in European materialism, while Indian civilization has a long hoary spiritual past encompassing centuries. But their linear view of history compelled them to reject the values and standards of ancient Indian civilization and adopt Western values and standards in the name of progress and modernity. The Indian "collective unconscious" to use Jung's concept, was not ready, and is still not ready, to adopt itself to these Western values. As a result, the development efforts have not produced any desired result though experiments after experiments have been taken recourse to. The half baked and vicillating policies of development have produced what is called 'uneven development'. There is a wide disparity between urban and rural sectors and regions. Metropolises like Mumbai, Delhi, Chandigarh and Bangalore, have become the abodes of the comprador class and big business houses and the rural India is still mired in illiteracy, poverty and darkness. This uneven development is the natural consequence of social Darwinian liberalism and totalitarian Marxism. An analysis of the actuality of liberal democracy and Marxist classless society may make clear their unsuitability for the country of the Third World.

Despite the changes in capitalism and its corresponding political formations, social Darwinism has remained its fundamental underlying principle which manifests itself in consumerism, libertarianism, commodification of human values and ideas and the advocacy of the functional utility of the social conflicts and competition. With these 'liberal' values the industrialized capitalist countries of West are trying to subjugate the economic and political sovereignty of the Asian and African countries. Many of these countries have already become "dependent states" with "dependent economies". With these two concepts, the theorists of the 'Dependencia school' of Latin America have analysed the capitalist exploitation of the Third World countries and the political and economic restructuring of these countries under the influence of the so-called liberal States under the leadership of the USA. The dependent States of the Third World have been forced to follow the dictates of WTO, IMF and World Bank to redraw their economic policies which serve these liberal capitalist countries and their multinational corporations. These dependent States are governed by new 'State class' or a plutocracy consisting of big business houses aligned with foreign multinational corporations, technocrats, managers, journalists serving in the newspapers controlled by business houses and other hangers on. This analysis decisively locates the place of the Indian secularists in this plutocracy.

Analysing the nature of dependent States and their dependent economies John D. Nagel writes: "Dependent economic development is tied to social and political dependency, the creation of clientele or comprador social elites whose influence comes from serving powerful foreign interests. This comprador stratum includes the local bourgeoisie, too weak to compete with multinational corporations, but able to act as a junior partner in middle-men and service roles. It includes the higher bureaucracy which allows the multinational activity, suppresses local dissent (for example, attack by secularists added and abeted by Indian bureaucracy on Swadeshi Jagran Movement) and militant union activity, and provides a tiny island of luxury consumption through the pilfering of State funds and bribes from the multinationals. These islands of affluence can be seen in nearly every Third World capital city, rising out of the cardboard and tin-can shanty towns that surround the capital."

In India these cardboard and tin-can shanty towns, called *chals* (slums), are mostly inhabited by rural poor who come to town for better wage and better standard of living but find themselves surrounded by social Darwinists who, through their agents, the secular journalists and so-called activists, exploit their labour and encourage further exodus from villages by publishing inspired articles and editorials against the higher castes and landowners in the so-called leading national newspapers owned and controlled by big business houses like Birlas, Goenkas and Tatas.

The Marxist secularists have further weakened our agriculture economy and social bonds by creating frankensteins in the name of Naxalite movement. The various groups of Naxalites have created havoc in the rural areas by killing innocent people branding them as big landowners and members of higher castes. Bihar, especially central Bihar, presents a grim picture of Naxalite violence which is perpetrated in the name of the emancipation of rural poor. But this is a ruse. They are casteist adventurists and criminals as the objective social and economic situations do not warrant their ideological claims and violent activities. Some examples from Naxalite infested Jehanabad District of central Bihar can be cited to substantiate this conclusion. Ever since this district was created in April 1986, violence in this region has only grown resulting in human slaughter in one after another encounter. The Naxalites wage caste war in the name of social justice and economic emancipation. But the facts belie their claim. In 1987, a survey was conducted by the then collector of Jehanabad to assess the degree of land alienation among poor people of rural areas and the concentration of the same among the members of the so-called high caste. The survey report revealed that except for dozen families none owned over 50 *bighas* of land in the district. Nearly 80 per cent of the people (both higher and lower castes) had not more than 1 to 5 *bighas* and the rest having 5 to 10 *bighas* each. Even these holdings have mutated so much so that to say that landlords still exist in the area is a travesty of truth. These Marxist adventurists are still following the moth-eaten theory that with the inevitable growth of capitalism in the countries of the Third World the agriculture sector will also be industrialised creating the two classes of haves and have-nots who will wage class struggle in the rural areas and create base for eventual take over of the country by the communist vanguards. The application of this theory in various ways by the communist extremists in south and central Bihar speaks of its own bankruptcy. They have declared peasants, having only subsistence level of land ownership, as landlords, made them targets of attacks inviting counter-attacks in which innocent people of both castes (higher and lower) are killed mercilessly while State-protected owners of industrial houses in metropolises like New Delhi, Mumbai and Bangalore, etc., are enjoying the traits of what Marxists called the "surplus value by playing second fiddle of the American multinationals."

Conclusions: The *Sanatan* Alternative

The present leadership and the secularist propagandists serving the interests of comprador class have brought Indian social order on the brink of destruction by aping Western values and social Darwinist ideologies. In the name of secular humanism, they have created a licentious middle class in the metropolises and unscruplous caste mobilizers in the rural areas. Both of them are eating into the very vitals of age old Indian values and ideals. They have made a fetish of secularism, thus creating, what Raymond Aron has called, 'orthodoxies without doctrine.'

These secularists have no idea of an integral human life which *Sanatana Dharma* provides and which aims at a complete harmony between man and nature and between man and society. The *Sanatanist* view of integral life is based on ideas of *Atmwat Sarv Bhuteshu* and *Sarv Khalwid Brahm* (The entire world is guided by the one ultimate power and therefore every being, conscient and non-conscient, are his creation). As such we must treat all beings as equal. The *Sanatan* view does not accept the Darwinian view of struggle for existence and survival of fittest on which both liberalism and Marxism are based. It advances the idea of *Sarve Bhawantu Sukhinah* against the so-called technological rationale and the Biblical doctrine that "man is the measure of everything", which have paved the way for merciless exploitation of nature. The *Sanatana* view advances the idea that whatever is available in this world for your consumption is the gift of God. Therefore, man must enjoy these gifts presented by God not out of greed but to sustain one's life. Nature is not for collection of riches and exploitation. She sustains us like our mother. These are not mere ideal verses. They can form the ideological pillars upon which a real egalitarian and peaceful society can be created.

No doubt religion and politics are two distinct modes of life, former an expression of *vita contemplativa* and latter that of *vita activa* yet two are hierarchically related. Accordingly, politics is governed by religion (in the sense of righteousness). It follows that to separate the political realm from the sacred and to make it sovereign is necessarily a politics of exploitation and oppression. Gandhiji has summarised this view in a single sentence:"Politics without religion is a soulless machine." So long as the Westernizing elite and secular propagandists continue to swear in the name of secularism and attack our *Sanatana* values and principles, India will remain afflicted by the organised anarchy which we are witnessing today.

Notes and References

1. All quotations are from G. Parthsarthy and S. Gopal, "Jawaharlal Nehru and Quest for a Secular Identity", *Occasional Papers on History and Society* (New Delhi: Nehru Memorial Museum, May, 1987).
2. Gautam Sen, *Indian Express* (20-11-1993).
3. *Ibid.*
4. Eric Fromm, *To have or to be* (London: Penguin, 1990).
5. *Ibid*, pp. 12-14.
6. *Ibid.*
7. Golo Mann, 'History and Historiography Today' *Universitas*, Vol. 19, No. 4 (1977).
8. *Ibid.*, p. 263.
9. *Ibid.*, p. 259.
10. Marx, *Selected Writings* (Moscow: International Publishers, 1962), Vol. 1, pp. 350-51.
11. Karl Marx in *New York Diary Tribune* (August 8, 1853) Quoted in R.G. Peffer, *Marxism, Morality and State* (Princeton: Princeton University Press, 1990), p. 401.
12. Engels in Marx and Engels, *Colonialism* (Moscow: Progress Publishers, 1987), pp. 306-07.
13. J.D. Sethi, *Gandhi Today* (New Delhi: Vikas Publishing House, 1978), p. 46.
14. Ved Mehta, *Mahatma Gandhi and His Apostles* (Middlesex: Penguin, 1976).
15. John. D. Nagle, *Introduction to Comparative Politics* (Chicago: Nelson-Hall, 1985), p. 230.

16. Mathew Mammen, "Political upmanship behind carnages" *The Hindustan Times* (21-3-1999).
17. Anand Coomarswamy quoted in D.P. Singh, "Something concerning the roots of our crisis" (Presidential Speech delivered to the forty-second Indian Political Science Association at Jodhpur, 1984).

13

Inadequacy of Democracy

S.E. Bhelkey

> Democracy works only when there exists a higher principle of social good which is followed by all. This is *Dharma* as enunciated in our tradition.
>
> *Editor*

From Hobbes to Rousseau we come across various views and theories of human nature which stand at opposite poles. For Hobbes "the life of man is solitary, poor, nasty, brutish and short." (Leviathan Pt. I, Ch. 13). For him, "the condition of man is a condition of war of everyone against everyone, in which everyone is governed by his own reason." (Ch. 14). Against this, for Rousseau, man is good by nature and born free (vide, a discourse on the Origin of Inequality amongst Human Beings and the Social Contract). Both these philosophers proposed a contract theory for the formation of the society. The liberal positivist tradition developed democracy as a form of government in England in which Hobbes' theory of social contract had a considerable contribution. Rousseau advocated democracy as the best form of governance. Both these traditions have opposite conceptions of the human nature. Even then both advocate the theory of social contract and democracy as the best way of life in the modern times. However, it should be noted here that the great Greek philosopher Plato had condemned democracy.

The basic idea involved in the ideals and operations of democracy is not totally new to the Indian tradition. Nevertheless, the present form of democracy practised in India is adopted from the Western tradition and ideas. For India and Indians the democratic outlook and the democratic values consist of the ancient heritage which was observed even when the State was ruled by a king. The idea of a king as a ruler of the State was unique in the Indian society. In spite of king being the sole ruler of the State the freedom and dignity of each individual was preserved as an important value. The will of the people was reflected in the rule of the king, though it was managed through a different kind of mechanism. However, there is a rupture in the Indian tradition, especially since the Mughal era. When the Britishers invaded India the Indian society and polity was totally different. This was the period when Indians and the Indian tradition was exposed to the ideas, and way of life which was totally alien to its original psyche. The social, political and cultural situation compelled Indians to accept and imbibe modernization which was truely speaking Westernization. This opened an era of an exposure to the modern Western liberal tradition of thought in the various walks of life. In spirit, the Western democratic way of life shared with the ancient Indian values the foundations and presuppositions of the democratic values, though several forms of their expressions were exotic and repugnant. One should not believe that the democratic values of the modern world are foreign adoptions to the Indian culture. In this background we have to reassess the practice and applications of the democratic values and forms in our social and political life of present India.

Let us first try to understand the spirit or the essence of the concept of democracy in a philosophical way. Democratic way in essence accepts a possibility that one's own point of view is inadequate or even wrong and the other's point of view may yield truth and correctness. In this way the democratic mode establishes consistency, coordination and compatibility amongst varied views of those who live together forming one body politic. The democratic outlook, thus, arranges the men in the society in such a way that they cooperate with one another instead of entering into conflicts. In democracy, disagreement is honoured and a general consciousness is developed in spite of the disagreements without denying any of the disagreeing views but accommodating all of them into one whole. It creates a cooperative organisation of various views to work in a unity in a unified way. Democracy means the rule of the people. It is the participation of the people in the process of arriving at decisions which are meant for the State. The various views of the people are to be taken together to form a decision.

However, once a decision is taken, it becomes obligatory on the part of the people to execute the decision whole-heartedly. This is a part of the discipline without which democracy gets no meaning. Democracy grants a privilege to the people to participate in the process of decision-making and at the same time demands that the people hold the decision responsibily, and accept the consequences of the decision willingly. Although, democracy is called as the rule by the people, it does not mean that people are only rulers; in fact, the people who rule the society are ruled by themselves. Thus, democracy turns out to be a self-rule and it is the self-rule which is the best rule. A mature understanding of the people makes them aware of their duties and responsibilities. Any ruler has to be strong, since he has to control and regulate people. The strength of the citizens in a democratic State lies in their mature understanding of their duties and preparedness to face the consequences boldly. Democracy, thus, demands a self-restraint.

The process of arriving at a decision is a complex one. It is not expected that the views of each member are included. The main view which is in the interest of the society needs to be convinced to all the members. Thus, in every decision, there is a consent of each citizen, irrespective of his personal views and position. The democratic process thus evolves a general consensus not by force or temptation but by conviction. The differences amongst the various views of the people are not to lead to conflict and friction in the society but to resolve them into a wider frame where each view has its individuality to supplement and complement each other. Democracy thus creates an accommodative platform where individuality is not curbed. In a democracy, each individual enjoys freedom; it is the freedom within the social context and which is not against any individual or society but in the interests of other individuals and society.

The most delicate and misunderstood element of democracy is the freedom of an individual. This freedom is to be used not as a right but as a duty. The obligation 'right' is person-centered which treats the agent as an end and the society as a means, while the obligation 'duty' is society-centered which treats the agent as a means and society as an end to which the agent also belongs to as one of the members. In fact, this norm needs to be accepted and practised in India to strengthen the democratic rule. The Indian way of life needs to be oriented towards achieving social goals through collective endeavour instead of the personal pursuit of self-excellence. Adopting the ideal of democracy would help us in this direction and creating such a society-oriented awareness will make our democracy meaningful and fruitful. The process of arriving at a decision is a democratic way which involves freedom and participation of all citizens and the process of executing the decision demands discipline, commitment and restraint on the part of citizens. The essence of democracy does not lie merely in freedom, equality, and participation but also in discipline. In fact, freedom is not possible without an order within it and discipline takes care of the order due to which freedom becomes possible. Freedom suggests that there are no external restrictions or compulsions but without regulation it would become a chaos.

Democracy is a form of government in which the same agency plays both the roles, viz., that of a ruler and that of the ruled. This characteristic of democracy is its virtue which makes it much more than the form of a government. It becomes a structure of society and also a way of life. To rule and to be ruled turn out to be just functions which arise out of the social interactions amongst men when they live together to achieve a common goal. Democracy is a structure of self-governance which leads to practically no-governance. This is the ideal state of freedom in the social life. Nevertheless, the practice of democracy as a form of governance follows a chain of procedures.

Today, we practise representative democracy and not direct democracy since the size of the society has become very big. Although democracy is understood as a self-rule, we are practically ruled by our representatives. Certainly there is a considerable gap between the aspirations of our rulers and our own aspirations. This gap is creating problems and tensions in our social and political life. Freedom implies less constraints, less controls and less compulsions. This fact has mismanaged the role and behaviour of the representatives who rule the country. What we need, to begin with, is to make a distinction between regulation and restraint and also between discipline and chaos. In the social sphere, the worst type of conflict is between individual or personal interests and social interests. The items which are to be avoided or eliminated in the social life are brought under constraint. This is not curbing freedom but closing the avenues to go astray. When freedom and discrimination becomes indiscrete in a democratic set-up some regulations must be brought in as a part of discipline. In the present Indian context, this is relevant and more true.

It must be remembered that Plato, the philosopher who had advocated the idea of a philosopher king, has condemned democracy saying that it is the worst form of government. What he wanted was the rule of wisdom. The idea of a rule of a king has become obsolete and in no way it is desirable to revive it. Nevertheless, a society needs a rule and of course such a rule which does not become oppressive to any of the sections of the society. A rule is meant to regulate and not restrain, and a rule is to be such that it does not cause either slavery of shame or inequality amongst the members. When a rule is used for vested interests, it becomes atrocious. Hence a way is suggested that the source of control and exercise of a rule will remain with those who are to be ruled. This ideal of self-rule takes a political expression in the form of democracy. But for practical purposes the rule of the society does not remain with citizens in a representative democracy. The danger has occurred because the rulers who are representatives of the citizens do not represent the will of the society but work for their 'individual will' and petty interests. Unfortunately, the operations and exercise of an 'individual will' in the social affairs are not condemned and are not prohibited. Once the representatives get elected, they do not reflect any the social interests. The representatives have a responsibility and a responsibility implies regulation and discipline. In the true sense, the representatives have no accountability for any of their deeds or decisions. By getting elected, they get power and as soon as representatives get power, citizens become helpless and play to the whims and indiscriminate indulgences of their power.

Democracy stands for freedom, equality, justice and participation. All these principles demand responsibility. Responsibility comes out of regulation in attitudes and behaviour. In fact, democracy is understood as a form of self-rule and hence the regulations required for its rule, too, are expected to be self-imposed. However, if the society is not mature enough to behave so responsibly, we should think of bringing some modifications in the structure and functions of democracy. We must evolve some mechanism which will make rulers more responsible to the society. It is desirable to introduce some regulative principles which will prevent some of the undesirable modes in performing the roles of rulers. When citizens realize by majority that their elected representatives do not reflect their will, citizens should have the right either to direct effectively their representatives to follow the 'general will' or to call them back and also disqualify them for a certain period to serve as representatives.

It is seen that our democratic pattern allows the rule of a party and most of the parties are guided and led by either a charismatic personality or a small group of persons. In both these cases neither the will of the people nor the welfare of the people is reflected. It is true that a good and strong leadership is desirable for leading the nation successfully. However, such a naturally good and strong leadership is available exceptionally. Hence, collective leadership becomes the best alternative. It is seen that in many occasions either the minority or the might rules. In both these cases the general will is not guaranteed. The pattern or the mode which cannot obviously guarantee the rule of the general will should find no place in a democratic set-up.

In fact, what is referred to above is one paradox of democracy where the formal procedure is democratic and still the general will does not reflect in decisions and their execution in such a democratic set-up. There are some more paradoxes of democracy. When people elect their representatives to rule the country, people do it at their own cost. It is the public money which is spent for the electoral expenses. People also expect a stable, just and reasonable government which observes its primary concern as the welfare of people and the progress of the nation. But now none of these expectations are guaranteed. The elected members belong to the same nation, share the similar aspirations of national interests and still cannot show unity and solidarity amongst them. On the contrary, their personal aspirations and individual will prevails over every social consideration they are supposed to have and the security and welfare of the entire nation is at stake. When the elected members cannot work together in the interest of the nation, even then a democracy allows them to rule the country again and again. The disagreement amongst members or parties, the shifting commitments from one interest to another in the name of ideology makes the nation to pay for through the unbearable cost of elections. And the members who are responsible for all these have no accountability. When the people honestly and intensely feel that their representatives show responsibility and work for the welfare of the society following the general will, they are helpless, they cannot do anything. This is a paradox of democracy. There should be an arrangement that the elected members complete their term in a fairly good manner. In fact, the conscience of the elected representatives should be sharp and strong. However, it cannot be activated by any external means. And hence instead of expecting it and waiting for it, we should evolve some mechanism which will regulate the performance of the representatives. One can think of evolving an organisation consisting of chosen wise people of the country who are beyond any constitutional institutions and political organisations to control the representatives. In fact, the President also can serve this function but only with the help of a small group of persons and not singly to avoid any distant possibility of dictatorial tendencies. Leaving a decision at the hand of one individual is dangerous and forming a group of individuals is futile since it delays the matters and renders the decision ineffective.

Time is the most crucial factor which affects the individual and social life. Any benefit or gain, if it is untimely, becomes meaningless. If the decisions are to be taken and if they are to be executed in a democratic set-up, procedures are to be followed. However, the procedures are to be made time-bound. It will be a serious folly if we ignore the role and significance of time in social life. The span of human life and various achievements in human life are time-bound and time-dependent. If time-frame gets specified in the matters affecting social life, the sense of responsibility will increase. This is true in the juridical matters. Judiciary can keep a check on the political mismanagement provided the judicial decisions are taken and executed in a reasonable span of time. Our nation is suffering from inefficiency in social life, although by nature and in personal life, Indians are reasonably efficient. Efficiency is correlated with the factor of time, especially in the social life. Hence not only democracy but judiciary and all social institutions should recognize the time factor and follow it seriously.

The history of Indian people has shown that Indians are good by nature, although there have been several shameful events. The natural inclination of man is towards goodness and a free atmosphere allows the blossoming of the natural traits. Democracy creates a free and open atmosphere. However, the democratic pattern should be organized in such a way that it will generate self-regulating principles which will check the role of an individual will in the social life and promulgate the role and significance of the general will. A democratic pattern should show more regulative principles than constraints. A democracy should function in a balanced way, i.e., both the citizens and representatives should discharge their social obligations responsibly. It is only a self-regulating principle which can protect democracy from its internal paradoxes and external threats. A firm faith in the goodness of man and a strong belief in the freedom of man can save, correct and strengthen democracy, especially in the present Indian context.

14

Politics and the Social Good

M.N.V. Nair

> Democracy can survive only if poverty and under-employment are removed which, in turn, is possible only if the elected representatives cease misusing their power. This can happen only through a social consensus or *dharma*.
>
> *Editor*

The foundation of Civil Society is the Rule of Law. There are Statutory Laws enacted to implement government policies, Natural Laws reflecting the principles of natural justice and Social Laws embodying the values of society. An essential condition for the effectiveness of any system of laws is the determination of the community to uphold and defend them even though particular laws may be perceived as hostile to any individual or group. Two instances will illustrate this.

In the US, President Roosevelt and Congress were elected on a New Deal Programme wherein they enacted a number of legislations to implement them. The Supreme Court found them ultra vires of the Constitution and declared them void. To overcome the hurdle, the President sought to pack the Supreme Court with judges sympathetic to the New Deal. The Congress though committed to the New Deal refused permission to the President to violate the spirit of the Constitution and thus upheld the rule of Law.

In Pakistan, on the other hand, Gen. Zia-ul-Haq characterised the Constitution as just "a booklet of 10 to 12 pages. I can tear them up and say that from tommorrow, we shall live under a different system. Is there anybody to stop me?" There was none and he ruled until he died in an air accident.

In the long run, people will respect a system of laws only if it contributes to their welfare. In Pakistan, there was a general perception that the civilian rulers were manipulating the system for their personal and sectarian ends. Hence they meekly succumbed to military take-overs.

At the same time, India except for a brief aberration in the Seventies, has been able to uphold the Rule of Law and function within a democratic framework. It may be mentioned that India is one of the few multi-ethnic States which has been able to strengthen its unity and deepen the democratic processes while other States like the USSR, Yugoslavia and Pakistan have disintegrated. It is a tribute to the Founding Fathers of our Republic that they gave us a Constitution which has had the resilience to provide stability while enabling change in a peaceful manner. The re-organization of the States on the basis of language, the tackling of the demands for a Dravidian State in the South and Punjabi Suba in the North-West are classic examples of the dynamism of the Indian State structure and its ability to solve such problems peacefully within the existing constitutional framework.

This has become possible because the Indian Constitution is built on the assumption that people will obey the laws only if they are legitimate. And legitimacy is dependent on their ability to respond meaningfully to the articulated aspirations of the people. To ensure this, the Constitution has made it obligatory on the Governments to renew their mandates periodically. They have also provided an institutional framework for the making of laws, as well as their administration and adjudication in the event of disputes. They were in fact laying the foundation of a social revolution.

The Founding Fathers were aware that the State they were shaping on the principles of equality was resting on a fragile foundation of a society with centuries' old institutionalised social inequities and economic inequalities. They sought to mitigate the problem by providing for affirmative State action to reduce the inequities. This made it possible for the State to provide for preferential treatment to the Scheduled Castes and Backward Classes though such actions may militate against the principle of equality.

The Government since Independence has been pursuing a strategy of development designed for economic growth and the elimination of poverty and unemployment. Though it may have not been actually intended, the focus of the programme was on those endowed with the faculties to take advantage of the policy initiatives. Consequently, the strategy has primarily benefited the better-off sections of society. The hope that the benefits will trickle down to the poor and deprived do not appear to have occurred to any significant extent.

This situation would have been tolerated, as it has been for centuries in India, if the people believe it is natural with no hope of liberation. Their entry into the political process has made them aware of the possibilities of change and the role of governments in effecting them. The effort of political parties to win their support for securing power has given a further momentum to this process. They now realize that their votes matter and with every election, they are becoming more aggressive in its use.

Elections help this process in two ways. In the first place, they become conscious of their rights. In the second place, political parties are forced to formulate programmes to win their support.

The concerns of the upper sections of society are different from those of the poor and deprived. They can afford to have a long-term perspective and may be prepared to forego some of the gains of the present for the rewards of the future. Though it may be only skin-deep, they at least pretend to have commitment to the liberal philosophy of the Constitution. They are against corruption, criminalisation of politics, and use of power as an instrument of patronage. They are votaries of good governance, effective enforcement of the laws and political stability. They believe that merit should be the criteria for admission to educational institutions and recruitment to jobs.

The blinkered vision of the upper classes ignore stubborn social realities. They support the laws because they protect their interests. They support merit because merit gives them an advantage over those sections of society which did not historically have the institutional facilities to acquire them. They believe that social institutions are natural, permanent, and unchangeable. Therefore they appear to be justified in imagining that their privileges are natural and their interest coterminus with the interests of the society.

It is also a fact that their support to the philosophy behind the present system is also tenuous. They will have no hesitation in manipulating it if it gives them personal or sectarian advantage. They do not find any conflict of principles in supporting educational institutions where money and not merit is the criteria for entry. If money can buy the qualifications for entry into jobs, what happens to merit as the criterion for selection? They will also not hesitate to take to the streets if they perceive that a government policy, even though initiated as a product of a positive electoral mandate, will alter fundamentally a system of interests from which they benefited. The so-called liberation movement in Kerala in 1959 which resulted in the dismissal of a government enjoying a clear mandate when they tried to reform the land relations; the violent demonstrations which broke out in parts of North India in the early part of this decade following the decision of the government to implement the Mandal proposals for which it had a clear electoral mandate; and the violent efforts being made in Bihar to prevent the effective implementation of land reforms are clear examples of such attitudes.

The concerns of the poor and deprived are different. Their immediate problem is the present. Future has meaning for them only if they can survive until then. They find the laws of the system tilted against them. They see a ray of hope when they find that they, through the political process, can change the laws and the people who administer them. Therefore, they support the parties and leaders who promise such changes. Even if they do not always deliver, they still get support because the very assumption of power by them is perceived by the deprived as an assertion of their entry into positions of power and authority. They will ignore if such people accept bribes for giving of a license or awarding of a contract because they do not think that such things will affect their immediate interests.

When an African dictator made white men carry him sitting on a decorated chair, to the liberals of the West, it was a vulgar act but to the blacks who suffered slavery for centuries, it was an assertion of their power and authority.

This phenomenon has a negative effect on politics. Parties with populist programmes and extravagant promises which they have no intention of fulfilling emerge on the scene and vie for the votes of the poor. The poor may vote for them. The assertiveness and identification which they feel on the exercise of their franchise will give them a feeling of achievement. The increasing participation of the poor in the electoral process is an indication of this trend.

Some of the political parties which have cropped up recently are taking advantage of this trend. Many of them have no clearly worked out strategy for meaningful change which will confer benefits on the poor on a sustained basis. Herein lies the danger. When once their appetite is wetted, and steps are not taken to satisfy them, disillusion may result. It can have disastrous consequences.

Another danger is the tendency for political parties to undermine the institutions of State for sectarian and partisan ends. The state has enormous power of patronage. The Constitution guarantees the impartiality of the administration and the independence of the judiciary to ensure that control of State power is not used to distribute patronage and manipulate laws for partisan ends. There is a conscious effort to change this. The impartiality of the administration is being undermined to serve partisan ends. Merit and impartiality are not becoming the essential qualifications for judicial appointments. And above all, criminalisation of politics has grown to dangerous proportions. The number of people with criminal records in the Parliament and sometimes even in the Government are evidence of this trend. In this environment, institutional arrangement carefully constructed by the founding fathers have become important to play their designed role.

The danger to our democratic institution and the Rule of Law is primarily from two sources : (1) Inadequacy of the strategies of parties to effectively solve the problem of poverty and unemployment, and (2) The growing tendency to emasculate the institutions of State for personal and partisan ends.

If these two factors are ignored by the public, and the intelligentsia in particular, it may not be long before the people willingly submit to an end to the democratic process. The primary problem of the country is not instability but the misuse of power. The apparent instability is a symptom of the inability of the political parties to address themselves to the fundamental issues. The people have given their signal loud and clear. To ignore them and provide a technical solution to instability by giving a statutory life to Parliament or Government is the surest way to invite disaster and an end to the Rule of Law.

Democracy will survive only if it is able to address the fundamental problems of poverty and opportunities to the deprived. The Constitution has given a framework for addressing such concerns. It is the function of political parties to articulate policies and programmes which can meaningfully address them. The Constitution and the laws are not empty words but the abiding expression of our commitment to a civil society. Civil Society will survive only as long as we defend and uphold them.

PART II
HUMAN RIGHTS

15

Duties Before Rights

Mala Pyasi

The only right is the right to opportunities for self-development. There is no concept of other rights in Indian tradition. Only duties are stressed.

Editor

"Assemble here, O *stotas*! May you all sing the hymns in the same way in harmony. May you all be of same mind. Just as the gods are of same mind when they come to *Yagna* to gather the offering, so too you all be of one mind and collect your shares from the *Yagna*."

Rigveda 10/191/2

This hymn prays for realisation of those human rights which have been assured to the mankind at the global level only in the twentieth century.

The ordinary citizens are provided certain facilities through the medium of the State. These facilities constitute what we understand by the term '*rights*'. Human rights, such as right to equality, freedom, respect, etc., are essentially related to his existence as a man and are in no way affected by his sex, creed, colour or race. These rights, therefore, include the right to education, medical facilities, a dignified life and protection against torture or insult. Every human being is entitled to avail of such opportunities which are necessary for his proper development and realise his potentials as becoming of a man.

Thus, we see that rights are necessary ingredients of the social life. Without them, an individual cannot develop himself into being of use to the society. It is in fact impossible to conceive of the existence of human life in the absence of these rights.

The Constitution of India as well as the Indian culture incorporate many shades of the human rights. The Vedas constitute the foundations of the wisdom and culture of India and they have been on the forefront in espousing the cause of humanity. The Vedic society viewed peace and prosperity as true aims of life. All the Vedic prayers and *yagnas* were performed with such objectives. A typical hymn in this context says "O Indra of mighty fame ! Please save us from destruction. May Pusha who knows all and who feeds all grant us happiness. May Taksha with his unbreakable and unfailing weapon grant us well being!" (Rigveda 1-89-6).

The vedic man in fact also prayed for friendship and amity with all beings. "May all creatures see me as a friend and may I too see them all as friends" (*Yajurveda* 36/18).

Vedic *samhitas* are full of prayers and preachings. Analysis of the prayers made by a society can provide us with valuable insight into the aspirations of its individuals. In the Vedas, we find that all those attributes which were considered essential for happiness in life became the chief objects of prayers. Simultaneously they also spread the message of love and friendship. It can be reasoned that these messages also reflect the ideal objectives of the Vedic society. The feeling of friendship towards all is possible only when everyone shares such feelings and there is a meeting of minds.

Human rights were not documented in writing in the Vedic era. They were an intrinsic part of the social make up. They were always there to be enjoyed, to be acted upon.

The usage of the word *Adhikaar* has been employed in a sense that is quiet different from its present meaning of 'a right'. According to the old dictionaries or *Kosha Granthas* the word is derived from the prefix *Adhi* and the root *kree* and means 'duty' or responsibility. The great poet Kalidasa has also used the word *Adhikaar* in the sense of 'duty' (*Meghadoot* : 1). This is also true for vedic literature where we see that the notion of 'rights' is contained in the concept of *dharma* and duty. The *Purusha Sukta* (*Rigveda* 10/90/16) declares *yagna* as the principal *dharma* since it is the basis of human happiness, prosperity and in fact, of his very existence.

The idea of viewing the entire world as a single family has existed in India since very ancient times. The issues related to the welfare of a single individual have been considered in this broader context. 'Rights' as such have not been emphasized much in the vedic period. In fact, one does not come across a well-defined concept of this term. Mention is made of duties alone and that too in the form of *dharma* of the mankind.

In the Indian thought, the word *dharma* as a synonym of 'duty' has been employed in a very broad sense. *Dharma* is derived from the root *dhru* which means to cause to hold, bear, support, etc. In *Rigveda*, the word *dharma* is used to mean a code of conduct or a fixed orderly arrangement. This meaning is also found in the *Vajasaneyi Samhita*. *Dharanat it Dharma*, i.e., that which holds together is *dharma*. If we reflect upon this, we find that the entire range of acts and tasks of life were based on the principles of *dharma*. It is the foundation of the personal and social life. *Dharma* is eternal. It is the greatest ideal. *Dharma* is that which enables everyone to exist and spend the life in an orderly and self-disciplined manner. *Dharma* helps men to achieve all round development of their personalities. It awakens their noble faculties and makes them aware of their duties towards their families, society, nation and the whole world.

The *Chhandogya Upanishad* (2/23), provides us with another very important meaning of the word *dharma*. *Dharma* has four branches.

1. Yagna, study and charity *(Grihastha Dharma)*.
2. Meditation *(Tapas* or *Vanaprastha Dharma)*.
3. *Naisthu Brahmcharitva* (to stay in the hermitage of the *Guru* till the end).
4. *Bramha-satya* (The ultimate truth—*Sanyas Dharma*).

Here the word *dharma* is used in reference to the various *ashramas* or stages of the individuals life span. *Dharma* is about the overall duties of men, their bonds and relationships, the code of conduct of the *Aryan* people, the division of life into various *ashrama* with their distinct characteristics and the duties in accordance with their *varna* or social category.

The duty of every person and his place in the society was determined in the *varna ashrama* scheme by taking into account his individual traits or qualities. Equal importance was thus accorded to the society and the individual in this manner. This social order reflects a very wide perspective and aims at maximising the welfare of the individual and the society in a wholesome manner.

This meaning of *dharma* is also reflected in *Taittairiya Upanishad* while addressing the students, i.e., *Satyam vad, Dharmam char:* speak truth, follow *dharma. Bhagawat Gita's* says *Svadharme Nirdhanan Shreyah,* i.e., it is preferable even to be poor in one's own *dharma.* According to *Manusmriti,* the sages had requested Manu to educate them on the *dharma* of all *varnas.* This meaning is also found in *Yajnavalkya Smriti.*

It is clear from the above that the notion of dutiful conduct held the highest position in the Vedic era. In the vast canvass of the welfare of mankind, the welfare of the individuals automatically finds a due place. The Vedic society was so advanced and prosperous that there was hardly a need to specially grant rights to the common citizen. The rights were contained within the network framed by the respective duties of all the classes of the society. The Vedic man was so enlightened that the rights had become a secondary issue. Everyone continued to traverse the path of his duties in a just manner and it created a situation where there was no necessity of seeking or granting rights to anyone.

Rights Confered as Human Rights

As the time progressed, the word *dharma* came to be employed in a more and more restricted and narrow sense. Likewise the rights which lay within the womb of duty also diminished in the same proportion. Nonetheless, the fact remains that whether the rights are contained within a framework of duties or they are recognised as Human Rights, they are ultimately linked to the basic issues of human existence.

The rights which have been specifically declared by the United Nations Declaration were very much present in the ancient times in the best possible way. In order to illustrate this observation, certain rights along with this relevance in the given context are mentioned here.

There are five basic necessities of a man – food, clothes, house, medicine and education. Every citizen has a right to acquire them. Arrangement was made in the Vedic period to ensure that these basic necessities of life were available to every citizen.

1. Right to food. It is a king's duty to make arrangement for providing food to all the citizens to the extent it is required. He must always strive for developing agriculture. 'O Indu, may we be equipped with food and wealth with your help' mentions the

Rigveda (1-53). The quality as well as quantity of the food are important so that 'our sons who eat them become healthy and strong' (*Rigveda* 1-12-11). This is a prayer made to *agni*, i.e., fire.

2. ***Right to clothe oneself.*** The *Vedic* thoughts are similar to the above on this. Everyone should have enough to clothe himself as per his needs. This provision should also be overseen by the king. *Twashta vaso vyaddhat*, i.e., the god Twashta made the cloth. A king is but another form of Twashta. He finds ways and means to protect the people's body from the extremes of the weather and seasons.

3. ***Right to a home.*** The State should make arrangement for ensuring airy and well-lit houses to all the citizens. It is a king's duty to satisfy himself with all such details before he grants permission for construction of the house. *Indro Brihaspativni Minotu Prajajan* (*Atharva Veda* 3-12-4) is a prayer seeking the able guidance of *Brihaspati* and others in the construction. The prayer further seeks that the house should be strong and lasting. It should be capable of absorbing the shocks of earthquake. The king should be happy to see the quality and beauty of the house (*Atharva Veda* 3-12-1).

4. ***Right to medical facilities.*** The Vedas are one in saying that the king is duty bound to see that his nation is free of all diseases and proper facilities are in place to look after the health of the citizens. 'O protector and caretaker of the houses, Vayan ! You are the destroyer of diseases. You are our friend and you give us happiness (*Rigveda* 7-55-11). This hymn reflects the medical and health provisions made by the king for his people. There are many other hymns in the *Rigveda* which suggest that the king made special arrangement for this purpose (*Rigveda* 1-12-7).

5. ***Right to education.*** Literacy amongst the people is an important characteristic of a developed society. Several hyms are found in *Rigveda* concerning the spread of education. These hymns pray to the king to make proper arrangements for imparting education relating to speech and the *Brahma Vidya*. The word 'speech' or *vani* is used in the Vedas in the sense of science in many places. The reason is that speech was the primary medium for transmission of knowledge during that period. *Yathemam Vacham Kalyanim*, this mantra clearly equates speech with the knowledge of Vedas. Since the prayers are made to the king, it can be easily

concluded that he was supposed to take effective steps for creating the facilities for imparting education. The *Brahma Vidya* knowledge is also in reference to the Vedas and actually means *Ved Vidya. Ved Vidya* is an extensive phrase and includes statecraft, code of behaviour, medicine, physical sciences, astrology, mathematics and philosophical concepts.

While teaching men about the importance of spreading the education, they have also been advised that they must never allow it to stop in their society. Education creates scholars—Vasu, Rudra, Aditya, etc. (*Rigveda* 8-10-15).

This is a directive to the king that the progress of education should never cease.

Education is really relevant only when the women are also given the right to educate themselves on a par with the men. In our country the female literacy is just about half of the male literacy level despite all the provisions and facilities offered by the government in terms of compulsory education, free education, adult education, etc. This is truly a sad paradox in a country that once boasted of such scholarly women as Gargi and Maitreyi. In fact, the level of literacy today amongst the rural, Scheduled Castes and tribal women is even lesser.

That the girls and boys had equal access to the opportunity of educating themselves and develop their personal character is a common knowledge. The *Brihadanyak Upanishad* (4-4-18) has even described the ritual for begetting an intelligent and learned daughter. Women resided in special hostels called *kshatrishala* (6-2-86). According to *Atharvaveda* (11-5-8), young girls lived in the *Brahamcharya Ashram* to hone their abilities by acquiring knowledge.

6. Right to marriage in adulthood. Marriages were solemnised in the Vedic era when the boys and girls had fully grown up and became youth. As *Rigveda* mentions, when a girl is beautiful and decked up, she is able to find her partner in a group of men by herself (*Rigveda* 10-27-12). Only such girls could be married in whom the desire for marriage has arisen from within. This desire is seen only in youth (*Rigveda* 1-22-9). Women also enhanced their prospects of marrying qualified men by developing their abilities (*Atharvaveda:* 11-5-8). The *mantras* recited in the marriage also make it clear that the married women were not little girls but fully adults.

7. Right of a candidate to campaign. The citizens should not be kept in dark about the capabilities of one whom they may select as a king. In order to make it possible, a candidate had full rights to campaign for himself (*Rigveda* 7-98-5). In this hymn, Indra, the man of the people seeks to describe the old and the new. He tells how he has battled with the baseness of mind and heart. He has emerged a victor and is now a great person. This mantra clearly echoes the idea that the qualities of the would-be king must be presented before the people.

8. The right to express views in the Assembly and Councils. Rule making *Sabha* and *Samiti,* i.e., Assemblies and Councils are necessary to help the king or the State in executing duties and also to keep a check on arbitrary decision making. This idea occurs in several places in the Vedas. There is a particular verse in *Atharvaveda* (7-12-1) which has been said on behalf of the king and addressed to the members of the Assemblies and Councils. It has expressed his views on the kind of mental attitude which the members should possess while articulating their opinions in the deliberations—May the *Sabha* and *Samiti* protect me, may this *Samiti* educate me and I may be able to present interesting ideas in the *Sabha.*

9. Right to possess property. *Nityasyay Rayah Patayah Syam.* This mantra expressly clarifies that the wealth can always remain with one who has acquired it. In other words, he is its real owner (*Rigveda* 7-4-7). One who has acquired the wealth can also give it to his offsprings in inheritance. There is a prayer in *Rigveda* (7-32-3) that "may our scholarly sons who have acquired wealth in the tradition of 'from father to the son' live for hundred years and enjoy the bounties."

While we can see that the Vedas are clearly advocating that the common citizens be provided with all the necessities of life, it also stresses on the following three aspects :

1. Charity should be doled out as per the capacity for the welfare of others (*Rigveda* 10-107).
2. Wealth should not be accorded undue importance. Greed and attachment must be given up (*Rigveda:* 10-117-5).
3. The feeling of mutual love and universal brotherhood should be awakened in the spirit of *Visva Amritasya Putrah* (*Rigveda* 10-13-1).

It can be observed that the Vedic society was highly progressive. Yet it had also made provisions to take care of eventualities when any constituent unit of the society deviated from its duties and violated others' rights in the process. Certain duties of the State or the king have been specified for this purpose so that those who created such troubles were adequately punished. Courts too had been set up to deal with cases of violation of the rights. The crimes included aversion to Vedas and the branches of knowledge associated with them, to caste an evil eye on others, lust, anger, greed, drunkenness, etc. (*Rigveda* 7-104-12, *Atharva Veda* 8-4-12). The punishments were made progressively harsher. To begin with, the offenders were advised in many ways to give up their evil traits. If this could not reform him, financial and corporeal punishments were meted out. Death penalty was the last resort.

Vedas, however, did not view punishments in a favourable light. They can only stop the occurrence of crimes for a time. Crimes are only suppressed in this way. They are not rooted out in a real sense. An ideal society is one where the crime and not the criminal is eradicated. Vedas have also described the ways of creating a crime free ideal society—"O king Agni (fire) ! You are a poet. May you defend us in all four directions through your poetry" (*Rigveda* 10-87-2). Here the king is the poet and the knowledge is construed as the poetry. Poet is one who has knowledge and capabilities to see through the innermost essence of objects or events (*Nirukta* 12/2/12). If a king is able to make arrangements to spread all the knowledge that lies in his kingdom amongst all the citizens, the society would be secure from criminals and violations of rights since no criminal or violator of human rights would be produced by an enlightened society in the first place. Ignorance lies at the root when a man becomes a criminal.

Having thus recalled our past we must seek inspiration from it to mould our present and move towards a happier and brighter future.

16

Priority to Duties in Indian Tradition

Urmila Chaturvedi

> Though duties are specific to *varna*, there are some duties which are common to all varna.
>
> *Editor*

Human rights have been the most discussed about and the most pondered over subject of modern age. They saw their dawn with the very advancement of man. Without them he could neither live with dignity nor could he develop his civilization and culture. Respect to human rights is the touchstone of a country's cultural advancement. Awareness of these rights is expanding. Strangely enough, progress has attracted suppression of human rights. A constant fight against political, economic, social and cultural suppression is now being waged. Second Intercontinental Congress of July 4, 1776, French Revolution of 1789, Bolshevic Revolution of 1917, Lahore Conference of 1929, Karachi Conference of 29-31 March, 1931, sessions of Legislative Assembly on December 9, 1946 and January 22, 1947 did the spade work to prepare background for human rights. On December 10, 1948 the General Assembly of the UN adopted and proclaimed the Universal Declaration of Human Rights. Following the historic event the world body called upon all member States to adopt and implement these rights. Since then every year December 10 is celebrated as the Human Rights Day. This declaration displays the significance and importance given to dignity and respect of human beings.

Today humanity is crying under non-stop exploitation in almost all spheres of life and in all corners of the world. Inhuman incidents, cruel and heartless exploitation have made man indifferent to the efforts being made to safeguard human rights. He thinks it is his fate now to suffer. Nobody is serious enough to see that ordinary man should harvest the benefits imparted by human rights. Lip service is there but no serious effort is made. Officials responsible to implement these rights are engrossed in personal gains. Vicious circle of human exploitation, atrocities and suppression is expanding day in and day out.

Indian culture has by and large blossomed and sprouted under the shadow of human rights. In our culture clear-cut guidelines are enshrined for performing duties in place of enjoying rights for different segments of society. In this way an ideal picture of society is presented. In such a society, men cooperating with one another and marching constantly on the path of advancement can touch the zenith of progress and prosperity. Mahatma Gandhi laid utmost emphasis on the performance of duties and he rightly declared that rights follow automatically. In reality our duty is other's right. If we are aware of our duties, rights of other human beings would be protected naturally. No extra protection would be needed.

Dharma is a means for alround uplift and development of man. It does not mean any particular religion, creed or sect. It means the code of conduct where man individually as well as socially does his duties. In the Indian mode of living, *dharma* plays a vital role. It signifies a system which is comprehended through wisdom and intellect. Life circumscribed by intellect alone can free man from the bondage of nature and can usher in his spiritual development.

Vedas are considered to be the storehouse of *dharma*. They urge us towards a moral life. Three paths of *Karma Yoga, Bhakti Yoga* and *Jnana Yoga* are described for the spiritual aspirant to achieve his goal of self-realisation. Yoga is intimate means of spiritual knowledge. Non-violence, renunciation, Brahmacharya, nonstealing, truth are five *Mahavrtas*. *Smritis* emphasise moral qualities. Fearlessness, self-restraint, harmlessness, truth, wrathlessness, renunciation, absence of crookedness, compassion, uncovetousness, modesty, absence of fickleness, vigour, forgiveness, fortitude, purity, absence of envy and pride—these are divine qualities. Hypocrisy, arrogance, conceit, anger, unwisdom, harshness and wrathfulness are demonical qualities.

Triple is the gate of the hell—of the self-lust, wrath and greed. Man should renounce them (*Gita*). Scriptures should be the ultimate authority in determining what ought to be done or what ought not to be done. These divine qualities mentioned alone are for leading a tension-free life. These are propounded in *Mahabharata, Gita* and *Smritis*. To perform duties without malice, anger and greed is true *dharma*.

Ramayana and *Mahabharata* stress on the performance of duties and thereby realise welfare of the people. *Varnashrama* provides opportunities for each and every man to do his duties. Specific duties ordained in each *ashrama* make man perfect in performing his duties in the best possible manner. The observance of one's duty leads one to heaven and infinite bliss. When it is violated the world would come to an end owing to confusion of castes and duties. *Grihasthashrama* is the fountain head of all other *ashramas*, so it is the greatest. Duties performed well in *grihathashrama* lay the foundation of other *ashramas* firmly and it ensures easy march towards the greatest aim of life, i.e., salvation. Four labours are covered in these four *ashramas*. Accepting the importance of desire, lust and passion in man's life, Lord Krishna says in *Gita* – "In beings I am desire not contrary to duty." Regulated *kama* is *purushartha*. The subsistence of mankind is termed *artha* (wealth). That is why Kautilya has put great emphasis on *artha purushartha*. *Mahabharata* accepts that *kama purushartha* and *dharma purushartha* cannot be accomplished without *artha*. Creation, distribution and use of economic means are circumscribed by *dharma*. *Manusmriti* and Yagyavalkya smriti have described rules of selling and buying, i.e., trade. Wealth earned through righteous, genuine and incorrupt means is classified as *purushartha*. Wealth acquired otherwise is declared illegal and attracts punishment and wrath of the gods. *Mahabharata* advises to follow *dharma* while acquiring wealth because *artha* acquired otherwise breeds tension, loss of peace of mind and above all, man falls in his own eyes and when his conscience pricks him he repents but then it is too late.

In *Mahabharata, Raj dharma, Praja dharma, Jati dharma, Kul dharma, Varna dharma, Dal dharma, Moksha dharma, Stri dharma* are different forms of *dharma*. It simply displays that all departments of life, social, political, economic and religious have a tinge of *dharma*. *Dharma* sustains life and ensures all round development of human beings.

If we apply our discerning wisdom and intellect while performing our duties, different exploitations prevalent in society would die their own death. In that case we would be having no need to look towards foreign guidelines and declarations for human rights. We ourselves would be strong enough to re-establish the ideal of *Vasudeva Kutumbakam.*

17

Individualism and Materialism are Contra Human Rights

Hemant Namdev

> Materialistic and individualistic culture is inconsistent with human rights.
>
> *Editor*

The rich tradition of Indian thought has never given encouragement to exploitation of any kind in any form. *Sahanavavato sah-nan Bhunaktu Sahviryam Karvaveh*—this prayer desires that we should all progress together and we should all cooperate for each other's welfare giving full respect to the dignity of others. We recognise the entire world as one family.

"The narrow-minded persons can only think in terms of 'mine' and someone else's. The great liberal-minded people see the world as a family," says another famous verse. The concept of the world as one family takes shape as soon as the perspective is enlarged. When the perspective is developed, when it is ripe and ready to bear flowers and fruits, there is an automatic end to exploitation of any living being on the planet. Everyone would work towards the welfare of others and the necessity for safeguarding human rights will simply not arise. Nor would it be demanded from any platform.

The Indian tradition has laid greater emphasis on duties. This is based upon the thinking that if everyone discharges his duties with sincerety, there would not remain any possibility of the occurrences of human right violations. This perspective has been changing and today our thinking process is becoming increasingly self-centered. Man now wants to receive more and give less to others.

This is the biggest reason behind the cases of violence since others too react against this tendency. Conflicts, violence and terrorism are the natural outcome of this self-centrist way of thinking.

The remedy lies in reverting back to the ideal of *sarvajana-hitaya*, i.e., welfare of all. An exploitation-free society can only be possible when it becomes the dominating attitude. In other words, our thinking should not just revolve around the 'I'. Annie Besant writes in her book *Thought Power*, "all our troubles arise from thinking ourselves as separated units and then revolving on our own mental axis, thinking only of our separate interests, our separate aims, our separate joys and sorrows".

As the man today lies imprisoned in the confines of 'I', his vision is limited to seeing only that which is associated with the 'I'—my son, my brother, my mansion, my vehicle, my bank balance, and so on. He wants everything to be his and only for him. Nothing should belong to others. This is obviously a distorted perception which motivates to indulge in exploitation of other beings. This faulty perspective ensures that the man wastes away his life in accumulating all those things which are ultimately worthless. He spends a life time in running in a race in which there is no hope of reaching anywhere after all the effort.

The question arises as to how man lost his way despite being a wise and thoughtful creature. Quite possibly it is a result of the theory which was proposed by Charles Darwin in his book *Origin of Species*. The theory says that 'life is a struggle and he who is the best will survive'. This idea has given acceptance to the role of struggle and conflict in the society and introduced fierce competition. When it is one's ideal to be the best at any cost he could not hesitate in using others as a mere tool in his schemes. He will accept exploitation since he has developed a fear that if it stops, others would grow rich and endanger his very own existence. And why should he help other competitors? He would not like to increase the number of his competitors by offering help to those who are weak. Given such an ideology where only money and power take one to the top, the debate on human rights is a totally futile endeavour. Dushyant Kumar has perhaps rightly observed that

> There is no ground
> under your feet
> yet it is a wonder that
> you do not believe it.

Man has become materialist as a result of this belief which propels him to be the best amongst all. Since he believes that the goods which provide material comfort can make him happy, he has collected a vast array of the same. Happiness, however, has eluded him and he is getting farther and farther away from it. When money become the sole aim, life itself becomes meaningless. In all the din and noise created by the talk of money all the time and everywhere, no one is really prepared to hear the talk on human rights protection.

Market is the high temple of the religion of economics today. Money or currency is the God. An exhalted place is occupied by foreign currency and the dollar lies at the apex. The leaders of almost all the nations have no choice but to lie prostrate before the rich industrial nations. These industrialised nations are cornering all the resources through the device of free market. It is immaterial which government is ruling in which country. There is only one fate which awaits those who have accepted this order and that is economic slavery. Under such conditions, is it not a kind of delusion to talk about human rights ?

I seek your support
Though I do know that
Shout as you might
the stones will not listen.

According to the *Mahabharata* the *Sabha* should treat the sinner with contempt and he should be discarded. Otherwise the leader of that Assembly is deemed to have committed one-half of the sin himself. The real sinner has only one-fourth share while the rest of the members are deemed to have the remaining three-fourth share of the sin. Such a fine exposition on justice can hardly be found elsewhere.

Today, we all have to make attempts to seek a practical solution of this problem. We may begin by observing that certain civilized societies have forgotten the sanctity of means under the influence of the Darwinian theory and a money-centered system. Human beings lost their humanity as soon as purity of thoughts made an exit from this scene. When every human being decides to live just for his own self, he is insensitized to other's feelings and emotions. He does not think it necessary to fulfill his duty towards others. The moment a man ceases to perform his duties and responsibilities, violation of someone else's right begins to take place. There is a chain of rights and duties. That which is your duty is a right for another.

The neglect of duties has acted as one of the greatest obstacles in the path of human welfare. Society has been divided into two. On the one side live the people enjoying ultra-modern goods and facilities while on the other side live the ordinary citizens suffering from hunger and devoid of facilities for education and medical treatment. There are countries which throw away foodgrains into the sea because of surplus production. There also countless children who are trapped in the vicious cycle of hunger and poverty. They are looking towards us to seek deliverance from the painful sentence. But it is an endless wait for them.

Such a state of affairs has thoroughly shaken our thinking, our families and our social and political life. The conflict between the rights and responsibilities lies at the root of family break-ups. It can be resolved only by the knowledge which enlightens us and tells us to recognise each as soulmates in the path of progress and enables us to realize the spiritual unity in the shape of a larger family that is called humanity.

It is said in the *Yajurveda,* "May I see all as friends and may all beings too see each other as friends." The point is that we must change our way of looking at things. We will have to abandon the approach of the survival of the best and adopt the motto of universal welfare. We should chalk out the path of mutual cooperation instead of competition. We have to choose not just that which is desirable but that too which is good. We often fail to make this distinction. Achieving the object of desire gives us only pleasure but the 'good' gives us self-satisfaction. Both give us happiness but one is about enjoyment of physical senses, the other relates to the inner happiness. That which gives satisfaction to the soul constitutes what is good.

The Indian code of conduct is derived from a humane perspective. It specifies rules not for the welfare of the individual alone but for the benefit of the entire society. Its approach to mutual relation is also a humanitarian one. It believes that 'to forgive' is the greatest *dharma.* Establishing human value even in conduct of war reflects the same mindset. The current debate on human rights is a step in the direction of this thought process.

The highest aim of a moral life can only be personality

development or the upliftment of the soul. This development must have an all-round character. It should not be uni-dimensional. The ultimate of the behaviour lies in development of a wholesome personality itself.

The aim of the spiritual life is not to destroy our present life, but to enrich it, to make it fuller, more powerful, more effective. We must never think that we are neglecting anything, when we try to do right things towards our soul.

We ourselves will have or make efforts in this discition. If one wants to stand on his feet or if he wants to uplift himself, he will have to activate himself. A paralysed man may stand up for once with other's help but he will not be able to remain erect. The aim of the Indian way of life is not materialistic enjoyment but to achieve a spirit of sacrifice. As *Yajurveda* puts it, "*Ten Tyakten Bhunjithah,*" i.e., "You enjoy through sharing your enjoyment with others, by giving it to others." Human rights can be safeguarded only when we have all begun to think of the well-being of every creature. *Gita* has described the characteristics of the people endowed with the desire to seek truth. These include a spirit of non-violence, truthfulness, lack of anger, spirit of sacrifice for others, a love for peace, aversion to speak ill about others, kindness towards all, devoid of greed, feeling of shame towards evil deeds, a stable temperament, brilliance of mind and soul, readiness to forgive, patience, purity, absence of pride and an attitude not given to conflict and revolt. One who has succeeded in achieving inner purity, has learnt to keep his senses and thoughts under control and has achieved equanimity is a person who can never cause violence. Violence is possible only when a deep hatred lies hidden within. But when the inner self has become pure and the feeling of love has sprouted within, such evils as violence, anger, falsehood, greed and pride, etc., are automatically destroyed.

Thus, the theory of the 'survival of the fittest' is pitted against the ideology of "the whole world is but one single family." The former is looking for acquisition and quick satisfaction of desires. The latter teaches the virtue of dutiful actions without a sense of attachment. The selection has to be made by us. We are free to choose between the two extremes. On the one hand lies enjoyment with gay abandon, on the other lies a way of life dominated by the spirit of sacrifice.

It is only the principle laid down in theory of *Anasakta Karma* i.e., performance of duty without a sense of attachment which can guide our path so that we can shoulder our responsibilities without fail. There is a tradition of co-existence here. The 'I' is missing. Here, everyone is fulfilling his responsibilities towards others and heading towards the goal of universal welfare, toward a world full of happiness. Everyone is contributing his bit in the reconstruction of this great world.

Dr. Radhakrishnan writes, "Unfortunately we provide nourishment to the animal which resides within a man in our educational institutions. We train his mind but pay no attention to his inner-self". The need of the hour today is to take a vow to work in this direction with a sense of self-confidence. The Urdu poet Dr. Bashisbaddha writes :

We do not know our skills as
we are like a river
whichever way we move
the path would be clear.

18

Priority Given to Human Rights in Ancient Indian Tradition

Vidyanand Jha

> When every person works for others rather than oneself then other's rights are spontaneously secured. The ideology of cooperation and harmony has to be cultivated. *Editor*

For the unbiased, objective and disinterested review of any particular subject, it is essential to peep into its present and past picture or identity. The present alone is incomplete in itself because today's present passes into the realms of past by tomorrow. The hands of the clock are ever ticking. From the womb of the past and the present gushes out. We can visualise the identity of future only in the context and light of the past and the present. While reviewing the system of priority of duties we feel the necessity to review its past context along with the modern mode of thinking and established rule of conduct, customs, opinions and behaviour.

Traditions are not established in a day. Indian traditions are everflowing right from the dawn of civilization till today. They have shown the path not to India but to the entire world. They are the path finders. They are the beckoning light and have imparted vitality and wisdom to the world all over.

The tradition of giving priority to duties has been handed over to us right from the times of Manu. Indian traditions have peeped into rights and duties very minutely. Relation between the two has been given thorough pondering and discussion. From the point of view of etymology, the subject matter of action, comes under the ambit of duty. Duty predicates action. So the word duty is used comprehensively. Whatever man does for himself and for the sake of others comes under the class of duty. But Indian intellect does not consider work done for self as duty. Duty is that work which is for the welfare of others, beneficial to society and nation and the world. Even tiny insects perform duty to sustain and maintain themselves. But this duty is not adorable. Welfare of the entire humanity is the core of duty. In this tradition, duty gets the upper hand and rights occupy the back seats. But it does not mean to sideline rights at the cost of duties. Our traditions do give due importance to rights but these rights are exercised not for selfish ends but for the welfare of others and thereby for salvation consequently. The right which is only a means for selfish end and which burns others to ashes is meaningless. It is better to be without such a right. Indian tradition puts forward only one thinking in the context of right and duty. Duty and rights are inseparable. They are two sides of the same coin.

A human being is not inclined to do any work devoid of some motive or interest. Right is the reward and duty is its cause or means. There can be no work without motive or purpose. Means invokes no interest if there is no desire of fruit. So there is interdependence between right and duty. Right is result and duty the means. He who sows the seeds will have the right to harvest the crops. It is ridiculous and ironical if a person exerts his right on the crops though he has never been to the fields. Today we are confronting a very strange phenomenon. To gain our right we pay little heed to our duty. We see it in the shape of strikes. If we cut the very branch on which we are sitting our fall is sure. Duty done never goes fruitless. To fight squarely for right is not essential. Do your duty and the right follows naturally.

In the battlefield of Kurukshetra when Arjuna was oscillating like a pendulum between two extremes of right and duty Krishna told his friend, "O Arjuna ! Right is inherent in doing one's duty. Right has no identity without duty. So you perform your duty." So priority of duty is convincingly established.

The Vedas, the Puranas and the Smritis make us acquainted with the ancient Indian traditions. Root or source of the Puranas and the Smritis is the Vedas. Vedic literature discusses the subject matter of man's duty profusely. Vedic attitude is universal and all pervasive. Personal, household, social, national and worldly duties are stressed in the Vedas. *Rigveda* lays stress on pure and virtuous duty: "O God ! make me darling of all irrespective of caste and creed." To be darling of all depends upon our affectionate and pious duties. So man should do pious and virtuous deeds: "O God ! destroy that malice and hatred which inflicts me and others." Then there will be no hatred and malice. Not to speak of man but animals and birds are also not to be killed, dictate the Vedas.

Violence does not mean to kill. Violence is done even when we torture, rebuke and violate the human dignity through our mind, speech and body. Greed of wealth other than your own is not your duty. It is sin rather. Basic reason of wars waged so far in the world is either a beautiful woman or gold. *Yajurveda* has decried the greed for somebody else's wealth. That is why vedic sages pray to God: Let virtuously gotten wealth increase splendour of my home; I have destroyed the ill-gotten wealth." So the Vedas on the basis of priorities in the life have always given the first place to duties.

A small collection of human beings is called family. When all the constituents of family put their respective oblation of duties in the sacrificial fire a new all-powerful, united, prosperous and harmonious family takes shape. The *Atharvaveda* also propagates a family where there is complete harmony and oneness in the members and where their individual actions and deeds fructify the whole. When the wheel of harmony and love get stuck to the chariot of family it gets momentum. Addressing the bride *Rigveda* propounds: "O bride ! Be the centre of your in-laws. Be a darling of all and administer with affection." Ancient Indian tradition considers woman as the hub of a family. Each members revolves around her. The Vedas have presented love as the sacred thread binding the family. All the members of the family do their respective duties with dedication.

Men make a family and families constitute society. Society means to tread the path unitedly, to think harmoniously and perform duties with one voice. Vedic sages also advise and direct society to work rhythmically and unitedly. *Rigveda* says: "All human beings should live sociably; all should converse with one another with love and affection; all should have the feeling of unity in their hearts; all should have similar resolutions and similar aims; all persons should keep themselves submerged in knowledge and prayer to God as learned men being graced with knowledge by

God worship him." By cooperating with one another they should do their duties nicely and diligently.

Elements essential to keep a society alive are inherent in the *Vedic mantras*. Mind is the basis of bondage and salvation. Stability cannot come to a society until and unless our resolutions are pious and our mind is truthful, auspicious and beautiful. *Yajurveda* at the very onset directs us to pray to God to instil our mind with auspicious resolutions: "Mind, giver of knowledge, is rational, animate, steady and indestructible and illuminates the hearts of the entire humanity and imparts splendour. No work is possible without it. O God ! Fill that mind with auspicious thoughts." Such a mind would be impenetrable and impregnable. Natural order has created both the fathomless chasm and the high Himalayas. The rich and the poor are present in society and it is all natural. To keep the superstructure of society intact it is the duty of the rich to assist and aid the poor with open arms. *Atharvaveda* also propagates that man should distribute more than his capacity. He should not store things for his own use. He should earn with 100 hands and distribute with 1000 hands. This Vedic assertion seems to be a little bit unbalanced. How can a man with 100 hands distribute with 1000 hands? It simply means that rich people are less in number in society and the poor are in large number. A drowning man catches at a straw. So even a little help of aid to a poor man becomes a great impetus. The gulf between the rich and the poor would than be plugged to some extent. This process would keep the balance in society intact.

The nation is a big institution and its constituents are individuals, families and societies. Rigveda visualises a country devoid of all hunger and thirst. The king and the people should do their duties to nurture the nation. The notion to perform duties guilelessly and diligently by the ruler and the ruled instils extraordinary nationalism in the people.

Ancient Indian traditions visualise that the entire world is one family (वसुधैव कुटुम्बकम्). God is omniscient in all animate and inanimate things. According to *Vedic* sayings the earth is the mother, the cloud is father. All the worldly matters are made of five elements and so is the body. The earth and the cloud belong to the entire world. They are the parents. All human beings are made of the same five elements. They are brothers. The notion of universal brotherhood is based on solid facts. That is why Vedic sages want peace of the earth, of the sky and heaven along with their own peace. They desire peace in water, in herbs, in vegetation, in the entire world and even in God. Not to speak of well-being of others they want peace of peace. It shows the lofty ideas and pious notions of the sages and they thought it their sacred duty to pray to God for peace everywhere.

Vedic traditions depict a man performing his pious duties and praying to God to grant him a long life of 100 years. Irrespective of any human aspect they lay stress on duties. Right has no entity without duty. This idea permeates the ancient Indian traditions. Our *smritis* have successfully presented a thorough examination of right and duty. In them the importance of *grihsthashram* is well established over and above other *ashrams.* The reason being that there is more scope to perform duties in *grihsthashram.* All other *ashrams* are based on *grihasthashram.* In the ancient Indian tradition to perform five oblations is a paramount duty. Generally *brahmyajna, deoyajna, bhootyajna, pitriyajna* and *manushyayajna* are designed to be performed. In these oblations the ideas of worship of God and study of the Vedas, respect for forefathers, mercy for the entire world and magnanimity for mankind are inherent. These ideas are psychologically profound and they do influence the mind and the body. In the *bhootyajna* the offering is not put in the sacred fire but is placed on the washed hand and holy water is sprinkled on earth. Sacrifices are made to the gods Indra, Yama and Varuna in addition to birds, demons and the forefathers. Last of all offerings are set aside for dogs, crows, insects, etc., and are placed on the earth. *Bhootyajna* is the symbol of disinterested enjoyment. For men to cook food for themselves is considered abominable and vile. Enjoyment without renunciation is a sinful act. Our traditions advise a householder to treat a guest as god or a respectable person. It is incorporated in *Manusmriti* that service to the guest brings about wealth, long life and heaven for the host. According to *Vishnu Dharma Sutra* the guest transfers all his sins to the householder if he goes unsatisfied and takes away in return all his good deeds done. *Manusya yajna* is also based on these very beliefs and notions. Moreover, it is performed for the well-being of the entire mankind.

Priority of duties is referred to in *smritis.* In the eleventh Chapter of *Gautama Smriti,* a king is considered not fit to extract taxes from the masses if he does not perform his duties faithfully, diligently and conscientiously. Untold rights of the king are referred to in the *smritis* but he is taught to be aware of his duties at every step. *Manusmriti* denies the right to wealth to that elder brother who does not perform duties towards his younger brothers. So much so, he is deprived of his right of natural primogeniture and the whole wealth is put under the direct control of the king. All the brothers are deprived of their paternal property and wealth if they do not perform their duties righteously and faithfully. *Prashara Smriti* clearly opines that seeds should be sown only in the fertile land and only uprighteous sons should be given the possession of wealth and property. Thus, we see that duties come first and rights afterwards. We can undoubtedly say rights are the natural corollary of duties.

In our *Puranas,* relation between human beings and the earth, water, air, fire, vegetation and inanimate things, between man and animal and between woman and man have been surveyed. God himself has assimilated in the lives of animal and bird, man and insects as incarnations of boar, tortoise, Nrisimha, swan, horse and the like.

In the light of ancient Indian traditions, demanding of rights look small and insignificant before duty. Sri Rama's utterance is idealistic: "Not to speak of friendship, affection, compassion and all comforts but even while renouncing Sita for the service of the universe and for performance of duty I will feel any anguish and sorrow." Rama did what he said. The great battle of *Mahabharata* was fought to uphold the sanctity of duty. Nowhere in the *Gita* did Krishna ask Arjuna to wage a war to procure his rights. Perhaps, he would not have agreed to fight simply to procure his rights. Duty is that ideal before which all deep and strong relations look dwarfish, pigmy and insignificant. Bharata of *Ramayana* had got the right to the throne. Still to honour the public feelings towards Rama and to uphold his own duty towards his elder brother he performed his duty without wiles and with docility.

Ved Vyas has composed 18 *Puranas* but he has presented the gist of human duties in one word—*Paropkar.* Today the world is sitting on the heap of gunpowder, on a volcano which can erupt any time. Unrest is all pervasive, needless cut-throat competition, hunger, unemployment and many other maladies are looming large on our heads. We are clamouring for our rights and rights only. If we ponder over the assertions incorporated in our sacred books we can find solutions to our formidable and complex problems and in the doctrine that right is inherent in duty.

19

Varna and Equality in Indian Tradition

Bodh Kumar Jha

> *Varna* is only an operational classification to evolve a better organisation of society.
>
> *Editor*

According to the Indian tradition, the entire world forms a single family. One can see the image of the entire family in each member of the family. This is natural because it is the parts which make up the whole. If the parts are weak, the whole can never be strong. We can substitute a family in this argument in place of 'a part' and consider the entire world population as the 'whole'. The ideal of public welfare can be achieved only when the rights of all its individual are protected. It is important to maintain a sort of balance between the elements which confer a distinct identity to an individual and those elements which define his place in the world. A harmony is expected here.

Even though the individual by himself appears to be more important in the given context, his individuality will become a questionable if the factors governing the totality of his existence are ignored. In fact, an individual becomes meaningful only in the larger context. This is the basic idea behind the Indian concept of universal brotherhood. All fellow human beings are addressed as *Bandhus. Bandhus* are those who are bound together with each other through the bonds of duties or rights. Every individual has a specified and predetermined role in the maze of relationship which is thus formed. No one would accept interference and mix-up between the respective roles. Simultaneously, however, each one is also striving to look for his own image outside himself. And one who can see his ownself in others cannot inflict pain on them.

The Indian tradition embodies an ideal expression of the concept of public welfare. Its votaries feel satisfied if they receive little and give away fortunes. They would, though, not indulge in this to the extent of committing suicide. The soul must remain intact so as to contribute its bit towards the welfare of others. There is a total protection of an individual's rights in this tradition. But acquisition of a right in itself is not sufficient to achieve satisfaction. An individual would be fully satisfied only when he sees that the rights of others are also protected. He neither believes in going hungry nor does he want others to be starved. "I should have my food but the holy man who come seeking for food at my doorsteps must also not go back hungry."

Public welfare and individual rights are two essential pillars which support the temple of humanity. One half of the Indian tradition pertains to individual rights while the other half is related to public welfare. Or they may be construed as two-halve of a sphere. There is a very thin line which separates these two aspects. An action which is performed for one's own benefit is basically personal in nature but when it is performed for the sake of others, it belongs to the realm of public welfare. In our tradition, we are taught to see other women as we would see our own mothers. It also teaches us to view the wealth of others as mere dust. It calls one a learned man, i.e., a *pundit* when he can see his own soul in all beings. Lord Krishna says in *Gita* that the learned ones, view even dogs and heathens as they would view their own selves. The *Vedic* seers have addressed the sky as father and the earth as mother. Whosoever is related to these two is a brother. Under such a system of belief it is only natural to consider the entire world as one single family since this institution is based on the principle of equality. It is difficult to differentiate between one's own self interest and interests of others. An analogy can be drawn with the ocean water. There is total uniformity but when a sample of sea water is kept in a pot it assumes a kind of an individual identity. Likewise when we consider the question of rights from the viewpoint of protection of our own self interest, they are called individual rights. When the perspective becomes larger and covers the totality of the world, we arrive at the ideal of public welfare. The word *manav,* implying a 'human being' has a very wide connotation in the Indian thought.

A *manav* is one who possesses the attributes of humanity. Feeling of sensitivity, service, truth, sacrifice, spirit of non-violence, morality in action, etc., are implicit in the usage of this term. These are the very qualities which distinguish a true human being from a devil. All that is near to us and all that is far away and all that exists in the world as a living or non-living entity is *manav*. All that is necessary for the *manav*, all that enters into a relationship of give or take with him is also *manav*. When the vegetation or wildlife is destroyed, or hills, rivers and climate are disturbed, the humanity as a whole is hurt. If an earthquake occurs in Bhuj (Katchh), the entire humanity feels the painful vibrations. The Vedas which form the backbone of Indian tradition, therefore, repeatedly pray for peace to prevail on the earth and in the sky. Not just this, they pray even for peace for water, medicines and plants. They prey for peace in that which is minutest and in that which is the greatest. There is a full awareness that until and unless there is a sense of well being in all the constituents of the universe, humanity itself would remain sick.

Similarly, the meaning of the term 'human rights' is also quiet unique in the Indian tradition. The concept of human rights encompasses everything that is essential for qualifying as a true human-being. It is not just food that is required. Roses are also required as much. It includes everything that is needed to maintain the pace of the eternal cycle of creation. In the Indian tradition, a man not only desires to live for a hundred years, he also wants to be able to see, hear, and speak properly until he breathes his last. He wants to remain free from any devilish influence on his behaviour. As long as humanity remains wanting in this respect, the cries of agony caused by violations of human rights will become more and more shrill. The world would, in the meantime, continue to look for another god to incarnate himself on the earth and provide relief.

Whenever we discuss the question of humanity or human rights, our attention is immediately drawn towards the women. They constitute one-half of the mankind. In our tradition, a woman is not just a mere womb or a machine for giving birth. She does not exist solely for the sake of bodily pleasures. She is much more than mere body. She is a being who possesses a mind, wisdom and soul as much as she is in possession of her body.

In the *Vedic* literature, the relationship between a man and a woman has been compared with that which exists between the sky and the earth. The sky and earth are two complementary components of a single system. The clouds wandering in the sky brings rain and fertilize the earth and cover it with plants and fruit bearing trees. Man and woman are similarly related. Despite being two distinct entities, they are one. When a man and woman cease to register the distinction in each other, it is called marriage of the two. The *Vedic* hymns are quiet clear on this 'I am this, you are that. I am that, you are this. I am *Sam,* you are *Rik.* I am the sky, you are the earth' (*Atharva Veda,* 14-2-71, *Aitarey Brahmana* 8-27). The hymns of *Samveda* have been composed by modifying the hymns of *Rigveda.* Likewise man has been created by imparting additional modifying qualities to a woman. The analogy of the sky and earth has been selected to drive home the point that despite the apparent differences, man and woman require each other in a vital way and this dependence is rooted in the very construction of the universe.

Manu who founded *Dharma Shashtra,* i.e., the body of knowledge dealing with the precepts of *dharma* accepted these facts and established the theory that 'that which is man is also the woman' (*Manusmriti:* 9/45). One is fiery while the other has a moon-like coolness and beauty. One is strong and rigid, the other is soft and flexible. The *Satpatha* Brahmana states that a wife is definitely the other half of her husband (5-2-1-10). A man is not complete without a wife and the children begotten through her. *Ardhangini,* meaning one-half of the body, is a popularly used synonym for a wife in India. No act of man can ever be completed in our tradition without the involvement of his wife. In absence of Sita, Lord Rama had to place her golden statue in the *yagna* performed by him. Shankaracharya, who had defeated the scholars all over in religious and philosophical debates did not consider his victory over Mandana Mishra as complete until he had also won the debate with his wife Bharati. Such notions about the man-woman relationships are truly original hallmarks of the Indian tradition. There are no parallel to such ideas in the rest of the world.

Let us examine whether Indian tradition has accorded the right of studying *Vedas* to women. To assert that the woman must not be allowed to study *Vedas* on the basis of certain verses in the *Bhagwat Purana* (1-4-25) or *Apstamba Dharma Sutra* (2-11-29) which pointedly deprive her of that right would be an injustice towards the Indian tradition. Shankaracharya has clearly said that everyone is free to acquire knowledge. It cannot be denied to anyone through punitive laws. The question of a woman's eligibility to learn *Vedas* can hardly arise if we note that some of them have actually composed *Vedic* hymns. They were also seers a matter of fact. The illustrious list of such women includes Godha, Ghosha, Vishvawara, Apala, Lopagupta, Semsha, etc. If the Indian women were not allowed to study Vedas, sage Valmiki would not have mentioned the particular incident in *Ramayana* when Rama saw his mother Kaushalya reciting hymns in holy Vedic ritual of *havana* (*Ayodhya Kand* 20-15). When Hanuman entered the Ashok Vatika, he reasoned that Sita would surely come to the bank of river for performing *sandhya* or the evening worship. Tara, who is to be believed to be a monkey, was well-versed in Vedas. If a non-human creature learns and recites vedas, how can it be ever said women had been denied this right in ancient India? In Gargi, Sulabha and Maitreyi we find further evidence that they were learned *Vedic* scholars. In the *Shanti Parva* of *Mahabharata* (321-83) Sulabha describes herself as *Moksha Dharmacharini*, i.e., she is following the path of *dharma* to achieve ultimate union with God. The Neelkantha commentary further describes her as *Naisthik Brahmacharya Dharini*. This involved a disciplined life under the teacher and a compulsory study of the Vedas. All these examples offer sufficient proof that women did have the right to learn Vedas. Even Apastambacharya has stated in the concluding parts of his work *Dharma Sutra* that whatever remained to be said about *dharma* should be learnt from women of all classes.

We may also discuss the case of Sudras, now supposedly considered as belonging to the lower end of the Indian social order. Vedas are again quite explicit on this. The *Yajurveda* (20/2), seeks to enlighten everyone with the wisdom of Vedas including the kings, Brahmins, Aryans, Sudras and servants. The *Aitareya Brahmana* of Rigveda was written by a Sudra named Aitareya Mahidas, the son of Itara. In the Vedic Samhitas, the people belonging to the working class such as the charioteer, carpenter, potter, hunter, etc. have been saluted with honour in the rituals. In *Gita Bhashya*, Lokmanya Tilak has rejected the notion that the women and Sudras are born in sin.

The great Narayana is himself quoted in *Gita* as saying that the four *varnas* or the classes have been created by him on the basis of aptitude for various acts. If the notion of a sinful birth still persists, it would be in order to remember the words of the great Hindi poet, Ramdhari Singh Dinakar. He has said that if the almighty God himself was to pick up a handful of men and hurl them down from the heaven on the earth, they would automatically be divided into various castes and races upon their arrival. When the ground below has been partitioned, the seeds have no choice but to belong to one of the sub-divisions.

In the Indian tradition, no one is untouchable or worthy of contempt *per se*. If such was not the case, Meera would never have accepted Raidas as her teacher. Lord Rama would not have befriended the king of a lowly tribe called Nishads. He would also not have accepted the half eaten berries from a tribal woman. Lord Krishna would not have declined the offer of royal hospitality from Duryodhana and accepted the simple food made from green leaves in the house of Vidura. This is also why the sage Vasistha came forward to embrace the king of Nishadas while the latter was only greeting him from a distance. The Sudras are as sacred in Indian tradition as the river Ganga which like them has emerged from the feet of the Lord. No class discrimination is found in the Vedic texts. Of course, there are proofs of its existence at several places. The Indian tradition has, however, not remained a mute spectator to this evil. It has also endeavoured to heal this malady. There have been illustrious reformers in this tradition including Lord Mahavira, Gautam Buddha, Arvinda Ghosh, Raja Ram Mohun Roy, Swami Dayanand Saraswati, Bal Ganga Dhar Tilak and Mahatma Gandhi. All of them worked for the eradication of this evil from the society. There is actually no place for such a petty notion in the greatness of the Indian traditions. When an individual or a society takes up a challenge with a sense of detachment, the course of history, may, even the path of the constellation changes.

The real aim of the Indian caste system is to create the best possible environment for the welfare of the society as a whole as well as of its individuals. Proper running of the institution of the society requires contributions from all its people. Just as the government employees have been divided into four classes for the sake of operational efficiency and better management, division of the society into various classes was considered to be a natural and appealing idea in the olden times.

The notion of Brahmin, Kshatriya, Vaishya and Sudra are quite scientific. Even gods were categorised in a similar fashion. Agni and Brihaspati are Brahmins. Indra and Varuna are Kshatriyas. Marut, etc. are Vaishyas while Pusha is a *Sudra* god. Even inanimate substances like water have been addressed as Brahmin (*Aitareya Brahmana, Sayana Bhasya, 2/3*). Obviously, this was done on the basis of inherent qualities of the living or non-living objects. These four sub-divisions are like the four different parts of the human body. The four body parts are distinct and yet they work together for the benefit of the human-being. The creation of the classes is also based upon a similar expectation.

In this arrangement, personal rights are fully protected. Barring specific circumstances, interference in the sphere of activity of others is prohibited. Successful execution of an individual's tasks with a sense of devotion and commitment is the basic aim of the caste system. It not only works for the benefit of an individual but brings about overall social welfare. Since interdependence is implied in this system, there is a natural respect for the idea of overall public welfare. In this social order no single class can think of leading a wholesome life without the cooperation of others. The vitality of the individual as well as the society is sustained in this system through a process of mutual adjustment and harmonization of purpose.

The human life span has also been divided into four distinct *ashramas* or stages. This has been done on the basis of a thorough analysis of the physical, social, mental and spiritual aspirations of the mankind. The objective is to maintain a balance in each of such diverse aspects of the personality. Rejection of monotony in favour of a lifestyle leading to all round development constitutes the essence of this system. In the first stage of *Brahmacharya,* one acquires the basic knowledge and skills. In the next *Grihastha Ashrama,* he discharges his duties and asserts his rights to the best of his abilities. In the third stage of *Vanaprastha,* his focus is on learning to give up his desires and attachment. In the last stage of *Sanyasa Ashrama,* he hands over all his duties and rights to the righteous successor and devotes himself completely in seeking the Divine. He is a part of the eternal truth. The first two stages lay emphasis on individual rights while the last two are attempts to further the cause of public welfare. The Indian tradition believes it as an ideal that one should not go hungry and he should also not let others go hungry.

Poet Iqbal has said in his famous composition: "Greece, Egypt and Rome have long disappeared from the world stage, there is surely something special about us since we continue to retain our identity." What is it that imparts immortality to the Indian tradition? We can only conclude that the secret lies in our ideal of securing everyone's welfare. Our forefathers have taught us to obliterate even our own self for the sake of others. Sage Dadhichi gave away spinal bones for making a weapon to destroy the enemies. While discharging his duties as a king, Shivi offered his own flesh to a bird of prey for saving the life of a pigeon. A man can indeed exhalt himself into the rank of divine gods by adopting such noble ideals as commitments to duty, *dharma,* truthfulness and thorough belief in the message of love and piety. Yudhisthira had to bear many sorrows—he was cheated out of his great kingdom in a game of gambling. He had to tolerate the horrible insults inflicted on his wife Draupadi. Draupadi's rebukes to him were sharp and extremely painful. Yet he did not give up the path of *Dharma.* In order to enable Dasaratha to honour the promises made to Kaikeyi, Rama declared to the world 'It is possible that the world could become free of ice; Laxmi, the goddess of wealth could part ways with moon; The ocean may choose to cross its limits; He however would still not allow his father's word to be proven false'. For the sake of upholding the cause of truth, king Harish Chandra even sold his dear wife Taramati to an ordinary citizen. He even had to leave his only son to the mercy of fate. Yet, he did not deviate from his commitment. On the altar of piety, Bali gave away even his own self without sighing even once. Indian traditions are full of such noble examples. It is not possible to count them all in a life time. Hidden behind all such examples is the great ideal which seeks happiness for all and pain for none.

Such a lofty tradition is surely worthy of praise and worship. It deserves to be followed universally. However, we must not ignore the fact that Dadhichi's sacrifice was effective only because his bones were endowed with extraordinary powers. Shivi possessed flesh on his body to offer. Yudhisthira had a wife who could be gambled away. Rama possessed strength of mind and body. Thus, they would achieve dizzy heights of greatness only because they were in a position to give away something. But a person who possesses nothing is incapable of performing such great deeds. A hungry person cannot save others from starvation.

The concept of public welfare presupposes existence of people. Individuals are central to it. To think of the welfare of a society on the foundation of violation of individual's rights is an exercise in futility. Our great tradition reflected this truth quite well. If there is respect for Rama for what he did as a son or a king, he has also not been forgiven for his treatment of Sita which is a case of violation of individual rights. The Indian women will never condone Yudhisthira for treating his wife Draupadi as a mere object which could be gambled away even though rest of his deeds have earned him fame as the greatest exponent of *dharma*. The followers of Indian tradition waited for 14 long years for Rama to return from exile and reclaim the throne of Ayodhya which was his as a right. In a single instant the kingdom was restored back to him as if on a platter.

There were surely many cases of human rights violation in the days of *Mahabharata* but then, Kurukshetra turned into a sort of fiery inferno which destroyed everything. The *Devas* and *Danavas*, i.e., the gods and their foes had laboured together to extract the nectar of immortality from the depths of the ocean. They had equal rights on it. But the *Devas* cheated the *Danavas* and deprived them of their rightful claim. The result was terrible. Indra, the king of heaven had to suffer hellish torments for many years. Even Lord Narayana had to repent for this through repeated incarnation on the earth. In order to defend his right to freedom and be a true *kshatriya*, Maharana Pratap suffered all the miseries of life in wilderness. He even had to eat bread made from grass at times. Eklavya may have had to part with his thumb but he did set up a unique example for the world to see by asserting his right to education and learning. As for Dronacharya who had demanded the thumb, he remains guilty of a crime for which the historians of the glorious tradition of India will never grant him pardon. Not even if Dronacharya remained standing with folded hands for millennium.

To revert to the idea of maintaining a balance between individual rights and social welfare, it must be reiterated that it is a brilliant feature of the Indian traditions. It has set both the objective in a parallel position. If something is ideal for achieving public welfare then it is also the essence of individual rights. The underlying approach is such that an epic like *Ramayana* is composed by one who was deeply moved by the sight a bird shot dead by an arrow. On the other extreme is the case of furious battle of Mahabharata which were, in ultimate analysis, caused because of the unsuccessful attempt of disrobing a woman in full public view. The Human Rights Commission would do well to adopt such ideals of the Indian tradition. Rights and duties must be accorded equal importance. The Commission should also be given the powers of strengthening the government machinery for this purpose alongwith a greater role for the Human Rights Commission.

20

The Ideal of Social Good in Indian Tradition

Sridhar Misra

Rights are the limits within which one has to perform one's duties.

Editor

The vital source of Indian tradition is the Vedas. The knowledge of these traditions has come to us through *Smritis, Ramayana, Mahabharata, Puranas* and modern literature. Our *Vedas* are brimming with many instances of protection and nurturing of man, animal, insects and vegetation culminating in happy results. The doctrine of four labours—*dharma, artha, kama* and *moksha*—is propounded for human well-being and also to keep the animal kingdom intact and flourishing. In one verse of *Atharvaveda* man prays to God to bestow wealth on him in plenty because it is the means to keep the worldly activities in motion. In reality even *dharma* cannot be performed without money. Green pastures do not allure a hungry belly. He cannot concentrate on any subject. Hunger cannot be satisfied with scriptures and poetry cannot satiate thirst. Food and water are elixir and nectar for the hungry and the thirsty. An empty stomach shuns sermons.

To lead and live a comfortable and easy life the Indian culture does attach great importance to money. But this wealth should not be acquired through foul means, unjust deeds and unrighteous methods. Unscrupulous ways have no place in the Indian tradition. Money should be acquired through sweat of the brow. Moreover, wealth thus acquired should not be used exclusively for self but for the entire humanity. It should be used for *God, matter, sage and man*. Secondly, it should be used to nurture animal kingdom and insect world. *Rigveda* propounds that a person who does not help his friend monetarily is not a friend (*Rigveda* 10/117/4). A person who feeds himself alone is a sinner. *Manusmriti* also opines that he who cooks for himself alone swallows sin. It is clear that money acquired unjustly is censurable. Selfish attitude is wicked, says our ancient Indian tradition. Efforts are being made for the protection of animals all over the world. Indian culture tells us to worship them like deities. Killing of domestic and wild animals is prohibited. *Rigveda* attaching great importance to steed asks the worshipper to nurture it well and protect it from diseases to kiss victory in the battlefield. The cow is considered the best amongst all animals. It yields nectar like milk. Our scriptures direct us to have a cow-pen in our home and to nurture them properly. The cow supplies milk even after eating dry grass. It is venerable, cherishable and tamable. A distressed cow leads to distress in the family. A weak and undernourished cow spells weakness in members of the family. Likewise, the bird is also friendly and lucky for man. Indian tradition urges man to be friendly with the birds and look after them with compassion and love. *Yajurveda* speaks out that distinct birds protect man in different seasons in one way or the other. They should be looked after properly like animals.

Public welfare is accomplished on three levels—social, economic and political. On the social level it is performed by physical service, mental sympathy and economic assistance to those who are distressed and in dire necessity. Gujarat earthquake presents a glaring example. People from all rungs of society tried to save earthquake victims even at the cost of their own life. Wounded were given medical aid. Efforts are being made on social and political levels to bring the unfortunate brothers and sisters back to the mainstream. The *Rigveda* relates that people used to send their wards in their childhood to *Gurukuls* for study and for acquiring knowledge. He who failed to do so was punished by the king. If this is enforced everybody would be educated in due course of time. Girls too were sent to learned women for the same purpose. Knowledge was imparted according to aptitude and interest. Knowledge is of two types—worldly and other—worldly. Worldly knowledge was the harbinger of materialistic comforts. Other—worldly knowledge pertained to self-knowledge, self-thinking and self-analysis. The syllabus of worldly knowledge covered study of the Vedas, grammar, prosody, lexicography and astrology,

Saddarshna, Upnishada and Upvedas. Study of the Vedas was oral. Pupils used to listen to their Gurus; so this study was called Shruti. People used to traverse distant land for studies and the *Rigveda* is testimonial to it. Significance of education and learning made the teacher superior even to father. He was placed on a higher pedestal. Man is twice born—physically and educationally. Parents gave birth but it was the teacher who moulded the ignorant child and gave him knowledge. When a man became learned he was born once again. Rather it was his real birth. For this second birth the teacher was responsible. So he was considered superior.

Indian tradition lays much emphasis on discipline. Kautilya has said that pampering spoils children and discipline makes children. Pampering leads to obstinacy.

Many medicines were prevalent in ancient India to keep man and animal healthy. Rigveda tells that in man's body there are 107 delicate and vulnerable points which are more prone to diseases. To conquer diseases one has to take appropriate medicines. In ancient India, medicines prepared from fruits, flowers and creepers were easily available. Herbs were widely available in the Himalayas. Ayurvedic system of medicines tells everything about herbal treatment.

Natural calamities caused either by excessive rains or by scarcity of rains are inflicted on one part of the world or the other. Tornadoes also bring havoc and massive destruction in their wake. Natural calamities did inflict mankind in the past also. That is why men prayed for peace and discipline in all the elements of nature and that everybody-live a 100 years. Wish was also uttered for the proper functioning of all organs of the body to live a happy life.

> Sky should give peace to me; air should give peace to me; earth should give peace to me; all divinities should give peace to me; universe should give peace to me; may that peace come to me from every quarter.
>
> *Yajurveda* 36/17

> Through a 100 autumns may we see the bright sun; through a hundred autumns may we live; through a hundred autumns may we hear; through a hundred autumns may we clearly speak; through a hundred

> autumns may we live in comfort; through a hundred autumns may we live independent.
>
> *Yajurveda:* 36/24

To hear good and to see good was the universal wish. Such wishes can only emanate when the mind is pure. This mind of ours is unsteady. Strangely enough this very mind is the means to *moksha.* Purity of mind inculcates concentration in mind. Thus, purity of mind is supreme and most vital.

Now let us take the concept of personal rights. Indian tradition is very much clear as far as different types of rights are concerned. Rights are discussed in the Vedas and Puranas. Newly-born baby has the right to breast feeding. Wife has the right to perform her duties as per her own outlook. Old members of the family have the right to be properly looked after, serviced and respected by their offsprings. Its absence means violation of rights. These rights are more emotional than political.

When we thoroughly analyse the word 'Right' we realise that it depicts man's limits. So limited, he can perform his duties righteously. Whenever he has trespassed his limits there have been upheavals and turmoils in society and country. Its burning example is *Mahabharata*. Kaurvas trespassed their limits and tried to deprive Pandavas of their rights. Pandavas unwillingly had to fight to regain their rights. Arjuna expressed his unwillingness to fight with his own relations and *Gurus.* Krishna, calling this fight as *dharma yudh* to gain one's rights, compelled him to raise his weapons and said—"But if thou will not carry on this righteous warfare, then casting away your own duty and thine honour, thou will incur sin."

Division of rights is done to locate responsibility. Our ancient *Varna* system demarcated duties and rights according to periods in one's life. In *Brahmacharya Ashrama* man's duty was to acquire knowledge and to study; in youth to enjoy life; in old age to follow ascetic life and at the fag end of life to embrace *Sanyasa.*

A small group of human beings is called a family and a group of families gives birth to society. Family prescribes many duties and they are to be performed earnestly. Wrongly understood rights and duties inculcate disputes and unnecessary bickering in society and family. How can a person whose own family life is disturbed think about his society and country? Only feelings of compassion and love can eradicate this distress and trouble. *Atharvaveda* propounds that minds of husband and wife should be like air and smoke. Smoke flies along with the air. Husband and wife must have that feeling of love which we find in *Chakravateo Dampatti.* Today elderly persons are not getting the treatment which they should have received. In ancient India the right of the elderly persons to be looked after properly by their offsprings was well protected and respected. In our scriptures, description of elderly persons passing their life playing with their grand children and getting all attention from the young members of the family is very frequently found. Views of the elderly members were given due respect and weightage regarding festivals and social activities. Son used to obey his father's utterances and never tried to force his own views. Moreover, all the members of the family used to live in harmony. "Saraswati rests on thy tongue" – this dictum used to guide the conduct and behaviour of the members. *Atharvaveda* says so.

Vatsyayana's *Kamasutra* clearly postulates woman's duties. She is to be courteous to all the members of the family and her husband is her God. She should serve her father-in-law and mother-in-law. She is to be ever kind. The advice of sage Kanva given at the time of Shakuntala's departure for her husband's house is still relevant today. If it is followed, congenial and cordial atmosphere in the family is assured. Woman is not the property of man. She is not his slave and *chattel*. Our *shastras* have nowhere postulated any position of inferiority to the woman. Our scriptures describe the home like this – the mistress of the home is the home. In one of the verse of *Rigveda* she is asked to come and become queen of the household. Daughter is to inherit ¼ of her father's property; this is her right. No doubt *Manusmriti* says that the eldest son is to inherit his father's property because he has the right to do *Shraddha*. But he has been given the duty to look after and nurture well his younger brothers and sisters. A man who does not do so is deprived of the right to his father's property. An incompetent son loses his right to follow in the footsteps of his father.

Individual rights have been postulated so that all members live in harmony while enjoying their rights. Society guarantees methodical and well arranged life. Equality is the basis on which the superstructure of society stands steadfastly. Vedas ask all men to have respect for one another and not to yearn for the belongings of other people.

The *Varna* system has existed from time immemorial. This system is quality-based. The nature and quality of work determine the *varna* and not his birth. Lord Krishna says in *Gita*—the four castes were created by me, by a different distribution of qualities and actions'. A person born in Sudra *varna* if acquires the qualities of a Brahmin, he is Brahmin and not Sudra. Similarly if a person born in Brahmin *varna* indulges in vices he has no right to be called a *Brahmin.*

Duty gets priority over right. Our scripture and *granthas* lay stress on duty. Let us look at it from the political angle. The duties of a king are to nurture his people, to dispense justice and impart punishment. He is responsible for the smooth functioning of the State's affairs. All this requires proper training of a king. Manu says that a king should be well-versed in all sciences. *Sukraniti* postulates many duties for a ruler—he is to protect his subjects, look after the learned and the old, work for the uplift of all sections of society, apprehend the wicked and punish him. He should make liberal donations to the warriors and the learned to encourage them and to honour them. He should rule in concurrence with his ministers and spies. He is *Dandadhar* and he must wield his *danda* to bring to book all ruffians, rascals and unrighteous persons. He is four-eyed as he watches all the activities of the State through his spies. He is to assure complete coordination amongst different wings of the State and thereby ensure stability. It is the ardent duty of the ministers and the spies to feed the king with correct information. The performance of duty by the king alone ensures the rights of others.

21

A *Sanatana* Critique of UN Declaration of Human Rights

Bharat Jhunjhunwala

The UN Declaration on Human Rights is inconsistent with *sanatana* values.

Editor

The Universal Declaration of Human Rights is indeed a milestone in securing the welfare of human beings. But fifty years down the line many a shortcoming is visible. The Declaration sanctifies human inequality by ignoring the inherent psychological inequalities among human beings. It places an emphasis on 'rights' rather than duties. It sanctifies economic inequality between human beings by restricting economic rights within national boundaries. It ignores that the present Constitution of the UN Security Council is contrary to the principle of equality. The present Declaration is inequitous and needs to be thoroughly revised. India must prepare an alternate Declaration and present it before the United Nations.

Article 1 of the Declaration stipulates that all human beings are equal in dignity and rights. Article 3 stipulates that all have rights to life, liberty and security. Article 13 speaks of rights of freedom of movement. Article 26(1) provides for right to education. The difficulty is that no two of these many equalities can go together. If we were to secure equality of dignity between a weak and strong student in the class, it would be necessary to accept inequality of rights between the two. The right of the bright student to practicals would have to be restricted to provide equal dignity to the two. No two of the various equalities can go together. It was necessary to state upfront which would be the key parameter in which equality would be secured; and to acknowledge that inequality in all other parameters would be acceptable. The Declaration is a hotch-potch of mutually inconsistent equalities.

Our tradition has specified that equality will be secured only in 'opportunities of self-realisation'. Human beings are different in their *samskaras* (inner-tendencies) and capacities. Each should be provided with such opportunities which are necessary for his self-development. One who has the *samskara* of making money should be given the freedom to do business; but one who has the *samskaras* of kingship must be deprived of that very freedom. It is necessary to amend the declaration to say, "every human being is entitled to equal opportunities to realise his inner tendencies and that inequality would be accepted in all other parameters."

Men and women have different *samskaras.* There is no logic to giving them same equal freedoms and opportunities. Each must be given opportunities according to his or her *samskaras.*

Article 7 provides that 'all are equal before law'. This means that the weak and the strong have equal legal rights. Naturally the weak would not be able to enforce their rights. Our tradition asks for an affirmative approach. Yudhishtira was selected as *yuvaraja* because he awarded lesser punishment to the sudra and progressively higher punishment to Vaisya and Kshatriya. The principle was that punishment should be awarded in keeping with one's social responsibilities. This needs to be built in the Declaration.

Article 29 of the Declaration enables the rights of the individual to be limited for the 'general welfare of the society'. The problem here is that rights of the individual are primary. Only if they conflict with general welfare they may be 'limited'. The result is that individual rights of the terrorists are given primacy while the larger society suffers.

Our tradition puts general welfare in the Centre. It is said that 'give up one for the family, family for the village, and the village for the society.' The welfare of the larger numbers has to be secured proactively. The Pandavas burnt six unsuspecting villagers in the house of lac so that they could escape and punish the evil rulers. Lord Rama gave up Sita to secure the welfare of the society. It is necessary to amend this Article to say," Human Rights will be available only in larger social interests."

In Article 16 it has been accepted that the family is the 'fundamental group of society'. The 'group' should then have some autonomy to regulate the relationship between its members. The elders of the family would have greater authority. Thus our tradition demands that we respect the mother as God, respect the father as God. But other Articles of the Declaration require that equality be maintained between members of the family. Article 1 and 2 talk of equal rights of family members. Under Article 7 the weight of evidence of the grandfather and the grandchild are equal. Article 16(1) provides equal rights for the dissolution of family irrespective of the impact on other members. It is necessary to amend this Article to say, "the rights of the individual shall be subservient to those of the family."

Article 29(1) mentions that "everyone has duties to the community." But the discharge of these duties is not compulsory. These are empty advices without teeth. Article 26(2) says that education shall strengthen 'respect for human rights and freedoms.' It does not say that education shall strengthen the respect for 'duties to the community'. Article 18, 19 and 20 provide for freedom of thought, expression and assembly. These are not contingent on one discharging his duties to the community. The result has been that human beings do not discharge their duties. This leads to an ever increasing violation of the rights of others. Our tradition, on the other hand, speaks only of duties. *Gita* says "duties alone are your right." The Declaration should be amended to make rights contingent on the discharge of those duties.

The Declaration endorses the present Constitution of the Security Council which is based on inequality. But the Article 29 (3) says that nothing shall be said against the principles of United Nations.

The civil and political rights of all human beings stipulated in Articles 4, 5, 14(1), 15, 16, 19, etc., have universal applicability. But the economic rights are restricted within the borders of nations. Article 13 restricts the freedom of movement to "within the borders of each State." If all human beings are entitled to equal rights then why should one human being be restricted from movement into another country? Article 21(2) provides that the right of equal access to public services will be applicable only within 'his country'. Pray, why? When civil rights are universal then why not access to public services? Article 22 limits the right to social security 'in accordance with resources of each State.' Why should then political rights be universal? The result of these provisions is that the industrial countries can interfere in the affairs of the developing countries in the name of political rights, but the developing countries cannot interfere in the industrial countries to secure their economic rights. It is necessary to make these economic rights universal.

It is high time that we draw up a more just and equitable Charter of Human Rights and present it to the UN General Assembly for adoption.

22

Eternal Values and Justice

Sri Krishna Aggarwal

The modern system of court room based justice depends on evidence produced and is flawed. The ancient system of *Panch* was better.

Editor

Sanatana means eternal. Values are the ideal principles and processes which are pathfinders for humanity. Entire world is a family—this lofty feeling lends sincerity and meaning to our life style. *Sanatana* values saw their dawn along with the development of human civilisation and culture. Beliefs and faith constitute culture, conduct and behaviour according to this civilisation. Besides India, these eternal values have sprouted and blossomed in many countries of the world. Egypt, China, Greece, Rome particularly were the cradles of these values. Different classes and followers of different religions have their own values and ideals. Setting aside the controversy regarding the entity of God and rituals, we realise that different principles incorporated in all religions are eternal values.

Fundamental principles of justice are inherent in eternal values. Years have rolled by but values have not lost their lustre and grandeur. They are body and soul of justice. Speak truth and follow *dharma*—these principles are corner-stones of the edifice of justice. Listen to your conscience and do not inflict injuries on anybody and shun killing in any way. These are efficacious *mantras* for the protection of body and mind. One value leads to another. Nonstealing, renunciation and attitude of detachment are also lofty principles.

The guiltless and innocent should not be punished in any

way. Protection of the innocent sometimes increases the chances and possibility of the acquittal of the guilty. But this is tolerable. Natural justice plays a vital role here. To hear the complainant and the respondent properly, to give plaintiff full opportunity to protect himself, to assure kindness in the acknowledgment of guilt and impartial investigation are some points covered by natural justice. Statutes, acts and rules are roots of justice. They cover rights and duties of individual, society, association, and so on. Statutes depict method to get justice and dispense justice. Procedure from filing a suit to its final disposal are elaborately dealt with. There is no chance of any ambiguity. Jurisdiction of different courts is thoroughly demarcated. Statutes and Acts cover almost all departments of life—social, economic, educational, and so on. Indian Constitution is the main source of statutes and laws. Verdicts of the Supreme Court also become established laws of the land.

A correct interpretation of the Constitution, Acts and Laws is very important. Wrong meaning deduced by the party can change the whole perspective of the case. A wrong man always argues his case very forcefully and effectively. It may mislead the court and tilt the balance of justice. So the intentions of the legislature, past references, constitutional objectives and comprehensive justice are relevant in this context. Under the cover of elaborate principles guilty person creating a procedural labyrinth tries to misuse them.

Expenditure to be incurred in the dispensation of justice has tremendous significance for the plaintiff and the respondent. Big expenditure is an impediment in the way of judicial process. A poor man cannot afford costly medical treatment and he dies. In the same way costly judicial process compels society to undergo pangs of injustice and it makes the whole system diseased and sick. So expenses should be minimum. In labour disputes this expenditure is nominal and it is a good trend. Distance does matter. Distant locations of the courts creates unnecessary burden on the parties and increases the expenditure. Moreover, it constitutes loss of time and energy also. When the parties fail to turn up new dates are given for the hearing. So this complicates the whole procedure. After the first verdict the losing party or the convict goes in for appeal against the verdict in the superior courts. Ever-increasing number of appeals, and distance of the designated courts further increase the expenses. Moreover, it creates mental tension also. Time of justice gets prolonged. Evidence is all important. It can be purchased and repurchased. This also delays justice. Justice delayed is justice denied. Justice should be easy, quick and less expensive. Many things depend on legislature or executive and not on judiciary to set the system on right track. So there should be coordination between the legislative, executive and judiciary, the three organs of government. It is most urgent in a democracy.

Judges occupy a very significant place in the judicial process. They are the brain of judicial body. Time, place, expenses and credibility count much. Decisions by the *panchayats* have been very renowned and acceptable. Verdict by the elected *panches* by the disputing parties is always beneficial. This system is a boon bestowed on us by our ancient Indian tradition. It is suitable to Indian thoughts and values.

Judicial set-up was as per Indian requirements in the past. Judges of lower courts command no respect because in the eyes of the general public judges are blind. Present judge can hear. The verdict depends on the quality of hearings. His personal knowledge is generally of no use. If one side fails to participate in the discussion or is prevented from appearing in the court by money power, muscle power, cunningness and fraudulent means the judge is deprived of hearing the case and is bound to pronounce the judgement but strangely enough he is not bound to dispense justice. Knowledge collected and earned through study of law and proper apprenticeship is cleansed through experience. When the judge uses this knowledge and applyies his discerning intellect, justice can be expected. So right selection of the judges is very important. It demands a minute scrutiny of the character of the person to be selected to occupy the seat of judgement. Wrong selection casts an indelible slur on the fair name of judiciary.

Verdicts should assure justice. It is the quality and aim of good judicial system. Verdicts should be brief, clear and transparent. Clear views should be recorded on disputed points. Conclusion and judgement should be based on reasons and be rational. Interim injunction before the final order can be given to safeguard the interests of the plaintiff and maintain a status quo. Incomplete, ambiguous, vague and double meaning judgement create future legal disputes, complications and appeals. This delays the final judgement and increases expenses for nothing. An unwanted twist given to laws should be discarded. Moreover, judgement should be deterrent to falsehood and further disputes. It should discourage litigation. In criminal cases it should be full of compassion, softness and tenderness. Cruel, arrogant and obstinate culprits should be given exemplary punishment but it should not smack of revenge or malice.

Appeal can be entered against the verdict in a higher court of law. This process is adopted to ensure any ratification, if needed. But as far as possible these appeals should be minimised. They should be settled in the minimum possible time.

Implementation of the judgement should be assured within a fixed time period as far as possible. Unnecessary delay causes heart-burn and shakes the confidence of the victorious party; it also creates some doubts. Judiciary should be vigilant and intervene if need be and see that the executive implements it properly.

Judicial system is so comprehensive, one cannot even imagine. Does it assure justice? Does it safeguard the *sanatana* values of truth, good conduct, non-violence and tolerance? Proper judgement does indicate these values and preserve them. Present judicial system fails to deliver right decisions. Our Constitution has elaborately described the rights and duties of individuals, society and associations but their performance is not satisfactory.

The complainant and respondent misuse the provisions meant for the protection of the innocent persons. False statements, false evidence and false affidavits are presented to create obstruction and to prevent truth from coming to light.

In ancient India personal knowledge and enquiry of the jury and judges and the system of record of evidence by them did prevent to a great extent the parties from telling lies. Present judicial system is based on English Law. Justice does look explicit, unprejudiced, fair and lucid; but all that glitters is not gold. Interference in evidence affects decision. In France and some other countries judicial process is better. The witness is not cross-examined by the parties but the judge himself asks relevant questions. This system does resemble the ancient Indian system.

Intervention by the elders to dispense justice in family disputes should be re-established. The tragedy is that our elderly persons keep aloof from it for their personal comforts. Moreover, they do not want to incur the displeasure of one party or the other. The job to dispense justice should be assigned to *panches* and *panchayats*. This will certainly protect our *sanatana* values. Government is doing a lot in this direction and it is a good sign for good things.

23

Classification of Human Beings in Indian Law

Tarkesh J. Molia

Indian Law admits of equality only between similarly situated persons. This is the same principle as of *varna* classification.

Editor

Introduction

The notion of equality has intimate association with a great movement in human history. The concept is a difficult one and discussion of its meaning is often laden with emotional overtones. The word 'equality' is incapable of a single definition as it is a notion of many shades and connotations. Attempts to identify such attributes are likely to lead to far ranging discussion—of the relation between equality and justice and between equality and liberty.

A Jurisprudential Analysis

To say simply that men are equal would raise a host of troubling issues. In ordinary use of the term men are very often unequal. What then can we make sense of the notion of equality? The notion belongs to the sphere of values. It is used in moral judgement to the effect that equality is a good, that ought to exist, and that this is so in spite of the obvious ways in which men are unequal in strength, talent and intellect. Most philosophers have not wanted an equality which is total. The claim that men are equal is a claim in a fundamental respect.[1]

Rushdell advances the principle that every human being is of equal intrinsic value and is therefore entitled to equal respect. He, however, points out that the principle does not require that every person be given an equal share of wealth or of political power but rather equal consideration in the distribution of the ultimate good.[2]

Now, there is a variety of ways to express the idea of equality and different writers tend to emphasize some form of equality to be of over-riding importance such as equality before the law, equality of basic human rights, economic equality or equality of opportunity. *'Every man to count for one and one to count for more than one.'* This formula contains the core of the doctrine of equality. This formula is ambiguous but it constitutes the irrevocable minimum of the ideal of equality.

Equality, as a principle, amounts to no more than that men should all be treated in the same way save where there is sufficient reason for treating them differently.

An argument for *"equality before law"* need not entail a belief that equality is unrestricted. Thus the citizens may be said to have an equal right to public education in a country, but this need not mean that once enrolled in schools they deserve to recieve equal grades without regards to their performance.

Laski observed "equality, therefore, involves response to primary needs. And that is what is meant by justice. We are rendering to each man his own by giving him what enables him to be a man. We are, of course, therein protecting the weak as well as strong. Grant, as we may well grant, that this involves a payment by society to men and women who limp after its vanguard, the quality of the State depends on its regarding their lives as worth preserving. To act otherwise is to regard them not as person but as instrument."[3]

Concept of Equality Enshrined under the Constitution of India

Article 14 of the Indian Constitution deals with right to equality. It reads:

"The State shall not deny to any person equality before law and equal protection of laws within the territory of India."

This Article guarantees to every person the right not to be denied equality before the law or equal protection of the laws.

The first expression "equality before law" which is taken from the English common law is a declaration of equality of all persons within the territory of whole India, implying thereby the absence of any privilege in favour of any individual.

Prof. Dicey, while explaining the concept of legal equality as operating in England, said "with every official, from the prime minister to a constable or a collector of taxes, is under the same responsibility for every act done without any legal jurisdiction as any other citizen."[4]

The second expression 'The equal protection of laws', which is rather a corollary of the first expression, is based on the last clause of first section of the fourteenth amendment of the American constitution, directs that equal protection shall be secured to all persons within the territorial jurisdiction of the Union in the enjoyment of the rights and privileges without favouritism or discrimination.

Srinivas Theatre vs ***Government of Tamil Nadu.*** The court classified that even if there is much common between the two expressions in the Article 14 they do not mean the same thing. The word 'Law' in the former expression is used in a generic sense—a philosophical sense, whereas the word 'Laws' in the later expression denotes specific laws.

Underlying Principles Under Article 14 to Ensure Equality for Equals and Not for Unequals

The Article proceeds on the basis that men are unequal in many respects. The equality of treatment before law enjoined by the Article does not require that things different in fact be treated in law as though they were the same. It only requires that those who are similarly situated should be similarly treated. As different persons they should be treated differently.

Satish Chandra **vs** ***Union of India.***[5] The guiding principles of the Article is that all persons and things similarly circumstanced shall be treated alike both in privileges conferred and liabilities imposed.

Reasonable Classification

As a matter of fact, all persons are not alike or equal in all respects. Application of the same laws uniformly to all of them will therefore be inconsistent with the principle of equality. To avoid that situation law must distinguish those who are equal and to whom they must apply and those who are different and to whom they should not apply. It is accepted that a person may be classified into groups and such groups may be treated differently if there is reasonable basis for such difference. Hence it can be concluded that reasonable classification is permissible under Article 14. The Supreme Court held in *Kedarnath Bajoria* vs. *State of West Bengal:*

"The equal protection of the law guaranteed by the Article 14 in the Indian Constitution does not mean that all the laws must be general in character and universal in application and that the State is no longer to have the power of distinguishing and classifying persons or things for the purpose of legislation."[7]

Test of Valid Classification

The power of making classification is not without a limit. The classification to be valid must always rest upon some real and substantial distinction bearing reasonable and just relation to the needs in respect of which the classification is made. In order to pass the test of permissible classification, two condition must be fulfilled namely :

1. The classification must be founded on an intelligible differentia which distinguish a person or a thing that are grouped together from other left out of the group.
2. The differentia must have a nexus or a rational relation to the object sought to be achieved by the statute in question.

To illustrate, Under Section 11 of the Indian Contract Act, 1872 persons, who have not attained majority cannot enter into contract. The two categories of classification are adult and minor. The basis for classification is age. The basis obviously has a relation to the capacity to enter into the contract. Hence, the classification is valid.

New Approach to Reasonable Classification

Since early 1970, equality in Article 14 has acquired a new and very important dimension. Till then, as we have noted above, the requirements of Article 14 were met if a law or a administrative action satisfied the reasonable classification doctrine based on the nexus test. Towards the end of 1973 however J. Bhagwati, Chandrachud and Krishna Iyer J.J. in a concurring opinion in *E.P. Rooyappa* vs. *State of Tamil Nadu* propounded a new approach to Article 14 in the following words:

"Equality is a dynamic concept with many aspects and dimensions and it cannot be cribbed, cabined, and confined within a traditional and doctrinaire limit. From a positive point of view, the equality is authentic to arbitrariness. In fact, equality and arbitrariness are sworn enemies, one belong to the rule of law in republic while the other to whim and caprice of the absolute monarch. Where an Act is arbitrary in it that it is unequal both according to political logic and constitutional law and is therefore violation of Article 14."[7]

***Central Inland Water Transport Corporation* vs *Brojo Nath Ganguly*.** The court invalidated Rule 9(1) of the corporations rules which provided for a termination of service on a three months notice or on a payment of three months salary in leu of notice. Holding the corporation to be State within the meaning of Article 12 the court decided.

"Rule 9(1) is both arbitrary and unreasonable and it also wholly ignores and sets aside the Audi Alteram Partem rule. It therefore violates Article 14 of the Constitution."

Some Basis for Classification

As such there is not a unique basis for classification but the Supreme Court by the way of judgement has contemplated various kinds of reasonable classification based on geographical situation, nature of person in favour of States, object of laws, tax laws, etc.

R.K. Garg vs. *Union of India* **(Bearer Bond Case).** It is a glaring example of tax related law having being upheld under Article 14. The special bearer bond (Immunity and Exemption) Act, 1981, which in order to channalise black money for the productive purpose authorised investment of such money in a bearer bond with full immunity and exemption under the income tax, wealth tax and gift tax as well as from disclosure of source to the investors was upheld among other on the ground that it was reasonable classification between those who had and who did not have a black money and that this classification had a nexus with the object of the law, mainly to channalise black money for a productive purpose.[8]

Prohibition of Discrimination

The language of Articles 15(1), 15(2) and 16(1), 16(2) prohibits State for discriminating its citizens only on the ground of religion, race, caste, sex, place of birth or any of them. Further it cannot be subject to any disability, liability, restriction or condition with regard to the access to shop, public restaurant, hotel and place of public entertainment and be ineligible for employment or office under the State.

Protective Discrimination

Based on John Rawls theory of indifference and in furtherance of third generation right with reference to Indian Constitution we can state as follows:

Civil and political rights are first generation rights whereas economic, social, and cultural rights are the rights of second generation. At present, the claims are made to recognize the third generation rights. The third generation rights are right to peace, right to development and right to solidarity.

Prof. Rawls developed the theory of indifference. According to him, there are two interests in the society, namely Burden and Benefits. Some people are having more benefits and some less. Vice versa some people are having more burden and some less. Therefore, there exists indifference and inequality in the society in enjoyment of their rights. It is the duty of State while distributing burden and benefits, to take consideration principle of justice, that is, social and economical inequality should be removed by rearrangement. While rearranging one should see that the benefit goes to the lowest benefited people or group.[9]

The third generation rights speak about the development rights, thereby mean that additional opportunity should be provided to weaker sections to lessen the inequality and to cope with others for the claim of equality.

This is justified in the Indian context where large number of diversities exist in the enjoyment of these rights. Hence the Constitution incorporated the provision of protective discrimination for development of Scheduled Castes, Scheduled Tribes, social, economic and educational backward classes of the citizens of India. Articles 15(3), 15(4) and 16(3), 16(4), and 16(5) mean that nothing shall prevent the State for making a special provision for women and children, Scheduled Castes, Scheduled Tribes and social, economical and educational backward classes of the citizens of India.

Indira Sawhney Vs. Union of India (Mandal Case). The Supreme Court overruled the judgement of Balaji case regarding the classification of backward classes and more backward classes. Classification can be made in backward classes, viz., creamy layer and non-creamy layer. Further, it propounds that 50 per cent limits of reservation can be exceeded in a special situation but it needs special precaution in doing so.[10]

Conclusion

The concept of equality in the Indian constitution has both dimensions—negative as well as positive. Rights confered under Article 14, 15(1), 15(2), 16(1), 16(2) are of negative nature and the State has nothing to do with it. But so far as Articles 15(3), 15(4), 16(3), 16(4) and 16(5) are of affirmative nature, especially for the elimination of inequalities, is one of the dominant force in our current constitutional development. Hence, it can be concluded that the principle of equality is fully enshrined under our Constitution.

Notes and References

1. Deininger: *Problem of Social and Political Thoughts*, p. 256.
2. Rashdell: *The Theory of Good and Evil*, Vol. 1, pp. 223-24.
3. Horald J. Laski: *Grammar of Politics, Chapter on Liberty and Equality*, p. 160.
4. Prof. Dicey: *Law of Constitution*, p. 193.
5. 1953, S.C.R. 655.
6. 1984, S.C.R. 30.
7. A.I.R. 1974, S.C. 597.
8. A.I.R. 1981, S.C. 2138.
9. Prof. Rawls: *Theory of Justice.*
10. A.I.R. 1993, S.C. 477.

24

Human Rights in *Mahabharata*

Anil Kumar Sinha

Dharma mean social good, not religious denomination.

Editor

Sanatan dharma means eternal laws. *Sna* means always; *tan* means present. The ordinary word 'religion' is not the equivalent of *dharma* because it is not all pervasive and all permeating. *Dharma* is that special property which is inherent in every matter. It is natural and not superimposed. It is the nature of fire to be hot and water to be cold. Why is the water hot? It is not naturally hot because heat is not the natural property of water. Hot water kept for a considerable time cools off. It will be as it was. It will resume its natural property. Thus, it is proved that cold is the permanent quality of water. Similarly joy is the natural quality of man. Sorrow is acquired one. Happiness is his *lakshana* and sorrow *uplakshana*. So *dharma* is natural activity (phenomenon). So any set-up or system opposite to human nature *adharma*. Nature of man is to be ambitious, to abandon his beastly state and embrace godly state. This is his *dharma*.

Knowledge manifests itself. It is like the table in the wood or like a toy in the mud. Education draws out this knowledge which is always there. So knowledge is another quality of man. The word *dharma* occupies a distinct place in Indian culture. *Dharma* is which holds. It prevents us from falling, from ruining ourselves. It uplifts us. It is the harbinger of all round welfare, progress and prosperity. The utterance of the Sage Vyasa defines *dharma* in this way. According the Sage Kanaada: the thing that causes progress and salvation is *dharma*. The three labours—*artha, kama* and *moksha*, come under the umbrella of *dharma*. According to the sage Jaimini," that which causes the welfare of humanity is *dharma* and *dharma* is inspired by the Vedas. Its impulse is the Vedas." It lies in the acts and deeds ordained by the sacred Vedas. Deeds prohibited by them are to be given up. Above all, use of *dharma* is for common well-being. So Vedas are the basic *granthas* and anchor of *dharma*. Manu considers them the source of all knowledge and sciences.

Dharma is eternal, indivisible, comprehensive and has no beginning and end. Past, present and future are assimilated in it. Moreover, it has no alternative. It takes us from beastly to manly qualities. Vedas are the direct utterances of the Almighty. They are His direct commands. To follow them is the sacred duty of the entire humanity. Any violation of these commands attracts God's wrath. Thus says Lord Krishna in *Gita* :

> Whenever there is decay of righteousness and there is exaltation of unrighteousness then I myself come forth for the protection of the good, for the destruction of evil doers, for the sake of firmly establishing righteousness, I am born from age to age (Gita 4/7, 8).

Is Dharma meant for a particular society or for the entire humanity? The Vedas propound that *dharma* is natural. Being a social being, man is bound to a social set-up. He cannot remain aloof. If he can, he is a beast or a demon. Social system influences him. Still this influence is like changing robes. Man cannot give up his natural *(dharma)* under any circumstance. He is born with it and dies with it.

Sanatana dharma does not denote any community. It is symbolic of religious duties and righteous conduct. According to Sripad Ramanujacharya, *sanatana dharma* is beginningless and endless. It denotes those laws which cannot undergo change. We cannot separate heat from fire and cold from water. In the same way natural properties of man cannot be separated from him. *Sanatana dharma* is eternal part of human being. Human service is the gist of life, the only reality. All creatures are parts of God. In *Gita,* Lord Krishna says – A portion of Mine ownself, transformed in the world of life into an immortal spirit (*Gita* 15/7). The great Lord showed to Arjuna His supreme form as *Ishvara,* Deity of Deities. 'Thou are lofty beyond all thought, unperishing, Thou, treasuress-house supreme, all immanent; eternal *Dharma's* changeless Guardian, Thou, as immemorial Man I think of thee,' says Arjuna. All men being parts of God remain engaged in serving one another. We come across many types of services. Service inculcates a bond, a link. This creates cooperation and association, the prerequisites of service. To serve others is man's natural religion. Today society is segregated into many creeds and sects. This segregation is based on individual faiths, time and circumstances. But it hardly makes any difference because service is the aim of all creeds and sects. *Sanatana dharma* is not affected in any way.

Patience, forgiveness, endurance, no desire to possess belongings of others, purity, subjugation of senses, steadiness of mind, discerning intellect, truth and wrathlessness are ten instruments of *dharma*. By these means righteous deeds done bring about righteous knowledge and this in turn leads to bliss, *parmananda*. This is eternal truth. Where lies the difference between man and animal? *Dharma* elevates man and makes him the roof and crown of all the creatures. It makes him superior to animal. Therefore man is a beast without *dharma* according to our *shastras*.

Knowledge of Sanskrit language is indispensable to read correctly the scriptures and *shastras*. Shallow knowledge may lead to prejudices and wrong impressions. Once these wrong impressions leave stamp on one's heart it would be practically impossible to erase them and it would let loose wrong attitudes and wrong thinking. So Sanskrit language is not the language of a particular segment of humanity. It is of the entire world. Mysteries of the universe would be revealed when we would be able to read *shastras* correctly.

Mahabharata occupies the loftiest place in our scriptures. The age and life depicted in it are full of antagonism and conflicts within and without. Struggles and complications inflicted the general public. In the Vedic times Aryas used to fight the Anaryans unitedly. But the picture was altogether changed in the *Mahabharata*. Adversaries were both Aryas. They were engaged in endless quarrels and fights to cut short the life span of their own brothers and relations. Rivalry was not between two opposing civilisations or cultures. People proud of the same civilization and same culture were at war. Can there be a more tragic thing than this?

Yudhisthira and Duryodhana are symbols of righteousness and unrighteousness respectively. Yudhisthira, the administrator of law, himself was bound by the deep uncertainty and doubt when he could not come to any conclusion even after knowing various properties of *dharma*. His insatiable yearning for knowledge goaded him to ask Bhishma again the question about which is the supreme *dharma* so as to be free from the bondage of the world? Bhisma explains:

> Freedom from bondage is within the innermost recesses of the human heart. Freedom is attained through constant worship of the Almighty. Then evil thoughts evaporate into the thin air. Ill feelings cease and the soul mingles with God. In this way man attains salvation, freedom from the cycle of birth and death.

Religions may vary and their symbols may be different and there may be contradictory statements, but all creeds and sects are one as far as moral values are concerned. The moot point is that man should uplift himself to great heights so as to reach the ideals propounded by moral values. The needs of the hour is to reject beastly tendencies and to put oneself whole-heartedly into continuous effort so as to tread the spiritual path convincingly.

The proclamation of *Mahabharata* that labour is the only means to attain desired ideals is vital for the society which has gone dormant, lustreless and idle. Labour can be righteous and unrighteous. Desired ideals gained through unrighteous labour do impart pleasure but it is transitory and insignificant. Righteous labour is the harbinger of eternal grandeur, dignity and eternity. Look at the labours of Rama and Ravana. Rama is worshipped while Ravana is always disgraced. This displays the difference between righteous and unrighteous labour.

25

The Perpetual Conflict between Good and Evil

Shweta Srivastava

> There will always be some person in the society who will trample on rights of others. The war between good and evil is perpetual. *Editor*

The phrase 'human rights' is a modern concept but its roots are steeped deep into the fathomless chasms of history. In the golden age *dharma* was present in all the four *varnas.* But with the passage of time *dharma* lost its grandeur and anarchic conditions prevailed. Golden age stands for that era when human rights were given due respect and recognition. Old order changed yielding place to new. When the golden age saw its nadir, 'might is right' pushed brotherhood in the background. Survival of the fittest came into vogue. The poor and the weak could not lead life with dignity and respect. Chances were ripe for the society to crumble down. Brahma himself intervened to improve the condition and to establish the rule of the *dharma* on this earth and to maintain dignity of life. Manu was made the king. Manu came forward to scatter the clouds of barbarism and bring about an era of stability and peace embracing all departments of life. Coronation of Manu displays that with the establishment of righteous rule, dignity, pride and respect and rights of man were assured.

Only a conscious society can think about human rights and their progress. Dr. S. Radhakrishnan was of the view that only in a well governed society where security, peace and tranquility are well-guaranteed sensible and meditative brains and minds can visualise the rise and progress of arts and science. Society infested with turmoils and tribulations, upheavals and unrest, cannot boast of developed culture because in such a society the question how to fill the belly is supreme and poverty, paucity and scarcity force people to embrace death to get rid of sufferings and tortures. Fortunately India has been a blessed land where nature's bounties were in plenty. The lofty Himalayas and the gigantic sea helped a lot in keeping India out of the reach of the invaders for a long time. God's benevolence showered benedictions on the people of India specially and kept the land full of the things necessary for leading a comfortable life. The idea that the world is a battlefield never tormented the hearts of the Indians. Life was a smooth sailing here. It went on for years together. In such a favourable atmosphere society, its culture and its administration flourished. Indian minds remained engrossed in comprehending the problems and complexities of higher life. Aided by their scriptures our sages and men in general created and flourished the concept of *'Satyam, Shivam, Sundram'* and by nurturing the lofty ideals of non-violence, world brotherhood, welfare and happiness of all guaranteed prosperity, progress and dignity of people. These concepts have in their bosoms the resolutions of human rights.

Let us peep into our past when a demon-like father violated the human rights of his son Prahlad. God himself descended as Narsinh and protected the rights of his devoted worshipper. Similarly when another demon king Bali took the entire earth in his possession and tread upon the rights of the people, *Vaman* incarnation took back the earth in donation and protected the rights of the people. Incarnations of God descended on this earth from time to time to protect the rights of the distressed humanity and to punish the unrighteous usurper of these rights. Parsurama destroyed the cruel exploiters of human rights 21 times. He helped the helpless and the hopeless to regain their rights. Vishwamitra with the help of Sri Rama eliminated the demons and protected *dharma.* In the same way when a helpless woman was abducted by the powerful king Ravana, Sri Rama punished him and in his adventure many others namely Jatayu, Hanumana, Sugreeva and countless monkeys joined hands with him. By abducting Sita Ravana had violated her rights. He had to pay very dearly for his unrighteous acts. Rama put Bali, the abductor of his own brother's wife, to death and protected the rights both of the husband and the wife. When the public cried under the cruelties of king Kamsa,

Sri Krishna killed him and protected the rights of the common masses. Kamsa had put his own sister and his brother-in-law behind the bars and had killed their offsprings by hurling them to the ground. God had to descend as an incarnation. When a serpent poisoned the water of Jamuna, Sri Krishna destroyed it. Similarly when Indra's wrath caused excessive rains and people cried for help, Krishna not only helped them but even the animals and birds. Indra tried to snatch the right to life from the people and other creatures but could not succeed in his attempt. When Duryodhana and Dushasana were pulling at Panchali's robes to dishonour her, Krishna protected her honour and to get rid of these rascals the battle of *Mahabharata* was faught. Krishna played a vital role in getting the snatchers of human rights kiss death. Mythological battles were fought to protect women and their rights. No other proof is wanted to ascertain the fact that in ancient India, human rights were well-protected and well-assured.

In the ancient State administration the king had the right to inflict severe punishment on the violaters of human rights and *dharma.* Before inflicting punishment on others the king had to observe many *vratas* fasts and perform his duties according to the code of conduct and ordinances of the scriptures.

Law of *varna* does not admit superiority and inferiority. But law of variation in biology holds good. The natural differences (physical, intellectual, moral and all round) are inherent in respect of individual temperament, taste, capacity and so forth. Unity does not postulate mechanical uniformity.

In the ancient Indian social set up man and woman are considered one. According to *Manusmriti* Brahma's body split in two exact halves resulted into man and woman, the right side representing the man and the left representing woman—*Swayam-bhuva Manu* and *Satarupa Manu* respectively. As regards quantity, man and woman form 50:50 of the whole. There is no difference between man and woman.

Difference in works creates a disparity and inequality in the context of abilities and capacities of different persons. Abilities and nature differ from man to man. So will be the rights. Human race is one but social and natural conditions create disparities. Work according to capacity is inherent in *varna* system. But in the context of pleasure, all men are equal. Even animal kingdom is on a par with mankind. On spiritual level also all men are equal. The same soul permeates in all human beings. So they are equal. The doctrine of freedom of thought and work creates a difference. Difference is on physical, mental and intellectual levels only.

Now we have adopted and enacted our own Constitution of free India and in the context of Universal Declaration of Human Rights we have included the right to equality, right to freedom and right to life and many sub-clauses related to different social and economic rights in part 3 and part 4 of our Constitution.

Man was free to act according to his calibre and competence. *Varna* system was consolidation of competence and abilities and it has got no relation with birth. Today man enjoys some fundamental freedoms. In the ancient Indian society also, citing many provisions of *Smritis,* man was given freedom to act according to his will and inclination. No doubt he was bound by his abilities and competence. Even the king was subjugated to the codes like his subjects. The king and the Brahmin being dignified and occupying high places in social strata were given more severe punishment than ordinary people. Judges too were subjected to punishment according to their degree of dereliction of duty.

In Manu's social set-up every segment of society enjoyed equal participation in State administration. Individual abilities and competence mattered the most. Man's duties enjoined on him the corresponding rights also. The moot question according to Vivekananda is to uplift the down trodden and not to pull down those who have been uplifted already. Devahuti has described that in the court of Harshvardhna there was a poet who was an untouchable, a *chandal* by the name of Martand. His presence in the court simply proves that lower social status cannot deprive a person from rising the rungs of progress and respect. Action is supreme.

It is said that traits of a person do influence his action and work. Goodness, wrath and wickedness play a prominent role in the acts performed by men. These traits can be changed and modified. Vishwamitra attained *Brahmanatva* like this. He graduated inch by inch for his lofty position. Place of a person in society did not become an obstacle in his way to lofty heights.

Delving deep into our ancient literature and then prevalent point of views we can conclude that the king was appointed to protect *dharma,* justice and human rights. He was never given the robes of a despot. Before political organisation there was no king so neither punisher nor punishment. People protected one another by following *dharma.* With the passage of time *dharma* lost its grandeur. Economic power and muscle power let loose untold miseries for the people. There arose the need to have a king and court of justice to mitigate the sufferings of the people and establish the rule of law and uphold *dharma.* Brahmdeva created *Nitishastra,* to dilute the problems and sufferings and made Virja, the son of Vishnu, the king to rule according to the provisions of that science of politics. But Virja embraced asceticism. His son Kirtimana and Kirtimana's son Kardam opted for renunciation and penance. Kardam's son proved to be a good ruler but his son Atibala became slave of his senses. His son Vena was a cruel king and sages eliminated him. Vena's son Prithu was a righteous ruler as in his reign the earth was filled with wealth and grains. It was the result of his staunch faith in *dharma.* A king is the centre of all powers and by their use or misuse he can be a despot but applying his discerning wisdom and sense of justice he can tame his own tendencies of becoming a dictator. Vena and Prithu are glaring examples. Ravana and Kansa did not check their dictatorial tendencies. The result was they licked dust and died a dog's death. On the contrary, Rama and Krishna were exemplary kings. Rama respecting the sentiments of his subjects renounced Sita. Had he wanted he would have awarded the appropriate punishment to the person casting aspersion on his wife's character.

26

Daya Bhaga

Urmila Srivastava

The Indian social and legal system was based upon the concept of *rina* or the debt with which one is born.

Editor

The word *Daya* denotes many meanings—gift, award, portion, inheritance, ancestral property, etc. But its meaning in technical terms is inheritance of ancestral property only. So any material received from the parents is called *daai* (दाय). He who receives this material is called *daiad* (inheritor).

The word *daai* perhaps finds its first use in the *Ṛgveda*. In *Nighaṇtu daai* means ancestral wealth to be divided. But in *Smṛiti Chandrikā* and *Smṛiti Saṇgrah daai* stands for that matter which is received both from the father and the mother. *Daya Bhaga* denotes division of father's and grandfather's wealth among sons and grandsons respectively. The basis of this division is relationship of the inheritor/inheritors with the deceased owner/owners. Manu has included even division of mother's wealth in *Daya Bhaga*. Manu has discussed about *Daya Bhaga* to be retained by the son, the grandson and the great grandson in detail; but he has recorded only passing remarks about the ancestral wealth to be given to women. He has discussed about this issue very briefly. This has given rise to a misunderstanding that woman is to get nothing out of the ancestral property or wealth. It is clear that selfish elements quote or misquote scriptures to suit their ends. Some scholars have given wide interpretation of the word 'son' as far as *Daya Bhaga* is concerned. They argue that this word 'son' embraces daughter also. They see no difference between the son and the daughter. Paṇ dit Ganga Prasad citing an incantation from *Ṛgveda,* substantiates this notion that the word 'son' used here stands for both son and daughter. According to him, both son and daughter are born out of the body and so there is no difference in their birth. So the word 'son' denoting both boy and girl is acceptable. Thus, without any discrimination both the son and the daughter are to be regarded inheritors. Yaska, a famous sage who composed the *Nirukta* also hints at the same meaning of the word son used in Vedic incantations. Both the son and the daughter help the family tree to grow.

In the discussion on *Daya Bhag* two facts are noteworthy : (1) What kind of things can a father leave after his death? (2) Who should receive these things?

According to the tenets of Indian culture, offsprings are indebted to their parents not for flesh and blood and bones but for qualities, learning, traits and language. These traits come to the son and the daughter equally. Other things to be inherited from the parents are—wealth, food grains and cattle. These things are divisible. This characteristic of the things to be inherited gives birth to clash of interests amongst the offsprings. In the joint family system such clashes might have less possibility to raise their heads. That is why Manu did not think it necessary to frame rules for the division of material inheritance.

The third thing is landed property. According to Manu, landed property should be inherited by the sons and the daughters should get dowry *Streedhan*. A father having no son of his own should keep the husband of his daughter in his own house and treat their offsprings as legal inheritors. Manu opines that only after the demise of the parents sons, can inherit the paternal property and in no case if they are alive. The word *Matusch* मातुश्च employed by Manu in this context depicts that the living mother and not the son. The son has no right to property so long as the mother is alive.

Yāgyavalkya considers wife and daughters the inheritors of ancestral wealth after the death of the sonless father. *Viṣhnusmṛti* and *Mitakṣarā* allow the wife and the daughters to be the first inheritors if there is no son. Manu considers the mother and the grandmother also the inheritors if the father dies without begetting a son. Bodhāyana and Vaśistha do not give right of wealth to wife and women respectively. *Śankhlikhit* does give the right to wealth to the wife but she is the last in the row. He thinks that the wealth of a sonless person first of all should go to his brothers and then to the parents and wife in case there are no brothers. Gautama too considers wife the last person in the row of inheritors. In his views relatives (allied by blood) and the wife can get the wealth of an issueless person side by side. Brhaspati opines that wife has the first right to inheritance because wife is the better half and shares equally the sinful and virtuous deeds. So till she is alive nobody else can be the inheritor. Yāgyavalkya and Viṣṇu too consider wife the first inheritor of the property of an issueless man.

The question is should wife be the inheritor? There is no meeting point even for the commentators of *Manusmṛti* on the issue. *Medhātithi* and *Kullakū* express contrary views. *Medhātithi* says that wife is not the inheritor after the death of an issueless person. Kullūk Bhatta thinks otherwise. According to *Mitāksarā*, *Kātyāyan* and Manu only issueless and virtuous widow has the right to property. Perhaps here they attach more importance to the word virtuous. *Mitāksarā*, favours equal distribution of property amongst many widows. Yāgyavalkya thinks that the father should give equal portions of inheritance to the wives and the sons. Bodhāyanā is against the inheritance of women because women are weak and sapless so they should not get any inheritance. *Mitākśarā* considers that the portion the wife is to get from the inheritance depends solely on the whims and wishes of her husband. Bṛahaspati expresses the view that a single wife should get an equal share but in the case of many wives there should be equal division of inherited property. Thus we see that religious instructors in general have not propagated the right to property for the wife. They have whispered but have not spoken loudly and openly in favour of the wife. She can be the inheritor only after the death of her husband and that too if there is no male son of the deceased. So wife is given a second class treatment.

Girls are not inheritors in the eyes of Vaśiśtha, Bodhāyanā and Gautama. But Manu argues differently. He is of the view that like the son, the daughter is also a portion of the father. She is also the soul of her father. So nobody else but the living daughter is to be the inheritor. Manu also says that in the case of mother's demise all the brothers and the sisters should divide the property amongst themselves. Daughter is the successor after the widow according to Yāgñavalkya, Nārada and Vishnu. Narad give the unmarried girl the right to live in the ancestral house and get nurtured there. Brhaspati considers wife the plunderer of her husband's wealth. She is *Dhanhari*. Gautam is of the view that priority should be given to married and poor girls in the matter of inheritance. Mitākṣarā has put the unmarried girl, poor unmarried girl and rich married girl one after the other in succession of inheritance.

Property of a woman is called *Strīdhan*. The word *Strīdhan* is technical. Manu opines six types of *Strīdhan* :

1. Money received from the father in front of fire;
2. Money received at the time of departure or send off;
3. Money received from the husband out of love;
4. Money received from the brother;
5. Money received from the mother; and
6. Money received from the father on different occasions.

In the *Smṛitis* a list of *Strīdhan* is given. No jurist or legislator has endeavoured to define it elaborately. Kautilya considers dowry, money given for nurturing, money given for maintenance and money given by relations as *Strīdhan*. Inclusion of gifts given by the guests, gifts given after the marriage, presents given by father-in-law and others in *Strīdhan* has widened its realms. With the passage of time *Strīdhan* covered movable and immoveable property received by the wife before marriage, at the time of marriage and thereafter from the parents, relatives, husband and family members of husband side. *Smṛtis* call this wealth received from the loving relations, *Strīdhan*.

Woman has unbridled right on her *Strīdhan* as this wealth is given to her by her relations to help her in her bad days. It is an acknowledged fact that on moveable and immoveable property received out of love, offsprings and sale woman has full and sole right. She can spend it as per her wishes and desires. The father, husband, son and brother have no right to spend it and divide it. If they take it by force or use it, they have to return it with interest.

All jurists are unanimous on this point that daughter is the first master of *Strīdhan.* Sons get *Strīdhan* if there is no daughter. *Mitākśarā* views that a daughter's body has more elements of her mother in comparison to the son. So ṣhe is given priority in the possession of *Strīdhan.* Possibly because of this reason that when the son does not recognise the right of inheritance to his sisters in the property of their father the daughters too have the same right in respect of *Strīdhan.* Thus, we see *Strīdhan* is exclusively the property of the daughter. Gautam is of the view that first claimant of *Strīdhan* is unmarried girl. Its second claimant is poor married girl and in the end comes the turn of married rich girl. Bṛhaspati and Pārāshar are also of the same view. Married girls do get a portion of *Strīdhan* out of love. Money earned by the married woman through crafts and handiwork and by the sweat of her eyebrow or the money given to her by other people is not included in *Strīdhan.*

The Right to inheritance can be availed by a woman from the husband, father and son and also from the mother and daughter. This is the opinion of Mitāksarā. All types of such property is included in *Strīdhan.* But the Privy Council has rejected this explanation of *Mitākśarā* for all provinces except the province of Bombay. Its directions to the court clearly forbid them to give weight to this explanation; but decide cases according to the prevalent traditions and customs in a particular province or place. Really speaking the subject of *Strīdhan* is very complex and intricate and laws universally acceptable are difficult to be framed. In the past laws were simpler regarding *Strīdhan* or inheritance. With the passage of time they became complex because of the commentators and additions made afterwards. Right to inheritance attached to *Mitākśarā* changed the very aspect of inheritance. Complete and total ownership of inheritance was restricted for women. In Hindu Code it is named as 'bounded wealth'. Hindu Succession Amendment Act, 1929 not only bestowed the right to inheritance on the widow, daughter, mother, grandmother and great grandmother; but also on son's daughter, daugher's daughter and sister. Hindu Women's Right to Property Act, 1937 upgrading the status of widow, her daughter-in-law and her grand son's daughter granted them the right to landed property like their dead husbands and living or dead son. It has brought about a tremendous reform and transformation in the plight of women. This act was a fundamental change in the law of inheritance. This gave the widow the right of ownership of her husband's portion and the right to divide it as per her wishes. But it was not an absolute right. She did get the right regarding the use of landed property and its nurturing; but right of transfer as to change the title still eluded her. In all other Indian courts except those of Bombay, rights of the widow and of the daughter were the same. So the daughter could use the property, but could not divide it. Her father's and not her own heirs could be the claimant to property after her death. In Mumbai the situation was different. There she got absolute right of ownership of her father's wealth and property. Her own heirs inherited the property and wealth after her death.

Hindu Succession Act, 1956 played a vital role to ameliorate the plight of woman. Its Clause No. 14 conferred total and absolute ownership of property, etc., received by her through any source before and after the commencement of this Act. Now she was at par with male members in the family. Conditions of chastity for the widow and fidelity for the girl respectively were done away with. Even remarriage could not render the right to inheritance null and void. This Act is applicable for entire India (except J & K) equally to all sects which accept inheritance and *Smṛti* and on the condition that the parents of the inheritor must be followers of Hindu religion (not Christian, Muslim, Parsi) and citizens of India to satisfy the provisions of the Act. Those widows, widow's daughters-in-law and widow's grandson's daughter-in-law are not covered by this act who have married before the commencement of this Act. The discrimination propagated by ancient *Smṛtis* between married and unmarried, rich and poor daughters is done away with and it has been established that daughter's portion is to be equal to son's portion and she is to have absolute and impenetrable ownership to inheritance. The condition of legitimacy is also not applicable. Now a daughter can be adopted and an adopted daughter has the same right as that of legitimate daughter. Efforts are being made to enact laws to assure portion of inheritance to the widow and daughters in the farm land along with the living sons. Such equal rights would certainly improve the lot of woman. But this is also sure that this equal right in rural property similar to that of an urban property would usher in a lot of disputes and litigation and land would get fragmented. It would harm the family system. It would hit the families economically and weaken them. In the long run it would not benefit the Indian society. Disintegration of families economically would hit and weaken the very foundations of Indian society.

27

Limits of Statutory Rights

G.S. Misra

> Dharma cannot be established merely by the government or the Constitution. It requires establishment of social values.
>
> *Editor*

A Brief History of Human Rights

The United Nations has its origins in the unfortunate backdrop of Second World War which engulfed almost the entire globe. The enormous loss of life and cruel suppression of human rights during the World War were extremely painful experiences for the mankind. In order to prevent a repetition of such mindless events and ensure lasting peace in the world, various nations felt compelled to sit together and explore new alternatives for managing global relations. The result was a decision to create a new institution called United Nations for realising this hope.

In accordance with its mandate, the United Nations announced the Universal Declaration of Human Rights on 10th December, 1948. The Declaration listed thirty specific aspects relating to this issue. It expected all the nations to take necessary steps to assure these rights to their citizens and that they would incorporate the features of the UN Declaration in their respective constitutions. This hope, however, failed to materialise during the next 45 years. Violations of human rights continued to take place in one or other part of the globe. The resulting concern paved the way for another Conference of United Nations in Vienna in 1993 for reviewing the whole issue afresh. Representatives of all the countries were invited. After a thorough and intensive debate which lasted a week, it was decided that the Declaration of 1948 would remain in place without any amendment whatsoever. All the countries, however, decided to undertake effective steps for its implementation. Since the Vienna Conference, the issue of Human Rights has also come under sharper focus with the media attention, discussions, etc.

The Origin of the Concept of Human Rights

Since the UN Declaration of Human Rights was a result of the initiative taken by the Western nations, there is a widespread notion that the very concept of human rights itself is Western in its origin. This is far removed from the truth. India has been spreading the message of human dignity and equality for thousands of years now. It is India that gave the world the noble *mantra* of *Vasudaiva Kutumbakam*, i.e., the whole world is one single family. Our religious and spiritual literature are full of passages expressing desire for world peace. The ancient *Shanti Paath* or prayers for peace form an integral part of our religious rituals. They have also been a source of inspiration for the whole world. India has not just desired peace in the world but actually worked for it. This is amply demonstrated by the fact that India has never tried to conquer other nations through the use of force even though it was mighty and powerful enough to do so in the ancient times.

The reason for this preference for peaceful conduct lies in the prime role of the concept of *dharma* in all walks of life in India. *Dharma* is supreme. It has been said in the *Manusmriti* (II, IV-176) that if one has to choose between *dharma* and pleasures of materialistic and sensual kinds, one should follow the path of *dharma* without hesitation.

The daily prayers also include a wish for happiness of all—*Sarve Bhavantu Sukhinah, Sarve Santu Niramaya.* It is, thus, quite obvious that India firmly believes that all human beings have a right to lead a life of peace and prosperity. If we observe closely, we would see that all the thirty human rights listed in the UN Declaration ultimately arise from the desire of all living beings to live in peace and comfort. In fact, the very aim of human right would be to bring happiness and prosperity to the human beings. It is also evident from this perspective that the concept of human rights had its origins in ancient India and it was only thousands of years later that it became a globally accepted objective through the medium of United Nations.

Several other examples can be given to further validate this view. India not only granted human rights to all the citizens but also made effective arrangements for this purpose. There was a close relationship between the human rights and the duties of the citizens. The rights were to be earned by discharging one's duties. All the references found in this context stress upon this relationship. The underlying idea was that in a scenario where everyone is acting in accordance with the tenets of *dharma,* the human rights concerns were automatically taken care of. Respecting the rights of other citizens is an integral part of the social system designed on the principles of *dharma.*

To illustrate this, we can take up the issue of equality as a fundamental right. *Manusmriti* has laid down that a king should treat all the citizens as equal without any discrimination. It says "just as the mother earth feeds all living beings residing in its bosom, a king should also look after the needs of all its citizens without any distinction." When the king himself was duty bound to see every one as an equal, the fundamental human right of equality came into existence on its own.

As for the right to security, *Manusmriti* clearly mentions that it is the foremost duty of a *Kshatriya,* i.e., the person of the warrior class, to secure the well-being of the people.

In order to secure the right to education, it was necessary for everyone to pay the *Guru-Rina* or the debt due to the teachers. In other words the society was considered actually indebted to the teachers for their contribution. It also meant that the right to receive education also belonged to everyone.

Ancient India accorded highest respect to the women. According to a famous saying, gods choose to dwell only in a place where women are worshipped, i.e., they are held in high esteem.

It is only when each and every aspect of the society is governed by *dharma* that human rights could be achieved. No government, Constitution or law is sufficient in itself to deliver the rights. It has been said that in Sat Yuga where 'there was no kingdom and no king. There was neither crime nor criminals. Every one lived according to the limits of *dharma* and thereby each one defended everyone else.

Kautilya has given directions to the kings in *Arthashastra* to follow their duties: "The happiness of a king lies in the happiness of the people and his own welfare lies in their welfare." A king would not judge what is good or bad according to his personal interests but according to the principle that whatever is good for the people is good for him too.

Moral conduct and obligation to discharge one's duties was considered essential for both king and the people. The spirit of devotion to duty was therefore instilled in all the citizens in various ways. It was done not only through education but also by making it an integral aspect of the traditional value system which were absorbed even while one was growing up. A society which was built upon such foundations inherently guaranteed the human rights. These were the very notions which made India a land of true action or *Karma Bhumi* and not *Yoga Bhumi* as that would have made India devoted to only pursuit of spirituality at the cost of all other obligations. What is deemed as a basic right of an individual was made into a duty of another one. In fact it would not be wrong to state that in ancient India the citizens had been granted their basic rights only in terms of duties assigned to each one of them. The famous dictum of *Gita, Karamanyev Adhikaraste,* meaning that a man is only entitled to the right of performing action, confirms this.

It is evident from the above analysis that in the antiquity, the citizens automatically earned the rights by performing their duties. Simultaneously the kings also facilitated it all by discharging their assigned duties towards the citizens.

It would be proper to clarify here that the rights and duties are two sides of the same coin. Neither can exist without the other. What constitutes the right of one individual is a duty enjoyed upon the other and the rights of others automatically become the duties of each individual. Hence, if we really cherish our rights we will have to do justice to our duties towards others. Human rights cannot be ensured without fulfilling this precondition.

When people want to only safeguard their own rights without showing any commitment to their duties towards others, the net result is instability, chaos and conflict in the society. One path leads to peace, the other to violence. It is evident that India chose the path of love and peace by accepting to earn rights by discharging the duties.

It also needs to be pointed out that there is a fundamental difference between the Indian approach and the Western thinking on human rights today. The Indian wisdom suggested adoption of the principles of *dharma* as that itself would be sufficient to safeguard human rights in a peaceful manner. The Western nations have, however, treated the issue of rights in isolation. The citizens are expected to secure their rights through a process of struggle against the rulers. Hence conflicts and agitations are inherently present in this approach. Clearly the path chosen by India is more preferable to the Western one.

Values of life, in fact, mean nothing but *dharma* or duties. For example, the spirit of tolerance towards another is an important element of the value system of life. Simultaneously, it is also our duty to be tolerant towards the belief and rituals of all religions.

A brief account of those duties or values which should guide our conduct for acquiring basic human rights corresponding to the entries in the UN Declaration is given below:

- The right to freedom and equality is the *first* of the listed rights. The *second* one is the right to non-discrimination. This right can be acquired by accepting the values of a love for justice and universal brotherhood in our lives.
- To achieve the *third* right of security and the *fourth* right of freedom from slavery requires a spirit of non-violence and justice in our conducts.
- Recognition as an individual in the eyes of law is the *sixth* right.
- The *seventh* is the right to equality before law. The *eighth* is the right to protection of fundamental rights by the judiciary. *Ninth* is the right to safeguards of the courts in case of arrest. *Tenth,* the right to free and fair trial in case of criminal allegations. *Eleventh,* the right to be considered innocent until found guilty by the courts. *Twelfth,* Right to privacy of the individual, family, house and non-interference in communication, postal correspondences, etc. *Thirteenth,* right to reside and move about within the territorial limits of one's country. *Fourteenth,* right against persecution and seek asylum in another country. *Fifteenth,* right to acquire nationality and change it. *Sixteenth,* right of an adult to marry in spite of restrictions imposed by the nation, class or caste, religion, etc. In order to acquire these rights, we will have to accept truth, justice, non-violence and spirit of tolerance as essential values guiding our way of life.

- *Seventeenth,* the right to ownership of property. *Eighteenth,* the right to freedom of thought and religion. *Nineteenth,* the right to freedom of expression. *Twentieth,* the right to conduct a meeting peacefully. To acquire these rights we need to incorporate the values of trust, truth, non-violence, tolerance, non-covetousness in our lives.
- *Twenty-first,* the right to participate in the governance, right to vote and the right to employment. *Twenty-second,* the right to make use of the institutions and facilities of the State. *Twenty-third,* the right to receive equal pay for equal work and the right to form trade unions. *Twenty-fourth,* the right to fixed hours of work and rest. *Twenty-fifth,* the right to receive proper nutrition, food, residence, and medical facilities for ensuring proper standard of life. To acquire these rights we have to adopt the values of truth, justice, etc. and the duty to serve and work. *Twenty-sixth,* the right to education. *Twenty-seventh,* the right to be a partner in the development of art and sciences. *Twenty-eighth,* the right to a social international mechanism for securing the human rights. These rights demand that we should adopt such values as *dharma,* truthfulness, love for justice, etc., in our lives.

  The *twenty-ninth* and the *thirtieth* rights are duties in themselves.

The way of acquiring human rights. Human rights can be acquired in two ways. One is the way of ancient India where rights are conferred automatically through a commitment to duty. Education for imparting human values and creating a duty-bound society play important roles here. The importance of rights and governments is less. The second is the present Western way where rights have been given special emphasis. Struggle and conflict are advocated as a tool and the rights are given by the government or administration. The role of duty is greatly reduced here. The first is the path of love, peace and devotion, the second is all about conflict, resistance and a breakdown in peace.

Present position. Unfortunately most countries nowadays are adopting the second path. This is an important reason behind the troubled and violence prone State of affairs in many parts of the world. One can see that the reason the governments resist acceptance of more and more human rights for their citizens is that they are self serving in nature. These rights reduce their own gains and comforts while increasing their responsibilities. Indians are is also striving today to secure rights not through the path of duty but through conflicts. The courts are flooded with litigations as a result. It is also proved by the tendency of its government to impose more taxes rather than reducing the governmental expenditure. Many governments in the world today are more busy violating the human rights rather than granting these rights to their citizens. It is very difficult to expect protection of human rights from governments engaged in corruption, exploitation and self-serving activities.

It appears as if all the citizens of USA, Great Britain, France, Japan and some other rich nations have acquired human rights. However, the level of economic disparities existing in these nations tells another story. If the citizens are more prosperous in these countries, the reason lies in their exploitation of other countries and the policy of self-promotion at all costs. This exploitation is sometimes achieved by existing military pressure and by economic pressure at other times. Such acts appear quiet contradictory when these countries preach about universal brotherhood and morality all the time.

It is evident from the above that the human rights can be secured, and promoted in the world only when each citizen of every country adopts the right kinds of values for guiding his conduct. He should always be striving to secure human rights by discharging his own duties towards others. He should adopt the motto of 'simple living and high thinking'. He should always be ready to serve others and he should do it of his own will. There is, therefore, a need to readopt the ancient India's way of life and the system of *Gurukul* with necessary modification in order to inculcate such qualities in the citizens. If India was called a golden bird and also seen as a teacher of the world in ancient times, the credit goes to the purity of conduct, constant endeavours, and sense of duty which characterised its policies.

28

Basic Human Rights Transcend Human Differences

Uma Singh

Some rights are common to all human beings. These transcend differences in capabilities of individuals.

Editor

Humanity is like a beam of light which has left its source and is flowing away into the unknown towards the infinity. The concept of Human Rights contains in itself the feeling of universal brotherhood, happiness and beauty. It means providing an environment of assured basic human rights and thereby making it possible for a man to proceed forward in life with a sense of duty. The term 'Human Rights' applies to all such incidental circumstances which must ordinarily exist to ensure all round development of people. Thus, the way of life adopted by a society, its philosophy towards life and its overall value system play a decisive role in identifying the constituent elements of human rights.

When we analyse the premises behind the idea of these rights with respect to the differing level of skills and capabilities, we are basically concerned with discrimination made on the basis of sex or class or caste. When the extent of discrimination begins to amount to downright and inhuman cruelty, the question of human rights arises quite naturally.

There are certain universal traits such as the desire to live or the instinct to propagate one's species. These are common to all living beings including the mankind. They transcend the petty and artificial barriers created on the basis of colour, appearance or the levels of material wealth. In a scenario where one has no control over determining his origins, sex, religion, caste or race, such distinctions conferred upon him can only be deemed as contributions of natural forces when seen from his individual perspective.

Nature on its own has also not created all men as equals. Hence no two individuals can possess identical capabilities or temperaments. There is a general phenomenon which exists not only in India but in all the known races of the mankind in the world. One may be black or white in colour, he may be giant like or tiny in size or he may be thin or fat. It is impossible to locate a nation where such differences in the looks are not to be found. Even animals exhibit such wide variations in their external looks within a given species. it should hardly cause any surprise when men differ in such manners. So far as the questions of attitudes and temperaments are concerned, one should also likewise not expect any uniformity to exist in these respects. If one person has been given a merry disposition by nature, another person may burst into anger on smallest provocation. People conduct their day to day affairs in a similar fashion. The emotions of love or hatred, preference for peace or conflict or the level of sensitivity in general can never be present in same degrees in different individuals. It would be quiet problematic if all the traits of the nature were uniformly present in all its creation. That would simply stop the development of nature itself since the purpose of a change would cease to exist. There would be no reason for any change to occur. If everyone possessed a violent temperament it would be impossible to even think about simplicity in behaviour and conduct. It leads us to conclude that notwithstanding all the variations in temperaments which occur naturally, men are essentially equal from the viewpoint of possessing essential attributes of humanity.

People are bound to have different levels of skills and capabilities. If one person can run for 20 kms, another person can cover 80 kms. One may be able to lift 20 kgs but someone else is capable of lifting 80 kgs. While one may be a skilled writer, other could be a mathematician. If one is a good pilot, the other is a good lecturer. If one is a good economist, another is a good politician. One can go on indefinitely with such comparisons. If everyone had similar capabilities there would be nothing specific or special about any individual. There would also be no reason for developing inter-relationships in a society made up of such men. The whole fabric of social formation would be destroyed as a result. There would simply be no necessity for formulating rules and regulations in a world where all men behave alike. No standards could be developed to compare people's behaviour in such a scenario. However, the real world does not conform to such specifications. There are wide variations between the capacities and capabilities of people.

Human rights of mankind are directly linked to its basic needs. These needs decide as to what would or would not qualify as a human right. Just as all men have blood of red colour, they also feel the sensation of hunger and thirst alike. All of them need a shelter to live and garments to wear. These needs are not influenced on account of the differences in their sex, creed, caste, colour, etc. National boundaries or linguistic differences become meaningless in context of the basic needs which have their origin in the vital forces of life or in the collective consciousness of the humanity. Human rights are about creating and sustaining an environment conducive to survival and growth. If there could be uniformity in this respect, each individual would be able to develop in the true sense of the word.

A mother may give birth to many sons who differ in their colour, appearance, nature or capabilities. She would, however, never discriminate between them on such grounds. She treats all of them equally and provides them with similar wherewithals to grow and develop themselves. She does not believe in the theory of the survival of the fittest. She can never bring herself to think along such lines.

It would, therefore, be highly desirable to associate the issue of the quality of education directly or indirectly with the issues relating to human rights. The objective behind making such a proposition is to help in creating an environment which provides human rights protection to everyone in the best possible manner. Moral education, for example, must be imparted in the schools. An education replete with moral teachings would go a long way in developing an attitude of healthy understanding and tolerance towards other fellow human beings. The feeling of sameness or the sense of equality would be strengthened. Education would not only lead to a greater discipline in the society but also help in developing a self discipline amongst the individual members of the society. In turn, these qualities would result in a greater respect and care towards the rights, responsibilities or duties. A society which consists of individuals sharing such qualities would not witness cases of violations of human rights and all its citizens would be free to develop themselves into achieving the best of their capabilities.

Human capabilities and temperaments differ significantly on account of the various physical or mental attributes. Nonetheless, all human beings have identical basic needs. Certain traits are common to every person in the world. The instincts of self-preservation and procreation are found in all. Such traits, instincts or desire are not affected by such considerations as whether one is handicapped, suffering from some incurable disease or belongs to a very backward community living far away from the mainstream of human civilization. The same consciousness pervades all human beings. These underlying uniformities in different individuals do not fail to manifest themselves despite the obvious differences in the external appearances. The desire for freedom also belongs to this category. No one would ever like to lead a life as a slave or spend his days under domination of others. Everyone yearns for freedom and strives to achieve it if it is denied to him. When the mankind possesses such similarities in feelings and emotion, any attempt towards discrimination in the matters of human right on the basis of externalities like race, caste, religion, etc., is patently wrong and without any justification.

This Indian philosophy holds quite clearly that the whole debate about whether this is mine or that is yours is entered into only by the petty-minded people. The truly noble people consider the entire world as one single family. Indeed it is the approach of the petty-minded ones which prepares the grounds for violation of human rights. It runs contrary to the fundamental reality of the universe that the single supreme consciousness is all pervasive and binds all beings together. When the God himself has not resorted to any discrimination in his grand scheme there can be no basis for man to make such attempts. The education system must sensitise every human-being to this truth so that they can decide for themselves that the petty boundaries drawn on the basis of politics, race, creed, etc., are worthless in the real sense. He would also learn to respect and protect others' rights as much as his own as he would have ceased to make distinctions on the basis of 'mine', 'his', etc.

29

Individual Rights Lead to Social Good

Ashu Pasricha

Human Rights are integrally connected with development policy. *Editor*

Technology has increased the gap between the rich and poor countries. The global restructuring of 1980s and the 1990s has structurally foisted newer and sinister forms of exploitation and further marginalization of Third World countries from the world economy with progressive decomposition of social and economic structures. India has not been left untouched by this process. Not only has Indian economy been weakened by this process and its development paradigm is undergoing a great deal of strain, but we are also witnessing the growing ecological and environmental malaise that is its bye-product. A natural and logical corollary of this process is that communities are losing their inalienable human rights to live and subsist the way they have done for centuries together. By implication, it is also denying individuals their personal right to a safe livelihood and right to make sanguine and personal choices of liberties and entitlements. Thus, globalisation has rendered the traditional relationship between the State and the communities outdated. The State, being subjected to the forces of neo-imperialism is being forced by the logic of development to impose 'anti-people' policies and exploitative politics on the community. National sovereignty has been replaced by new concepts of 'intellectual property rights', based on the interests of corporations (MNCs and TNCs) and the reality of social, economic and political organization of industrialized Western countries.

At the time of independence, India borrowed a colonial model of economic development. Modernization was identified with industrialization. The mega industries established in collaboration with foreign finance were presented as models. The Iron and Steel Company in Durgapur was established with British collaboration, the Rourkela plant with German and the Bokaro plant with Russian assistance. Besides there were other mega projects with foreign collaborations. Though the country loudly made pronouncements for a socialistic pattern of economic development, the model was capitalistic. With the process of globalization, the country has adopted the capitalist model both in words and deeds.

Human Right activists, concerned citizens and several NGOs are of the opinion that the country is for sale with the opening of the economy for Multinational Companies, Transnational Corporations and Business Houses. Laws have been introduced making it easy for foreign nationals to acquire land, property and carry on business. While foreigners easily become citizens on the strength of their capital, citizens are ousted from their houses and evicted from their colonies and slums in the name of development. The biggest human rights violations in India today are in the name of development. The globalized model of development is causing untold misery and hardships to the average citizens in the country.

The word 'develop' is a 12th or 13th century word. The Italian word, according to Oxford English Dictionary, is *velupare,* which means 'to unrap', 'to disentangle', and 'to rid free of'. The opposite of 'develop' is 'envelop' which means 'to hide', 'to cover up', 'to put constraints upon'—which is what we do when we envelop something. When we develop we do the reverse. We remove constraints whatever they may be. The word 'develop' maintains its original definition in photography. When we develop a film we reveal what is already latent in that film. We cannot put new things into the film and call it developed. Development is thus a process of revealing. That is to say, something more comes out of that which already exists. Rural development should proceed on this basis rather than blindly following the theories of development propounded by the Western authors. This is what the *Mahatma* preached.

How are developments—induced displacements—classified as human rights violations? Three examples from three states of recent so-called development projects have been given to clarify this doubt.

(a) Sardar Sarovar Project : The project is intended to bring drinking water to Kutch and other drought prone regions of Gujarat and to irrigate a vast area of that State as well as two districts of Rajasthan. But the dam will submerge 37,000 hectares of land in three States—Gujarat, Maharashtra and Madhya Pradesh. It will require approximately another 80,000 hectares of land, more than twice as much land as the submergence area. The Project when completed will be one of the largest water resource projects. The impact of the Project will affect a large number of people specially tribals. Majority of the oustees are tribals. Over a lakh of people who live in 245 villages in the area will be affected by the submergence. Another one lakh forty thousand farmers will be adversely affected by the irrigation system. The Department of Environment and Forests estimates the timber loss in the forest to be to the tune of Rs. 40,000 crore.

(b) The Rengali Dam Project in Orissa has submerged 265 villages and displaced 10,847 families in two districts, three subdivisions and nine blocks. The Upper Indravati hydroelectric project located in Southern Orissa has affected 97 villages with 67 villages fully submerged, 34 villages from Kalahandi, 18 from Nawrangpur and 13 from Koraput districts. Only 5,448 families have been assisted with rehabilitation. Majority of the affected are tribals.

(c) The two 1000 MW Nuclear Plants: Established in 1980 at Koodankulam in Tamil Nadu resulted in the immediate eviction of the people of the Koodankulam village itself, barely 3 kilometres from the reactor site and villages of Panjal and Perumanal, very close to the site. Over 25,000 people were evicted. The setting up of the nuclear plants has curtailed fishing activities in a belt of nearly 75 kms. This has posed a threat to the livelihood of nearly 3 lakh fisherfolk. Once nuclear radiation leak from the nuclear plants contaminate the sea, there will be no way by which the fisherfolk will be able to sustain their life. Besides, fishing activities around 10 kms have been severely affected. One lakh people were expected to be evicted and the livelihood of 5 lakh persons was threatened. Most of the people affected are Schedule Castes and the poor.

Displacement in India specially affects the already impoverished SCs/STs and other marginalised groups. They hardly benefit from the projects. Tribals of Sardar Sarovar have not been provided with rehabilitation. According to the government these tribals are 'encroachers' on government land although they had been cultivating the land for generations in accordance with their customary usage though without formal title.

Then there are people affected by the project. According to the Tribunal Award 1979 they were to be given land, house sites and short-term financial protection. There are no examples in India where the government has done this in any project. Land at times has been provided as an exchange. Very often compensation is given for house sites and land. In some places one job per family is provided to some families. Beyond that there are no examples of any other assistance.

Besides the project affected, there are those who are project dependent. They are primarily those who work as labourers, milkmen, tillers, harvesters, cow and sheep rearers and flower and vegetable vendors. They are not treated as a category in the rehabilitation package. When the government or any other Business company acquires large land for development purposes, these people lose their livelihood and their very life or existence is effected.

Unfortunately, the human rights movements in our country have confined itself to a legal positivist view of rights. A comprehensive understanding of development has never been its agenda. This has happened because a definition of rights has not emerged from the notion of rights of the people in collective. The new Indian middle class has borrowed the concept of human rights from the practices and experiments of the West. There have been attempts to have an Indian agenda, especially related to incidents of State violation of constitutional and other codified rights. So far, the natural rights of the people to livelihood and self-reliance have not come under its purview. This is one reason why the human rights movement has not gone below the first two layers of the Indian society. This inherent limitation persists because human rights discussions in India have continued to exist as an urban phenomenon. A vast rural hinterland of the country is left outside its domain.

The urban culture is basically individual-centered. The middle class is more concerned with individual rights and interests. This is one reason why human rights activists have responded primarily on the issue of police atrocities on individuals. In reality, the Indian State has been continuously violating the collective rights of the people using ways and means, which are, at times, diabolical. The development policies of the State, in fact, are the greatest violators of people's right to livelihood and human dignity, and more importantly, to life. The development policies have uprooted people from their traditional life system based on values, collective growth and sustainable development. They have dissociated people from their self-propelling growth pattern, based on indigenously evolved science and technology. Majority of them are then placed in an alien economic environment where their human dignity carries no meaning. That is why human rights is a community issue and a collective concern. Debates on human rights, therefore, should have dealt with the democratic rights of communities and various other collectivities of the marginalised people. This is necessary because the violation of human rights is a continuous occurrence against the poor and the marginalised sections.

People assert their rights through protests against State actions. Continuous dialogue between human rights groups of the country, environment experts and the grassroots activists is necessary to make human rights more meaningful and effective.

This interaction can become successful if human rights debates go beyond the domain of codified rights. Because by codifying laws the State intends to safeguard the narrow interests of its political system and sovereignty of its territorial boundary. People's interests, in fact, are much wider than those of the State. Therefore, different dimensions of deprivation of humans, including the lack of political freedom to individuals and absence of personal security must be incorporated in the understanding of human rights. Rights carry a meaning when an individual is free from stress and tensions and when there is space for him to enjoy life. An interface between growth of the country and the notion of life and liberty of human communities is, therefore, necessary.

Globalisation denotes the unchallenged authority of the transnational companies to determine the production process and consumption pattern of a nation and its people. This is colonialism no doubt, but different from that which we had experienced earlier. Capturing a nation-State physically, perhaps, is not the agenda of globalisation. 'Free' economic and cultural systems of a nation, however, are made to be regulated by the global marketing framework of the TNCs, the MNCs and the international financial institutions. This regulation takes away the capacity of independent growth of a nation and its people. Independent nations become vulnerable to this global power. Globalisation is thus not an administrative invasion. Rather, it is an economic penetration and a cultural subjugation. India is one of those countries which are becoming increasingly victims of the stratagem of change and modernisation fabricated by the global economic powers.

Globalisation negates plurality of culture and destroys the life systems sustained around different cultural milieu. Plurality is replaced by a monolithic and homogenised culture. Many of our value-based people-centred cultural heritage, which is the main strength of our societal bonds, are fast disappearing under the pressure of a global economy.

Human rights debates, therefore, need to reflect on globalisation as an urgent agenda for concern because multinational companies have been making all-out efforts to establish harmful chemical factories and, to experiment with hazardous bio-scientific projects in our country.

However, massive ecological disasters and crises of life have compelled us to rethink about the feasibility of large industries, big projects and rapid growth of consumerism in Indian society. Even though rejection of the present model of development is necessary, it does not mean turning back upon growth and prosperity. It also does not argue for going back to a primitive life system. Rather, it pleads for an indigenous development process. It emphasises the continuous innovation of science and technology and exchanging knowledge and skills between different societies on equal terms. What it challenges is the blind adoption of the model of growth of 'developed countries' as the solution to the backwardness or under-development of India.

The Indian politico-economic system has failed to look into the basic needs of the people from this perspective. Instead it has defined basic needs of the people from a limited notion which includes only shelter, clothing, food, education and health. Such an understanding is devoid of an environmental consideration because it does not assure pure oxygen, pure water and fertile topsoil as essential for human society.

Over the centuries, human communities in India have proved their tremendous power and capacity to advance in science and technology. People have grown along with the preservation of natural resources. An increasing number of people at the grassroots have started resisting India's present development model. True, they do not have many success stories so far. But, through each of their attempts to prevent this growth model they have renewed their strength and power to protect their right to life and livelihood. More importantly, they have understood the problems not from any specific ideology. It is their own experiences that have given them the theory for sustenance and human rights.

Human rights, therefore, can become instrumental in changing society if it integrates itself with the people's way of transforming individual rights into new collective and community rights. This will not only strengthen but will also safeguard human rights in its true spirit.

30

Sanatana Values and Indian Constitution

Shobha Misra

The Indian Constitution provides the basic framework within which *sanatana* values can be established.

Editor

Sanatana dharma is steeped deep in the idea of welfare of the entire humanity. It pervades and permeates every activity of ours. It goads and urges us to follow absolute and definite principles. It aspires for man's immortality. *Sanatana* values enshrine not only individual binding but family, social, national and international bindings. This process of binding and regulation is motivated by high ideals of uplift of the soul, justice, freedom, equality, cooperation, peaceful coexistence, national integration and universal brotherhood. To sustain this process a meticulously framed Constitution is needed.

The eight *yogic* practices of Patanjali's philosophy provide practical methods of *anasaktibhava* for every human being and pushing man on the path of salvation and for the prosperity of the entire universe. Five *Yamas* namely non-violence, truth, nonstealing, *brahmacharya* and renunciation and five *niyamas* namely purity, satisfaction, penance, study of scriptures and God worship are the basic elements of lofty edifice and superstructure of *sanatana* values.

Non-violence. It is the supreme religion. Dark clouds of violence, fear and war can only be scattered by non-violence. Being worshippers of non-violence we would have to be practical. For self-defence and for upholding national integration we can give up this lofty principle if need be.

Truth. Speak truth and uphold *dharma* thereby. Truth wins and there can be no impediments in its way. The sun of truth may get overcast by jet black clouds of falsehood, but not for ever. Ulimately the brilliant rays of truth come out triumphant. So don't speak unpleasant truth. Don't tell pleasant lies. Speak the pleasant, speak the truth. Mind, speech and action should depict and display truth. Truth is transparency but proper care must be undertaken in this regard because transparency does not mean nakedness. To torture human mind by naked presentation of truth is not desirable. Has the American society gained anything by exposing sexual exploits of its President ?

Nonstealing. This feeling restrains man from taking possession of the belongings of other persons by force or otherwise. Stealing even by proxy is a sin.

Brahmacharya. It imparts physical strength and mental exaltation. This *sanatana* value is capable of containing AIDS and other fatal sexual diseases. Where woman is respected gods reside there, this Indian maxim can go a long way in changing the attitude of society about sex exploitation.

Renunciation. It forbids excessive possession of worldly things and indulgence in them. It brings about simplicity in life. Air conditioning has made us intolerant to natural conditions of summer and winter. It has generated environmental pollution and ecological imbalance. Stealing, embezzlement, sexual exploits, scams and match-fixing are the replicas of hoarding. Officials, political leaders and players have been declared culprits and these poor souls could not even enjoy their ill-gotten wealth and property. Now they cannot face society. Stigma on their name and face is indelible. Ordinary citizens are better than these parasites and corrupt people because at least they can live with dignity in spite of their limited resources. Usurpers die many deaths before their natural deaths.

Purity. Within and without. Bodily purity does count but mental purity is supreme. Purity enhances virtues, compassion, mental concentration, control of senses and furthers man on the road of introspection. It is indispensable for social equilibrium.

Contentment. It is bliss. If this virtue becomes integral part of man's life many other virtues follow spontaneously. Even while living in society man can live the life of a sage and may find it easy to march relentlessly towards the ultimate aim of life, i.e., salvation.

Penance. It purifies body, mind and dilutes our sins. It prepares path to salvation.

Study of the Scriptures. Continuous study of *granthas* and scriptures brings man nearer to God and it ennobles his mind, body and soul. It gives us that knowledge which is essential to peep deep into the mysteries of this world. In the same way faith in God and the practice of *Asanas*, restraining of breath, restraining of the sense organs, firm determination, steadiness, meditation and suspension of the connection between the body and soul are also important parts of our *sanatana* constitution. It is tragic that this constitution in our possession has failed to make us self-disciplined and fetters of slavery bound us from time to time. To resurrect our moral ground and replant *sanatana* values we had to frame a new Constitution.

Salient Features of Indian Constitution

India is a sovereign State and sovereignty rests in the masses. Our democratic set-up is to guarantee commom welfare by nurturing the feelings of equality, justice, freedom and fraternity. India is a secular State. There is no State religion. All religions are treated equally. Our Constitution guarantees fundamental rights, namely, the right to equality, the right to freedom, the right to worship or freedom of religion, the right against exploitation, right to cultural and educational, right to property, right to vote and right to constitutional remedy. All persons are equally entitled to freedom of conscience and the right freely to profess, practise and propagate their religion. India has adopted socialism based on the concept of economic justice. We have opted for mixed economy to reap the benefits of both socialism and capitalism. Dynastic rule has been rejected. We elect our own President through indirect election and he administers, assisted and aided by his council of ministers.

These salient features of Indian Constitution provide opportunities to every Indian citizen to prosper while upholding *sanatana* values. Directive Principles of State Policy are aimed at securing social and economic freedoms. The State shall strive to promote the welfare of the people by securing and protecting a social order in which justice—social, economic and political—is to be realised. It shall strive to minimise the inequalities in income and endeavour to eliminate inequalities in status, facilities and opportunities. The fundamental rights and directive principles constitute the conscience of our Constitution. Dignity of the individual and national integration get priority.

Social justice. Our sacred Constitution makes relentless efforts to establish a coordination between individual well-being and social well-being to minimise disparities due to caste, race, creed, sex and status. The State shall make provisions for securing just and humane conditions of work and for maternity relief and to establish institutions for women and to reserve seats for them. The State shall also make provisions for free and compulsory education for all children until they complete the age of 14 years and shall make effective provisions for securing the right to work, to education and to public assistance in cases of unemployment, old age, sickness and disablement.

Economic justice. Under economic justice many facilities are to be provided for ideal growth to the citizens :

1. Right to an adequate means to livelihood.
2. Equal pay for equal work for both men and women.
3. To ensure that citizens are not forced due to economic necessity to enter avocations unsuited to their age or strength.
4. The State shall endeavour to promote cottage industry on individual or cooperative basis in rural areas and to secure living wage to the workers.

Political Justice. Political justice pervades each and every page of our Constitution.

1. Equality before law.
2. Equality in political matters to all citizens.
3. No arbitrary discrimination.
4. Adult franchise.
5. Right to election.
6. To organise village *panchayats* in order to encourage self-governance.

Thus, we see our Constitution has assimilated almost all the *sanatana* values. Fundamental rights and duties enshrined in the Constitution speak volumes of our eternal values depicted by our ancient *granthas* and scriptures. Fundamental rights are indispensable for all-round progress of man. Remedies are there to safeguard them if they are encroached upon or uprooted. Article 51A enshrines fundamental duties which are 10 in number. Citizens should endeavour to :

(i) Promote patriotism;
(ii) Uphold and protect the sovereignty, unity and integrity of India;
(iii) Value and preserve the rich heritage of our composite culture;
(iv) Ensure respect of women;
(v) Protect and improve the natural environment and natural resources;
(vi) Develop the scientific temper, humanism and the spirit of inquiry and reform;
(vii) Safeguard public property and to abjure violence;
(viii) Work for allround development of nation;
(ix) Abide by the Constitution and respect its ideals and institutions, the National Flag and the National Anthem;
(x) Cherish and follow the noble ideals which inspired our national struggle for freedom.

Enriched with fundamental rights, assured by Constitutional remedies, embracing new direction of progress as per the Directive Principles, Indian citizens performing their duties righteously and following the doctrine of *Panch Sheel,* can firmly establish the universality of *sanatana* Constitution.

If we read between the lines and try to comprehend letter and spirit of our Constitution we would realise that provisions enshrined in it at once transport us to the realms of ancient Indian culture when *sanatana* values dominated governance. We can also conclude that imitable *sanatana* eternal values cannot be ignored whenever a modern Constitution is to be framed.

31

Human Rights Transcend Cultural Boundaries

Alok Tandon

Basic Human Rights are common to all cultures.

Editor

With the end of the cold war the concept of Human Rights is slowly emerging as an alternative ideology. Though the idea of Human Rights is a modern one, in the historical and philosophical sense, its widespread acceptance indicates that it is related to certain fundamental and deeply felt needs of man. In fact, the philosophy of human rights is a truly great achievement of the modern thinking. The initiatives being taken at the international level are increasingly providing a concrete shape to the idea. The ongoing changes in the list of Human Rights recognised by the member states of the United Nations amply demonstrate that these developments correspond to the changes in the circumstances over time.

This ideological challenge has manifested itself in the shape of several basic questions. *Firstly,* what is the real significance of human rights for a man until his basic needs are not fulfilled? This is a particularly meaningful question in case of the developing nations where the majority of the population still lives below or around the poverty line. *Secondly,* doesn't our over-dependence on the State for giving a legal form to Human Rights really divert our attention away from those defects in the socio-economic structures which are responsible for the violation of human rights? *Thirdly,* is it proper to take recourse to violent methods for securing human rights when there is a use of force for violation of human rights? The question assumes further complexities when it is linked to the national security concerns and becomes very difficult to separate genuine human rights concern from the politics which is played in their name. We also face a bigger issue here. Whether human rights are merely a means of protection of self or they are an integral feature of the struggle for securing a better structure of the society? These questions have been discussed extensively in the past. The result has been that the human rights is now not merely confined to the civil and political rights, it has been expanded to include the social, economic and cultural rights. In fact, hardly any aspect of life now remains untouched.

However, globalisation and the advances made in the field of Information Technology have thrown up new questions and challenges. The policy of economic liberalisation is fast transforming the world into a free market place. Man has now no other identity except being a mere consumer. The process of rapid modernisation has not only brought various cultures face to face with each other but also laid bare their internal and external contradictions. Questions are being raised regarding the utility of traditional lifestyles. There has emerged a vacuum and it is not possible to fill it up by importing a consumer-oriented life style from abroad. As traditional societies go through a process of doubts, tensions, illusions, insecurity and adjustments, man has begun to look towards the ancient traditions to protect his identity. At some places, it has expressed itself in the form of conservatism or fundamentalism. But elsewhere, it has also meant acceptance of the true worth of the traditional way of life. This phenomenon, however, has also given rise to the problems of conflicts between different cultures which are viewed by some thinkers as the most serious problems confronting man in the 21st century.

Under such circumstances, the concept of the universality of human rights itself is now facing many questions. It is being asked whether it is really possible to successfully conduct the struggle for human rights as long as there is so much cultural diversity and mutual animosity? Is it possible to create an alternative global culture by achieving harmony among the individual cultures? Does the reason for the limited success of the human right philosophy lie in the ideological belief in the universality of such rights? Is the concept of human rights a purely western concept which suits its culture but cannot be successfully transplanted on the Eastern societies? Should we give up the idea of universality of human rights in favour of a concept of right derived from the individuality of each culture? And if the answer is yes then what meaning or shape would it have in India? This paper attempts to discuss these questions.

Human rights are those rights which accrue to a man by the mere fact of his being a man. They are not dependent upon such considerations as his religious creed, nationality, race or gender identity. Acceptance of individual personality and its inherent dignity constitute the source of all human rights. It does not mean to ignore the society but it does say that a man is a distinct individual first before he assumes any social or political identity. No social or political system should have the right to suppress his right to differ or express his opinion. Between the man and the society, it is the man who holds the primary position. This is why the chief objective of the State is to bring about development and welfare of its individuals. The individual is an aim in himself. He is not a mere tool for achieving some supposedly better objective. Acceptance of the individual's dignity is the true aim of human rights. Freedom and morality are its basic values.

From the historical viewpoint, the concept of Universal Human Rights and the related UN Declaration is an outcome of a Western thought process which has been evolving since the seventeenth century. It is linked to the development of industrial revolution, aspirations of the middle class and liberal political thought. One cannot ignore the contributions made by such events in the Western history as England's Bill of Rights of 1689, Declaration of Independence by USA in 1776, the French Revolution of 1889 or the contributions made by such thinkers as Rousseau, Jefferson, etc. Despite such Western origins, human rights have emerged as universal entities. One school of thought believes that the concept is practicable in the whole world. The other school holds that the concept of human right can only be determined by taking the individual cultural context into consideration.

The problem becomes acute when in the name of cultural relativism, an attempt is made to defend such practices which should be treated as cases of human rights violation as per the Universal Declaration of Human Rights. In order to resolve this conflict, it is necessary to examine the arguments forwarded by both the schools of thought. Let us first discuss the arguments against the universality of human rights by the relativist school.

(1) The notion of Universal Human Rights is false. This is so since the scale with which excellence in human behaviour is measured is relative to the society to which he belongs. Given the diversities amongst cultures and also considering that the level of morality in all cultures is not the same, one cannot consider the yardsticks for judging behaviour by one to be superior to that employed by others. Hence a Universal Standard acceptable to all is not possible.

(2) The present interpretation of human rights is West-centric. To impose it on non-Western nations is colonial imperialism. To accept them amounts to mental slavery.

(3) An ideology of individualism lies behind the European notion of human rights. It does not match with the cultural ideology believing in primacy of public welfare as prevailing in countries like India.

(4) Rights come first and duties are secondary as per the present concept of human rights. Indian traditions believe it is the other way around, i.e., the duties have been given more importance than the rights.

(5) The concept of human rights has been changing along with the developments in history. Hence, so long as economic, social and cultural differences existing between various societies are not removed, it would be futile to speak of a struggle for securing universal rights.

(6) It is an attempt to replace cultural diversities by a uniform culture.

(7) The responsibility of safeguarding human rights lies with the particular cultural tradition which has provided for such rights. The notion of universal human rights interferes with this role of the traditional culture. Over-dependence on the State and its laws for securing Human Rights can lead to emergence of a State that is not neutral towards cultural values.

(8) Collective rights find no place in the current interpretation of human rights whereas a person's moral development occurs only in the form of a member of various groups. It is therefore not clear as to what should be preferred in case of a conflict of interests between the individual and collective rights.

It would be necessary to understand the historical origin of the issue of cultural identity before an attempt is made to accept or refute the above allegations. It had become a tradition amongst the Western sociologists in the colonial era to believe that the culture of the colonised nation was inferior, wild and backward. This approach automatically accorded a higher status to the culture of the colonising nations. However the anti-colonial movements gained momentum after the Second World War. Many eminent sociologist such as Levi Strauss rejected this as a colonialistic concept and accepted that each culture had a distinct identity requiring independent evaluation.

It was quite logical to speak of the need to preserve respective cultural identities during the phase of the freedom struggle. It imparted strength to the struggle and helped in overcoming the slave mentality and thus contributed in achievement of freedom. Basically it was an expedient device through which the cause of national unity was promoted by according a due place to the cultural traditions in the national life. But when some nations began to employ this weapon for violating the rights of their own citizens, they cooked up an argument that all the cultures at par in terms of moral values. This was nothing short of a sentence of death for the universal values arising from a confused thinking which mistook cultural relativism as moral relativism. The arguments forwarded by the proponents of cultural relativism have been used by the rulers of many nations to restrict the freedom of expression, suppress the women folk and justify many other barbarous acts like cutting off of arms and legs.

Fundamentality of Cultural Relativism in Human Rights

Cultural relativism is a new instrument in the hands of the suppressors which enables them to cover their misdeeds by raising the bogey of Western imperialism. However, such political misuse do not make the concept of cultural relativism irrelevant at the philosophical level. Let us, therefore, examine the issue further.

(1) The idea of cultural relativism is not based upon facts. All societies believe that the human life is precious and none approves of mindless and unjust killing of human beings. Sexual relations amongst very close kins are prohibited in all societies and excessive or free indulgence in lust is not approved anywhere. They all support stability in sexual relationship and none recommends acts

of rape. All the societies prefer the social good over the individual interests and they all prefer justice amongst the men and groups. Hence, we can assert that all the societies underline the primary importance of universal moral necessities. We cannot, therefore, deny that there are universal human rights. Most cases of Human Rights violation occur not because of the culture of a society but due to their dictatorial rulers. Nonetheless some cultural traditions are indeed so repressive and cruel that even the staunchest of the believers in cultural relativism admit of the universality of certain human rights. It would be wrong, therefore, to consider all cultures as same. Presence of certain adjustable and evil features in many cultures cannot be ignored. Nor is there a case for treating such cultures at par with the advanced ones.

(2) The relativists nurture certain illusive ideas on culture. They are almost hypnotised by the idea of culture and images of a golden past. They forget that culture had never existed in such pristine forms. The truth is that the cultures have their own internal dynamics which cause them to change continuously. In fact, one can measure the creativity of a culture by noting how it copes up with its internal contradictions and also how it absorbs the external influences without losing the best of its own elements. Hence, it can be said that there is no direct relationship between the cultural changes *per se* and the issue of safeguarding human rights.

(3) The pace of change in the traditional societies has increased rapidly as a result of the revolution in information technology and the process of globalisation. These societies are now accommodating individualistic thoughts in their cultures as it is now easy to reach out to other cultures and judge them. Barring a few dictatonal regimes, most countries have accepted the UN Declaration of Human Rights. The awareness about such rights is fast becoming an integral part of their societies.

Now that the human rights have become an inseparable part of the international law, it is really quite illogical to raise questions about their universality.

(4) There also happen to be some relativist thinkers who have full faith in the aims behind the human rights campaign despite their disagreement over the universal interpretation of such rights. They do this by taking recourse to the belief in the ideals of human rights. Like a good human being they see it as their moral duty.

Thus, despite not accepting the theory of universality, they support the human rights as universal objectives.

(5) The campaign for Universal Human Rights is not an attempt to bring about cultural uniformity. It is only a struggle towards obtaining a legal backing to the most basic human values. They are a result of a consensus amongst the international community arrived at through strenuous efforts and have not arisen from a process of cultural colonialism. It is a new achievement for most cultures and, therefore, the question of replacing one culture by another does not arise.

(6) There is enough flexibility in the concept of human rights itself for protecting cultural diversities and identities. This has been brought about by agreeing to the theory of Minimum Human Rights and the Right to Culture. In other words, one is free to maintain his cultural identity and lead the life according to his culture but his cultural right do not grant him the right to violate other human rights in any way. It is a limited right in the sense that it opposes certain customs approved by some cultures. Many cultures have accommodated the custom of slavery but it cannot be recognised as a right. Similarly, the discrimination made on the basis of colour, race, caste, gender, religion, language, etc., cannot be supported in the name of cultural rights. They all constitute examples of blatant violation of Human Rights.

It should be clear from the above that the talk of relative human rights is quiet irrational. Traditional culture cannot replace the human rights. But we should also not forget that the struggle for establishing human rights should be based on specific conditions prevailing in a country. There are two dimensions here—institutional and cultural. The concept of Universal Human Right is linked to the international process of creation of democratic system of governments. The struggle for human rights requires a greater degree of coordination between the concept and various cultures. Rather than modifying the rights according to cultural patterns, the cultures themselves should be reformed to bring about agreements with the concepts of human rights. All cultures share certain basic values which aim at protecting the human life and the social organisation and oppose undue intervention of the State. They can be of great assistance. In most societies, many sub-cultures exist alongside the mainstream culture. One can tap these sub-cultures and seek their cooperation in supporting and strengthening the campaign for human rights. This would require an in-depth understanding of various cultures. We would be only then able to obtain wider social acceptance of a legalised human rights.

It is a mistake to consider human rights as being relative to the cultural norms, it would also not be appropriate to consider them as being anti-culture. The concept of Human Rights is a universal idea which is awaiting its due place in various cultures and this goal must be perceived seriously. Our basic approach should be to engage the different cultures in this task by making them a partner in the campaign. Human Rights can be definitely accepted as universal values notwithstanding the diversities found amongst each culture. Just as many systems of democracy are current today, it is also possible to adopt different working mechanisms for establishing human rights. The intellectuals of the respective societies would have to struggle for this. It is not enough to depend upon the State alone. There is also a need here to draw attention towards two dangers. While we must not shirk away from the responsibility of promoting human rights by invoking the fear of backlash from the supporters of indigenous culture, it is also to be seen that those influential groups and communities which are in control of the State do not use cultural arguments to suppress those who are opposed to the dominance by a narrow segment.

In these days of globalisation, most nations are adopting the policies of economic liberalisation and free market. As a result, new kinds of problems are cropping up. The traditional societies of the developing nations do not possess any solutions for such problems. A time has come to think about globalisation of human rights too for resolving their vices. It would be futile anyway to look for solutions to those problems which were never faced by the traditional societies within their own limited framework. During the struggle against colonialism, these societies did take support from many ideologies which were not indigenous to them. The form of Constitution which was adopted after gaining independence also happened to be different from the traditional culture. Further, even modernity has slowly found an acceptable place as a kind of tradition in such societies. It cannot be ignored or wished away any more. The justification for cultural renaissance was valid during the struggle against colonialism but not any more. To talk of cultural relativism of human rights is nothing but to reiterate those post-colonial lessons which are no more in tune with the post-modern period of today.

32

Legal and Social Dimensions of Human Rights

Dhruv Kumar Dixit

> The United Nations Declaration only establishes the framework of human rights. Unless it is backed by social values it will not be effective. *Editor*

The children are the wealth of a nation. The nation is as responsible for their proper care as the parents and other family members. Unfortunately, we find that the family as well as the nation has been neglecting their moral duty of safeguarding the interests of the children. The future of a nation lies in its children. Yet it is common to see many a children labouring through their precious childhood in order to face the hardships of life which ends in denying them the opportunities of development. They look forward to future without any sense of hope.

There are nearly 40 million child workers in India alone. Forced to eke out a living for their families, they never get to know what it means to have a happy and carefree childhood. Jabalpur city alone has more than 2,000 of such child labourers engaged in various activities. It is not difficult to imagine the kind of future a nation will have when it allows its children to work as labourers, indulge in crime or forced into prostitution.

A number of surveys have been conducted in this respect. About forty million children are working to support their families. The number of children involved in prostitution exceeds four hundred thousand. The growing involvement of children in criminal activities sends out a clear signal that our country has not been able to safeguard the future of its children. Of course, this state of affairs also amounts to a clear violation of human rights. "Children have not been brought under the purview of human rights laws alongwith the women. The declaration on human rights of children announced on 20th November 1989 by the United Nations gives a special emphasis to them. It has outlined the necessity of providing a helpful and supportive attention to the children in their formative years."[1]

A family is the basic unit of a society. A society must extend all support and protection to its members. It should pay particular attention to the development and happiness of children so that they become capable of shouldering their responsibilities in the later years.

Balanced all round development of a child can take place only if there is a healthy environment in the family. A child who grows up in a conducive environment becomes well prepared to live a distinguished life in the society. The UN Declaration clearly states that since the children are neither mentally nor physically mature, special steps are required to protect their interests. They must receive adequate legal protection not only from the time of their birth but even before that. Their living condition should be constantly improved keeping in mind the tradition and culture of the country to which they belong.

The Human Rights Commission is fighting to procure for the child the rights which are due to them as a member of the human society. The difference is that this battle now has legal dimensions, i.e., laws are being or have been enacted for the welfare of the children.

India has been a staunch supporter of human rights since ancient times. In recent times, Mahatma Gandhi put up a strong resistance to violation of human rights in South Africa.

Neglect or downright exploitation of the children, women and backward classes has become a very common phenomenon in the modern days. The growing popularity of consumerism in the society lies at the root of this evil. The origin of this trend is found in mankind's transition from being a mainly agricultural society to one based upon technology-driven production processes. The social transformations which have taken place as a result of this transition unfortunately include growing intolerance, conflicts, violence and suppression of fellow human beings. There is a general feeling of insecurity. No one's life is really secure under such circumstances.

The fundamental rights were guaranteed to the citizens of India through the Constitution. This is the most important measure undertaken after independence for protection of basic human rights. The Human Rights Commission was set up on 24 September, 1993 through an ordinance by the Government of India. The aim was to provide a strong impetus to the cause of securing the basic rights of the citizens. The ordinance also provided for setting up of Human Rights Commissions at the State level. The Commission has been provided with extensive powers in order to achieve its objectives effectively. Apart from safeguarding the basic rights of the citizens, the Commission is also fully committed to procure justice whenever it is approached with a complaint pertaining to violation of human rights. The Commission is presently paying special attention to upliftment and welfare of children as they happen to be amongst the most exploited sections of the society.

Recommendations for the Upliftment and Welfare of Children

Certain recommendations were made in this respect in a meeting of the Commission held on 24 February, 1998 and chaired jointly by Shri Virendra Dayal and Justice V.S. Maniath after a discussion on the problem of child prostitution in India. These included:[2]

1. The Government of India and the Department of Women and Child Development will take action to tackle the problem of child prostitution under a declared national policy.
2. Effective use should be made of Doordarshan and advertising agencies by the Department of Women and Child Development as well as the National Commission on Women to create proper awareness amongst the people.

"We have made extensive efforts as a nation to protect the interests of children in our country since independence. However, despite such efforts, the cases of child abuse and exploitation have become more widespread and organised than even before."[3]

If we reflect upon this problem, we would find that the rising incidents of child exploitation are actually results of the rapid erosion in the traditional values of our society. Our ancient traditions have been derived from an understanding of certain basic and eternal truths. The result was a cohesiveness and orderliness in our social set-up. There is a deep sense of respect for basic human values in these traditions. Exploitation of human beings and violation of basic rights do no figure in this scheme. Ample protection has, on the other hand, been provided to the women and children. Human rights have been assured in ancient Indian social set-up for the welfare of human beings. The caste system as well as division of the life span of an individual into four phases, called *varna* and *ashrama* system respectively have been created with the objective of organising the society and making it a value based institution. In the *varna* system, the society was divided into four categories comprising *Brahmins, Kshatriyas, Vaishyas* and the *Sudras*. Each of these classes had distinct duties and assignments to ensure that the society functioned in an orderly and efficient manner. Similarly, the *ashrama* system enabled an individual to do justice to his duties not only toward the society but also to the aim of spiritual development.

Brahmcharya ashrama was the first of the four stages and laid down the foundations necessary for successful completion of the remaining ones. The young children were prepared and trained in this phase for travelling on the difficult and complex path of life. They spent the days under a teacher in the *Gurukul*. The children also had to perform many tasks but there was no element of exploitation. The primary aim of the *Gurukul* was to bring about all round personality development in a child. Moral education and inculcation of human values occupied a very important place.

The right of self-development of a child was thus fully protected in ancient times in a well-conceived moral framework. This is quite different from the ongoing UN campaign which seeks to achieve similar objectives through legislative means. Societies and nations continue, however, to witness cases of human rights violation in spite of legal protections. The Indian society, however, could not think about such violations as that would have been considered downright immoral and unethical.

The family is the smallest unit of social order. Families will determine whether a society would remain united or head towards a break-up. The society can be only as healthy as the families that it is made up of. The Indian social set-up is primarily founded on the joint family system. People of three or four generations live together under the same roof as part of a large extended family. The joint family also serves as a training ground

where every individual learns and absorbs basic human values. Children are accorded particular importance in this system. Moral values are imparted to them in this environment of co-existence. In fact, they even pick up these values during their little childish plays. The family looks after the needs of its elders while receiving guidance from them while the younger adult members shoulder the important responsibilities. The children grow up under the watchful eyes of their elders who fully recognised their rights and paid due attention to their welfare. Far from being considered as means of earning a livelihood, their presence in the house was considered auspicious. They were a sign of its glory. In the absence of any undue pressure they were able to develop in a balanced manner. The decline of Indian traditions and values under the significance of the Western lifestyle has, however, upset this harmony. The children have been badly affected alongwith the women. Almost every member has to work now for earning a livelihood due to the economic pressures. Working under duress has meant an end to one's freedom as an individual. The socially recognised rights began to be denied to them. Faced with widespread incidents of human rights violation, the United Nations had to enter the picture to put a stop these evil practices.[4] However, it chose to restrict itself to only the legal side of the issue. It made no effort to understand the traditional moral values which had kept a check on human rights violations. The result is that such violations continue to be reported on a higher and higher scale.

The point is that unless a society is based upon moral foundations, and until its members are guided by moral considerations in their actions, such violations would not stop. There is a difference between self-restraint and legal prohibitions. Man by his very nature prefers to act under his own convictions instead of outside pressures. He has always resisted authoritarian controls.

Considering that it is the women and children who are bearing the brunt of such defective policies, it is necessary to once again revert to our moral roots. The strategy of relying on legal provisions has to be abandoned in favour of a strategy of creating awareness and enlightenment in the society and its individual members.

Notes and References

1. Puspendra Shastri—*Manav Adhikar Sabke Adhikar*, M.P. Human Rights Commission, Bhopal, 2000.
2. Ashoka Kumar Mishra, *Manav Adhikar Sabke Liye*, M.P. Human Rights Commission, Bhopal, 2000.
3. *Human Rights News Letter*, Delhi, March 1998.
4. *Human Rights News Letter*, Delhi, February 1999.

Index